∼

The AS/400 Programmer's Handbook
Volume II

The AS/400 Programmer's Handbook

Volume II

More Toolbox Examples for Every AS/400 Programmer

Mark McCall

MIDRANGE COMPUTING
IIR PUBLICATIONS INC.

First Edition
First Printing—April 2000

© 2000 Midrange Computing
ISBN: 1-58347-012-3

Midrange Computing
5650 El Camino Real, Suite 225
Carlsbad, CA 92008–9711 USA
www.midrangecomputing.com

For information on translations or book distributors outside the USA or to arrange bulk-purchase discounts for sales promotions, premiums, or fund-raisers, please contact Midrange Computing at the above address.

V4R4

To D'Anna, Andrew, and Kevin McCall.
Thank you for all your support and encouragement.

ACKNOWLEDGMENTS

I would like to express my most sincere appreciation to the following people for their assistance in the creation of this book:

- D'Anna McCall
- Chris Peters
- David Morris
- Jim Utsler
- Merrikay Lee
- Steven Bolt

CONTENTS

ᔕ Part 2: Database Examples · · · · · · · · · · · · · · 227

Chapter 5: DATABASE CONSTRAINTS · · · · · · · · · · · · · · · · · · · 229

INTRODUCTION

While collecting material for the first *AS/400 Programmer's Handbook*, I quickly realized that the sheer volume of information was far more than I could present within a single text. As time passed, I found myself thinking, "I wish I could have included database examples like SQL and trigger programs" and "I wish I had put in more API examples." I finally came to the realization that a sequel was in order.

When developing applications, I find myself drawing from a collection of coding examples as a starting point or template. Rarely will I begin writing a new application from scratch without having a previously written source member from which to draw on. This book is a collection of more than 70 prototypical techniques and coding examples that you can use and adapt for hundreds of potential applications. The material presented here encompasses the most useful and powerful features of the AS/400, and each example is backed by a thorough explanation of the techniques employed.

Each example begins with a quick synopsis that is followed by the supporting source code. This structure allows you to quickly get in, find what you need, and use the example code. If you need more information, detailed explanations of the employed technique are included.

Every effort has been made to make each example stand on its own. This makes some of the information redundant, but the last thing you want to do when you need an example is to have to read other chapters to build an understanding of the topic. Whenever possible, every example is designed to work as a standalone instrument to allow you get in, get what you need, and get back to work.

I hope you will find this book to be a useful and valuable programming tool.

Part 1

RPG Programming Examples

The vast majority of AS/400 application software continues to be written in RPG. However, the RPG of today is barely recognizable from that used several years ago. RPG has evolved from a language encumbered by its rigid structure to a far more dynamic and flexible tool. The advent of ILE RPG, sometimes called RPG IV, has breathed new life into a tired language.

ILE RPG allows you to do things you simply can't do with RPG/400. For this reason, all of the RPG examples presented here use ILE RPG. The contents of this section include:

Chapter 1: Modular Coding Techniques

Chapter 2: Built-In Functions

Chapter 3: Exit Programs

Chapter 4: Application Programming Interfaces

1

MODULAR CODING TECHNIQUES

In programming, much of what is done is redundant, a fact that seasoned programmers who have been in the trenches for many years are well aware of. By the time a programmer has been on the job for more than a couple of years, he or she probably does more copying and adapting of code that already exists than writing new code from scratch. It is simply more efficient to leverage work that has already been done than to start from scratch every time. This technique of reusing and reapplying work that has already been done can lead to tremendous gains in productivity.

Another major benefit of reusing software components is reliability. Modular components are easier to test more thoroughly than full applications. Once tested and verified to work correctly, a component can be reused without being fully retested.

When thinking about designing code that can be used and reused throughout an application, one must maintain a balance between achieving modularity and maintaining acceptable performance levels.

COMMON MODULAR RPG CODING TECHNIQUES

The introduction of the Integrated Language Environment (ILE) for RPG empowered the language with the tools necessary for building reusable component-based software. ILE allows you to call on services from external providers without suffering from the poor performance that plagues dynamic program calls. Prior to ILE, the ability to build component-based software relied strictly on dynamic program calls or methods of sharing source code.

This chapter presents examples based on a variety of modular or component-based design techniques. The following is a list of today's most commonly used techniques to reuse software in RPG on the AS/400:

- /COPY compiler directives

- Internal subroutines

- External subprograms

- ILE subprocedures

- ILE service programs

EXAMPLE

Using the /COPY Compiler Directive

This example employs the /COPY compiler directive to copy source code from a central repository, often called a copybook, into a desired program. This technique of reusing source code is one of the oldest available to AS/400 programmers. While this technique has become outdated for many applications, copybooks remain an effective tool for storing ILE Procedure Interface definitions. The example takes a common generic programming task, determining the day of week for a given date, and deposits the code into a copybook, where it can be used by multiple programmers in multiple programs.

WHAT THE EXAMPLE DOES

The example consists of three source members. Members MOD002R and MOD003R contain copybook source that determines the day of week for a given date. Member MOD001R employs the copybooks using the /COPY directive. The mainline program logic in MOD001R accepts a date as an input parameter, then uses the copied source to determine the date's day of week. The resulting day is displayed for viewing. Listing 1.1 shows the mainline program MOD001R, while Listings 1.2 and 1.3 show the copybook source members.

Listing 1.1: ILE RPG member MOD001R uses /COPY compiler directives.

```
D/COPY SOURCE,MOD002R
C       *Entry          Plist
C                       Parm                    DateIn
C*
C/COPY SOURCE,MOD003R
C                       Dsply                   DayOfWeek
C                       Return
```

Listing 1.2: ILE RPG member MOD002R D-spec copybook.

```
 *_____
 *   Field definitions for copybook MOD003R
 *_____
DLillianOut      S              10I 0
DDateIn          S               8A
DDateFmt         S               8A
DOutFmt          S              10A
DDayOfWeek       S              10A
```

Listing 1.3: ILE RPG member MOD003R C-spec copybook.

```
C*
C                       Move        'MMDDYYYY'   DateFmt
C                       Callb(D)    'CEEDAYS'
C                       Parm                     DateIn
C                       Parm                     DateFmt
C                       Parm                     LillianOut
C                       Parm                     *Omit
C*
C                       Move        'Wwwwwwwwwz' OutFmt
C                       Callb(D)    'CEEDATE'
C                       Parm                     LillianOut
C                       Parm                     OutFmt
C                       Parm                     DayOfWeek
C                       Parm                     *Omit
C*
```

HOW THE EXAMPLE WORKS

RPG provides a number of directives that perform specific functions when the program source compiles. As its name implies, the /COPY compiler directive allows you to instruct the RPG compiler to copy in source member records from a different member before compilation.

When creating source copybooks, you can isolate a generic segment of code into a source member. Because the member is usually just a snippet of code, or a specific generic function, copybook source is never compiled. It is simply a repository for common routines that are copied and included in the compilation of other source members.

Source statements copied by the /COPY directive are placed into the target member at the point the /COPY appears. Because of this, it may be necessary to divide a single function into multiple copybooks. For instance, the example code that determines the day of week for a given date consists of two parts: definition specs for the used fields and the calculation specs that do the actual work. These two portions of the code are divided into two individual source members. The code is divided because the definition specs need to be copied into the definition specs of the target source, while the calculations may be copied one or more times into various locations within the target member. It is important to remember that source copied into one member from another must still conform to the basic structure and sequencing requirements of RPG in order to compile.

The syntax of the /COPY directive can be explicit or implied. That is, you can provide a fully qualified library, source file and member name, a source file name and member name, or simply a member name. If a library is not specified, the library list of the compiling job is used. If a source file name is not specified, the system assumes the file to be QRPGLESRC. A member name must be specified.

Source members MOD002R and MOD003R are never compiled as standalone modules. When either the Create RPG Module (CRTPRGMOD) or Create Bound RPG Program (CRTBNDRPG) commands are used to compile the member MOD001R, the copybook members are integrated into the source prior to the actual compile.

The example employs two system APIs to derive the day of week. For detailed information about the use of these APIs, please refer to chapter 4.

EXAMPLE

Using Internal Subroutines

This example employs an internal subroutine to share code within a single module. Subroutines are grouped segments of code, usually performing a very specific function that can be executed from multiple points in a module. As a general rule, subroutines deliver the best performance of all modular-coding techniques. The primary weakness of the subroutine is its inability to export its services across modules or procedures. The example takes a common generic programming task, determining the day of week for a given date, and deposits the code into a subroutine where it can be executed multiple times within the same module.

WHAT THE EXAMPLE DOES

The example presents member MOD004R that uses an internal subroutine coding technique to determine the day of week for a given date. MOD004R accepts a date as an input parameter, then uses the subroutine to determine the date's day of week. The resulting day is displayed for viewing. Listing 1.4 shows the source member MOD004R.

Listing 1.4: ILE RPG member MOD004R uses an internal subroutine.

```
DLillianOut      S              10I 0
DDateIn          S               8A
DDateFmt         S               8A
DOutFmt          S              10A
DDayOfWeek       S              10A
 *
C     *Entry      Plist
C                 Parm                      DateIn
 *
C                 Exsr      GetDay
C                 Dsply                     DayOfWeek
C                 Return
 *=======================================================
C     GetDay     BegSR
C                 Move      'MMDDYYYY'   DateFmt
C                 Callb(D)  'CEEDAYS'
C                 Parm                      DateIn
C                 Parm                      DateFmt
C                 Parm                      LillianOut
C                 Parm                      *Omit
C*
C                 Move      'Wwwwwwwwwz'  OutFmt
C                 Callb(D)  'CEEDATE'
C                 Parm                      LillianOut
C                 Parm                      OutFmt
C                 Parm                      DayOfWeek
C                 Parm                      *Omit
C                 EndSR
```

HOW THE EXAMPLE WORKS

RPG subroutines are routines that can be executed from any point within a procedure's calculation specifications. Subroutines are coded after the main body of code in the calculation's specs. They are defined using a unique subroutine name coded with the Begin Subroutine (BEGSR) op code. The end of the subroutine is identified using an End Subroutine (ENDSR) op code. They are executed using either the Execute Subroutine (EXSR) or Case (CASxx) op codes. When executed, program control branches from the executing line of code to the first line of code in the subroutine. The subroutine code executes until the end of the subroutine is encountered or until a GOTO or Leave Subroutine (LEAVESR) operation is performed. Upon completion of the subroutine, control is returned to the line of code that executed it.

The RPG Subroutine

A subroutine cannot contain another subroutine, but it can execute another subroutine. A subroutine cannot execute itself recursively.

It is important to understand that subroutines share all the variables and memory space with the rest of the module. A field defined within the subroutine can be accessed and altered outside the subroutine. In addition, fields defined outside the subroutine can be accessed and altered within the subroutine. The subroutine is merely a technique used to organize source code to reduce redundancy.

The example presented employs two system APIs to derive the day of week. For detailed information about the use of these APIs, please refer to chapter 4.

EXAMPLE

Using Dynamic Subprograms

This example employs a dynamic call to an external subprogram to access a shared function from an external provider. Subprograms are isolated routines that perform a very specific function that can be called from multiple modules or programs. Subprograms called dynamically, that is those that are not bound to the program object at compile time, carry significant overhead. Because they are called dynamically, the location of the program is not resolved until the call is performed.

The user library list is searched until the called program object is located. It can then be loaded into memory and executed. As a general rule, subprograms called dynamically deliver poor performance relative to newer techniques employing ILE early binding. The advantage delivered by dynamic calls is their simplicity. Because the object is not resolved until run time, internal changes made to the subprogram object immediately impact the programs that call it without recompilation.

The example takes a common generic programming task, determining the day of week for a given date, and deposits the code into a subprogram where it can be executed multiple times from any module or program.

WHAT THE EXAMPLE DOES

The example consists of two source members. Member MOD006R contains source that determines the day of week for a given date. It accepts the date as an input parameter and returns the day of week as an output parameter. Member MOD005R calls the subprogram dynamically using the CALL op code. The mainline program logic in MOD005R accepts a date as an input parameter, then calls the program MOD006R to determine the date's day of week. The resulting day is displayed for viewing. Listing 1.5 shows the mainline program MOD005R, while Listing 1.6 shows the subprogram.

Listing 1.5: ILE RPG member MOD005R calls subprogram MOD006R.

```
DDateIn          S              8A
DDayOfWeek       S             10A
 *
C     *Entry      Plist
C                 Parm                        DateIn
 *
C                 Call      'MOD006R'
C                 Parm                        DateIn
C                 Parm                        DayOfWeek
 *
C                 Dsply                       DayOfWeek
C                 Return
```

Listing 1.6: ILE RPG member MOD006R subprogram.

```
DLillianOut      S             10I 0
DDateIn          S              8A
DDateFmt         S              8A
DOutFmt          S             10A
DDayOfWeek       S             10A
C*
C     *Entry      Plist
C                 Parm                        DateIn
```
→

Listing 1.6: ILE RPG member MOD006R subprogram (continued).

```
C                   Parm                          DayOfWeek
C*
C                   Move        'MMDDYYYY'        DateFmt
C                   Callb(D)    'CEEDAYS'
C                   Parm                          DateIn
C                   Parm                          DateFmt
C                   Parm                          LillianOut
C                   Parm                          *Omit
C*
C                   Move        'Wwwwwwwwwz'       OutFmt
C                   Callb(D)    'CEEDATE'
C                   Parm                          LillianOut
C                   Parm                          OutFmt
C                   Parm                          DayOfWeek
C                   Parm                          *Omit
C*
C                   Return
```

HOW THE EXAMPLE WORKS

Prior to the introduction of ILE, there was only one way to dynamically call one program from another. Today, RPG provides three ways to call one program or module from another, including:

- Dynamically

- Bound by copy (static or early binding)

- Bound by reference (late binding)

Dynamic Program Calls

Programs called dynamically are coded using the RPG CALL op code. All resolution of the program object are performed when the CALL executes. Details such as the number and type of parameters being passed are not checked until the program is called. The program being called does not even have to exist when the calling program is compiled. This adds significant overhead to each CALL operation. If you need to call non-ILE programs, they must be called dynamically.

Bound by Copy Calls

Modules bound by copy are coded using the RPG CALLB op code. Binding by copy simply means that two or more RPG modules are combined into a single program object by the Create Program (CRTPGM) command. All resolution of module details such as the number and type of parameters being passed are checked when the program is created. To create the program object, all the modules being bound together must exist in the programmer's library list. Binding by copy delivers the best performance of all calling options.

Bound by Reference Calls

Calls to modules bound by reference are coded using the RPG CALLP op code or an exported procedure name in an EVAL statement. Procedures to be called are combined into a special type of program object called a *service program*. Binding by reference simply means that one or more RPG modules are combined into a single program object with a reference to a service program by the CRTPGM command. All resolution of details such as the number and type of parameters being passed are checked when the program is created. Most of the overhead associated with the procedure call is experienced when the program activation occurs. Subsequent calls do not experience the overhead, as with dynamic calls.

The ILE RPG Example Program

The example program calls a second program, MOD006R, dynamically. If the program will be called repetitively, changing the CALL op code to a CALLB op code and binding by copy will significantly improve call performance.

When the CALL operation is encountered, program control switches to the program being called. The subprogram code executes until the Return op code ends execution. Upon completion of the subprogram, control is returned to the line of code that called it.

A subprogram called dynamically maintain unique variables and memory space from the program that called it. The only field values shared between programs are those passed as parameters. The example subprogram presented employs two system APIs to derive the day of week. For detailed information about the use of these APIs, refer to chapter 4.

EXAMPLE

Using ILE Subprocedures

This example demonstrates a call to an internal subprocedure to share code within a single module. Similar to subroutines, subprocedures are isolated segments of code, usually performing a very specific function that can be executed from multiple points in a module. The primary weakness of the internal subroutine is its inability to export its services across modules. ILE subprocedures can be exported, allowing them to be accessed outside the module in which they reside. The example takes a common generic programming task, determining the day of week for a given date, and deposits the code into a subprocedure where it can be executed multiple times within the same module.

WHAT THE EXAMPLE DOES

The example presents member MOD007R that uses an ILE subprocedure coding technique to determine the day of week for a given date. MOD007R accepts a date as an input parameter, then uses the subprocedure to determine the date's day of week. The resulting day is displayed for viewing. Listing 1.7 shows the source member MOD007R.

Listing 1.7: ILE RPG member *MOD007R calls subprocedure DAYOFWEEK.*

```
DDateInput        S              8A
DDay              S              10A
DDayOfWeek        PR             10A
D  #DateIn                       8       Value
 *
C       *Entry      Plist
C                   Parm                         DateInput
 *
C                   Eval       Day = DayOfWeek(DateInput)
C                   Dsply                        Day
C                   Return
 *===========================================================
PDayOfWeek        B
DDayOfWeek        PI             10
D  DateIn                        8       Value
 *_____
 *  Local Variables
 *_____
DLillianOut       S              10I 0
DDateFmt          S              8A
DOutFmt           S              10A
DWeekDay          S              10A
 *
C                   Move       'MMDDYYYY'    DateFmt
C                   Callb(D)   'CEEDAYS'
C                   Parm                         DateIn
C                   Parm                         DateFmt
C                   Parm                         LillianOut
C                   Parm                         *Omit
C*
C                   Move       'Wwwwwwwwwwz' OutFmt
C                   Callb(D)   'CEEDATE'
C                   Parm                         LillianOut
```

Listing 1.7: ILE RPG member MOD007R
calls subprocedure DAYOFWEEK (continued).

```
     C                    Parm                      OutFmt
     C                    Parm                      WeekDay
     C                    Parm                      *Omit
     C                    Return    WeekDay
     P            E
```

HOW THE EXAMPLE WORKS

Before delving into the example implementation of an ILE subprocedure, it is important to understand a few basic ILE terms and concepts.

Programs, Modules, Procedures, and Subprocedures

If you are new to the concept of ILE development, it is vitally important to understand the basic building blocks of an ILE application. Prior to ILE RPG, application development consisted of source members that were compiled to make a program. The concept of what a program is differs in an ILE application. Modules, procedures, and subprocedures are new concepts to RPG.

The ILE Program

Before ILE, the RPG code statements residing in a source member equated to an RPG program. In ILE, there no longer is such a thing as an RPG program. Rather, a program is an executable object independent of the language or languages used to create it. An ILE program is an executable object comprised of one or more modules. When you create a program, you specify the name of the module that contains the program entry procedure. This specifies which module is to be called first when the program is activated.

The ILE Module

The RPG code statements residing in a source member equate to an ILE module. A module is not an executable object—you cannot run a module. Rather, it is an important component of an ILE program. A module can consist of one or more procedures and data specifications. A module extends its capabilities through an ability to export and/or import data or procedures for use by other ILE objects.

The ILE Procedure

A procedure is simply a collection of RPG code statements that perform a specific function. There are two types of procedures: main procedures and subprocedures. A main procedure is the section of a module that can be used as an entry procedure. It is simply the main body of the module and can include H, F, D, I, C, and O specs. A module can have no more than one main procedure.

A subprocedure is an isolated section of code within the module that is enclosed in procedure specifications. Multiple subprocedures can be coded after the main procedure section of the module. It is also possible to create a module that consists only of subprocedures and does not have a main procedure. In this situation, the subprocedures are accessible only by other ILE objects. It cannot be used as an entry procedure for a program. Modules created without a main procedure are unique. When compiled, the normal RPG cycle logic you are accustomed to is not included in the object. This is why a module without a main procedure cannot be used as a program entry procedure. A subprocedure can include only P, D, or C specifications.

Subprocedures are called either using CALLB or CALLP op codes or as expressions on op codes formatted like calls. Op codes that can be used to call subprocedures include EVAL, EVALR, IF, WHEN, DOU, DOW, and FOR.

Scoping of Fields

One of the greatest features of subprocedures is their capability to scope fields to the subprocedure level. This means that fields defined within the subprocedure are hidden to the code outside the subprocedure. The fields are not recognized and do not exist to other subprocedures or to the main procedure. The scoping is thus considered local only to the subprocedure. If you desire specific field definitions and values to become enabled to other procedures, they can be explicitly exported. This affords you a great deal of control over the operating environment.

The ILE RPG Example

The example consists of a single module, MOD007R, that contains a main procedure and a subprocedure named DAYOFWEEK. The module's main procedure accepts a date as an input parameter, then executes the DAYOFWEEK procedure using an EVAL statement. Figure 1.1 shows the module's main procedure.

```
C           *Entry      Plist
C                       Parm                        DateInput
   *
C                       Eval        Day = DayOfWeek(DateInput)
C                       Dsply                       Day
C                       Return
```

Figure 1.1: The main procedure for MOD007R calls the DAYOFWEEK procedure.

The Procedure Prototype

To call a subprocedure, the subprocedure must have a prototype that defines the call interface. This interface specifies information such as the number and type of any parameters to pass and whether the parameters are optional or required. The prototype is checked
at compile time, resolving such errors before a program executes. Procedure prototypes
are coded using a special descriptor in the D specs. The prototype for the example
subprocedure is shown in Figure 1.2. It is coded in the main procedure of module
MOD007R.

```
DDayOfWeek      PR          10A
D  #DateIn                    8    Value
```

Figure 1.2: The prototype for the DAYOFWEEK procedure.

The prototype specifies that when executed, the DAYOFWEEK procedure returns a
10-character value. It accepts an input parameter that is an eight-character field and is
passed *by value*. Passing a parameter by value means that only a copy of the field is
passed. If the field is changed inside the procedure, the changed value is not returned.
This is a very handy mechanism to ensure that the contents of a parameter field are not
inadvertently changed.

Procedure Specifications

All subprocedures, coded after the main procedure if applicable, begin and end with a
procedure specification. All code between the two specifications is the logic of the
subprocedure. The example subprocedure, DAYOFWEEK, is shown in Figure 1.3.

```
PDayOfWeek         B
DDayOfWeek         PI            10
D  DateIn                         8     Value
  *_____
  *  Local Variables
  *_____
DLillianOut        S            10I 0
DDateFmt           S             8A
DOutFmt            S            10A
DWeekDay           S            10A
  *
C                  Move          'MMDDYYYY'     DateFmt
C                  Callb(D)      'CEEDAYS'
C                  Parm                         DateIn
C                  Parm                         DateFmt
C                  Parm                         LillianOut
C                  Parm                         *Omit
C*
C                  Move          'Wwwwwwwwwwz'  OutFmt
C                  Callb(D)      'CEEDATE'
C                  Parm                         LillianOut
C                  Parm                         OutFmt
C                  Parm                         WeekDay
C                  Parm                         *Omit
C                  Return        WeekDay
P                  E
```

Figure 1.3: The subprocedure DAYOFWEEK.

All subprocedures that return a value or receive parameters must have a procedure interface definition. A procedure interface matches the procedure prototype definition. A prototype defines the interface of a procedure outside the procedure, while a procedure interface defines the same information within the procedure. The procedure interface is coded using a special descriptor, PI, in the D specs. When the module is compiled, the attributes of the external prototype are checked against those of the internal procedure interface to ensure proper parameter definitions.

The DAYOFWEEK procedure employs two system APIs to derive the day of week. For detailed information about the use of these APIs, please refer to chapter 4.

EXAMPLE

Using ILE Subprocedures from a Service Program

This example demonstrates a call to an external subprocedure in a service program to share a common function. Similar to subroutines, subprocedures are isolated segments of code, usually performing a very specific function that can be executed from multiple points in a module. The primary weakness of the internal subroutine is its inability to export its services across modules. ILE subprocedures can be exported, allowing them to be accessed outside the module in which they reside. The example takes a common generic programming task, determining the day of week for a given date, and deposits the code into a service program subprocedure where it can be executed multiple times from any ILE object.

WHAT THE EXAMPLE DOES

The example presents two ILE source members, MOD008R and MOD009R. MOD008R accesses the DAYOFWEEK subprocedure coded in module MOD009R. MOD008R accepts a date as an input parameter, then uses the exported subprocedure to determine the date's day of week. The resulting day is displayed for viewing. This example differs from the previous example because the subprocedure does not reside in the module from which it is called. The subprocedure is coded into a separate module, where it can be compiled into an ILE service program. Listing 1.8 shows the source member MOD008R. Listing 1.9 shows module MOD009R.

Listing 1.8: ILE RPG member MOD008R calls subprocedure DAYOFWEEK.

```
DDateInput        S              8A
DDay              S             10A
  *_____
  *    Procedure Prototype
  *_____
DDayOfWeek        PR            10A
D   #DateIn                      8     Value
  *
C       *Entry      Plist
C                   Parm                      DateInput
  *
C                   Eval       Day = DayOfWeek(DateInput)
C                   Dsply                     Day
C                   Return
```

Listing 1.9: ILE RPG member MOD009R contains subprocedure DAYOFWEEK.

```
HNoMain
DDayOfWeek        PR            10A
D   #DateIn                      8     Value
  *
  *==========================================================
PDayOfWeek        B                    Export
```

Listing 1.9: ILE RPG member MOD009R
contains subprocedure DAYOFWEEK (continued).

```
DDayOfWeek        PI            10
D  DateIn                        8     Value
   *_____
   *  Local Variables
   *_____
DLillianOut       S            10I 0
DDateFmt          S             8A
DOutFmt           S            10A
DWeekDay          S            10A
   *
C                   Move      'MMDDYYYY'    DateFmt
C                   Callb(D)  'CEEDAYS'
C                   Parm                    DateIn
C                   Parm                    DateFmt
C                   Parm                    LillianOut
C                   Parm                    *Omit
C*
C                   Move      'Wwwwwwwwwwz'  OutFmt
C                   Callb(D)  'CEEDATE'
C                   Parm                    LillianOut
C                   Parm                    OutFmt
C                   Parm                    WeekDay
C                   Parm                    *Omit
C                   Return    WeekDay
P                 E
```

HOW THE EXAMPLE WORKS

Before delving into the example implementation of an ILE subprocedure, it is important to understand a few basic ILE terms and concepts.

Programs, Modules, Procedures, Subprocedures, and Service Programs

If you are new to the concept of ILE development, it is vitally important to understand the basic building blocks of an ILE application. Prior to ILE RPG, application development consisted of source members that were compiled to make a program. The concept of what a program is differs in an ILE application. Modules, procedures, and subprocedures are new concepts to RPG.

The ILE Program

Before ILE, the RPG code statements residing in a source member equated to an RPG program. In ILE, there no longer is such a thing as an RPG program. Rather, a program is an executable object independent of the language or languages used to create it. An ILE program is an executable object comprised of one or more modules. When you create a program, you specify the name of the module that contains the program entry procedure. This specifies which module is to be called first when the program is activated.

The ILE Module

The RPG code statements residing in a source member equate to an ILE module. A module is not an executable object—you cannot run a module. Rather, it is an important component of an ILE program. A module can consist of one or more procedures and data specifications. A module extends its capabilities through an ability to export and/or import data or procedures for use by other ILE objects.

The ILE Procedure

A procedure is simply a collection of RPG code statements that perform a specific function. There are two types of procedures: main procedures and subprocedures. A main procedure is the section of a module that can be used as an entry procedure. It is simply the main body of the module and can include H, F, D, I, C, and O specs. A module can have no more than one main procedure.

A subprocedure is an isolated section of code within the module that is enclosed in procedure specifications. Multiple subprocedures can be coded after the main procedure section of the module. It is also possible to create a module that consists only of subprocedures and does not have a main procedure. In this situation, the subprocedures are accessible only by other ILE objects. It cannot be used as an entry procedure for a program. Modules created without a main procedure are unique. When compiled, the normal RPG cycle logic you are accustomed to is not included in the object. This is why a module without a main procedure cannot be used as a program entry procedure. A subprocedure can include only P, D, or C specifications.

Subprocedures are called either using the CALLB or CALLP op codes or on an EVAL statement formatted like a function call.

Scoping of Fields

One of the greatest features of subprocedures is their capability to scope fields to the subprocedure level. This means that fields defined within the subprocedure are hidden to the code outside the subprocedure. The fields are not recognized and do not exist to other subprocedures or to the main procedure. The scoping is thus considered local only to the subprocedure. If you desire specific field definitions and values to become enabled to other procedures, they can be explicitly exported. This affords you a great deal of control over the operating environment.

The ILE Service Program

An ILE service program is a collection of procedures that can be called from another ILE object. Conceptually, a service program is like a library of related subroutines that have been grouped together for organizational purposes. A service program cannot be called like a traditional program. Further, its procedures are available for use only by other ILE objects. Non-ILE programs cannot call a procedure in a service program.

The ILE RPG Example

The example consists of two modules, MOD008R and MOD009R. MOD008R contains a main procedure that calls a subprocedure named DAYOFWEEK. The module's main procedure accepts a date as an input parameter, then executes the DAYOFWEEK procedure using an EVAL statement. Figure 1.4 shows the module's main procedure.

```
C         *Entry      Plist
C                      Parm                      DateInput
  *
C                      Eval      Day = DayOfWeek(DateInput)
C                      Dsply                     Day
C                      Return
```

Figure 1.4: The main procedure for MOD008R calls the DAYOFWEEK procedure.

The Procedure Prototype

To call a subprocedure, the subprocedure must have a prototype that defines the call interface. This interface specifies information such as the number and type of any parameters to pass and whether the parameters are optional or required. The prototype is checked at compile time, resolving such errors before a program executes. Procedure prototypes are coded using a special descriptor in the D specs.

The prototype for the example subprocedure is shown in Figure 1.5. It is coded in the main procedure of module MOD008R.

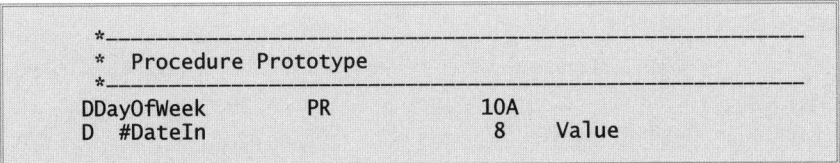

Figure 1.5: The prototype for the DAYOFWEEK procedure.

The prototype specifies that when executed, the DAYOFWEEK procedure returns a 10-character value. It accepts an input parameter that is an eight-character field and is passed *by value*. Passing a parameter by value means that only a copy of the field is passed. If the field is changed inside the procedure, the changed value is not returned. This is a very handy mechanism to ensure that the contents of a parameter field are not inadvertently changed.

The ILE Service Program Module

The example procedure, DAYOFWEEK, is coded in module MOD009R. Because the module is designed to be created as a service program, it is created without a main procedure. The module becomes more efficient because the RPG cycle logic is omitted from modules not having a main procedure. It is good practice to create modules without a main procedure if you know the module will not be created as a standalone program. The module's H spec defines it as not having a main procedure. The keyword NOMAIN provides this designation.

Because the module's procedure is to be exported to other ILE objects, the module must have a procedure prototype coded in the D specs. The prototype is identical to that used in the module importing the procedure's services. Figure 1.6 shows the procedure prototype coded within module MOD009R.

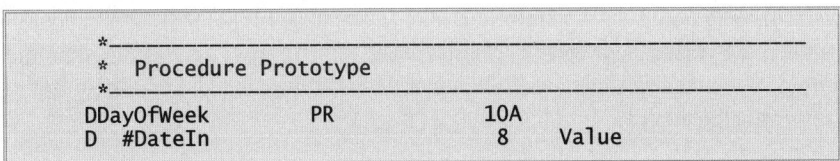

Figure 1.6: The prototype for the DAYOFWEEK procedure within module MOD009R.

Procedure Specifications

All subprocedures begin and end with a procedure specification. All code between the two specifications is the logic of the subprocedure. The example subprocedure, DAYOFWEEK, is shown in Figure 1.7.

```
PDayOfWeek        B                         Export
DDayOfWeek        PI              10
D  DateIn                          8    Value
 *_____
 *  Local Variables
 *_____
DLillianOut       S              10I 0
DDateFmt          S               8A
DOutFmt           S              10A
DWeekDay          S              10A
 *
C                 Move      'MMDDYYYY'      DateFmt
C                 Callb(D)  'CEEDAYS'
C                 Parm                      DateIn
C                 Parm                      DateFmt
C                 Parm                      LillianOut
C                 Parm                      *Omit
C*
C                 Move      'Wwwwwwwwwz'    OutFmt
C                 Callb(D)  'CEEDATE'
C                 Parm                      LillianOut
C                 Parm                      OutFmt
C                 Parm                      WeekDay
C                 Parm                      *Omit
C                 Return    WeekDay
P                 E
```

Figure 1.7: The subprocedure DAYOFWEEK.

All subprocedures that return a value or receive parameters must have a procedure interface definition. A procedure interface matches the procedure prototype definition. A prototype defines the interface of a procedure outside the procedure, while a procedure interface defines the same information within the procedure. The procedure interface is coded using a special descriptor, PI, in the D specs. When the module is compiled, the attributes of the external prototype are checked against those of the internal procedure interface to ensure proper parameter definitions. The EXPORT keyword specified on the beginning procedure specification denotes that the procedure is to be exported for use by objects outside the module.

The DAYOFWEEK procedure employs two system APIs to derive the day of week. For detailed information about the use of these APIs, please refer to chapter 4.

Creating the ILE Objects

The modules MOD008R and MOD009R are both created using the CRTRPGMOD command. To create a service program from module MOD009R, the Create Service Program (CRTSRVPGM) is used, as follows:

```
CRTSRVPGM SRVPGM(DATESERV) MODULE(MOD009R) EXPORT(*ALL)
```

After the service program is created, the program object for module MOD008R is created. To use the DAYOFWEEK procedure from the DATESERV service program, the program must bind to the service program as follows:

```
CRTPGM PGM(MOD008R) BNDSRVPGM(*LIBL/DATESERV) ACTGRP(*CALLER)
```

2

BUILT-IN FUNCTIONS

Before the introduction of ILE RPG, performing a function in an RPG program meant having to rely on the rigid format of RPG op codes. With the advent of the free-format extended factor 2 capabilities of ILE RPG, sometimes called RPG IV, the language gained the structural flexibility to support built-in functions. Built-in functions perform specific operations in a manner similar to op codes but with the flexibility of commands. Many accept parameters, called arguments, that can be simple values or complex expressions. Many shops have justified the advancement to RPG IV from RPG III simply because of the capability to use built-in functions.

With each new release of OS/400, IBM has aggressively added new built-in functions to RPG. The prevailing trend in RPG enhancements is to replace the fixed-format-dependent features of RPG such as indicator use and op code functions with more flexible built-in functions. This infuses RPG with flexibility and robust features enjoyed by more modern development languages. This chapter presents examples using most of the built-in functions available in RPG. The following is a list of the built-in function presented in this chapter:

- %ABS - Absolute Value
- %ADDR - Get Address of Variable
- %CHAR - Convert to Character Data
- %DEC - Convert to Packed Decimal Format
- %DECH - Convert to Packed Decimal Format with Half Adjust
- %DECPOS - Get Number of Decimal Positions
- %DIV - Return Integer Portion of Quotient
- %EDITC - Edit Value Using Edit Code
- %EDITFLT - Convert to Float External Representation
- %EDITW - Edit Value Using an Edit Word
- %ELEM - Get Number of Elements
- %EOF - Return End or Beginning of File Condition
- %EQUAL - Return Exact Match Condition
- %ERROR - Return Error Condition
- %FLOAT - Convert to Floating Format
- %FOUND - Return Found Condition
- %INT - Convert to Integer Format
- %INTH – Convert to Integer Format with Half Adjust
- %LEN - Get or Set Length
- %NULLIND - Get or Set Null Indicator
- %OPEN - Return File Open Condition
- %PADDR - Get Procedure Address
- %PARMS - Return Number of Parameters
- %REM - Return Integer Remainder
- %REPLACE - Replace Character String
- %SCAN - Scan for Character String
- %SIZE - Get Size in Bytes
- %STATUS - Return File or Program Status
- %SUBST - Get Substring
- %TRIM - Trim Blanks at Edges
- %TRIML - Trim Leading Blanks
- %TRIMR - Trim Trailing Blanks
- %UNS - Convert to Unsigned Format
- %UNSH - Convert to Unsigned Format with Half Adjust
- %XFOOT - Sum Array Expression Elements

EXAMPLE

Using the %ABS Function

This example employs the Absolute Value of Expression (%ABS) built-in function to eliminate the negative sign of a number, making it a positive integer.

WHAT THE EXAMPLE DOES

The example source member BIF001R performs a subtraction that results in a negative difference. If the difference is negative, the %ABS function is used to return the absolute value of the number. Listing 2.1 shows the source member.

Listing 2.1: ILE RPG member BIF001R uses the %ABS function.

```
DCreditLimit    S              7  2 Inz(10000)
DCreditAmt      S              7  2 Inz(11237.52)
DDiff           S              7S 2
 *
C                     Eval      Diff = CreditLimit - CreditAmt
 *
 *_____
 *  If difference is negative customer is over limit.
 *  Remove negative sign and perform an over limit process.
 *_____
C                     If        Diff < 0
C                     Eval      Diff = %Abs(Diff)
C                     Endif
 *
```

HOW THE EXAMPLE WORKS

The %ABS function accepts one argument, a numeric expression, and returns the absolute value of the argument. If the expression is negative, the function returns the value as positive. If it is positive, the value is returned unchanged.

EXAMPLE

Using the %ADDR Function

This example employs the Get Address of Variable (%ADDR) built-in function in a number of ways to demonstrate its capabilities.

WHAT THE EXAMPLE DOES

The example source member BIF002R performs three pointer operations to demonstrate the use of the %ADDR function. Listing 2.2 shows the source member.

Listing 2.2: ILE RPG member BIF002R uses the %ADDR function.

```
*
DCharacter            S          1    Dim(3)  Based(Ptr)
*
DPtr            S                *
*
DField1         S                3    Inz('123')
D*
DName           S                26   Inz('ABCDEFGHIJKLMNOPQRSTUVWXYZ')
*
*_____
* After pointer is set, array Character contains '123'
* Character(2) is '2'.
*_____
C                     Eval      Ptr = %Addr(Field1)
C                     Dsply                 Character(2)
*
*_____
* After value of Field1 is changed array Character contains '999'.
* The array is linked to the field because they share the same
* address.  Character(2) is now '9'.
*_____
C                     Eval      Field1 = '999'
C                     Dsply                 Character(2)
*
*_____
* After pointer is set, array Character contains 'ABC' because
* pointer is set to the beginning of the field.
* Character(2) is now 'B'.
*_____
C                     Eval      Ptr = %Addr(Name)
C                     Dsply                 Character(2)
*
*_____
```

Listing 2.2: ILE RPG member
BIF002R uses the %ADDR function (continued).

```
*   After pointer is set, array Character contains 'MNO' because
*   pointer is set to the beginning of the field plus 12.
*   Character(2) is now 'N'.
*_____
C                      Eval      Ptr = %Addr(Name) + 12
C                      Dsply                     Character(2)
 *
C                      Return
```

HOW THE EXAMPLE WORKS

If you have not used pointers in an RPG program before, they are simply a way to address a specific storage location in memory. A pointer is just another data type—like a character, packed numeric, or date field. Instead of holding text or a number, pointer fields hold an address location. A memory address is loaded into a pointer variable using the %ADDR function.

Using Pointers

Pointers are commonly used with data structures to parse the data addressed by the pointer location into individual subfields. When coded on a data structure or standalone field definition, the RPG BASED keyword specifies that the data structure or standalone field is to be loaded with the data residing in the address provided by a pointer. Setting or changing the value of the pointer causes the contents of the data structure or standalone field to automatically change. Further, if you use a pointer to assign the same memory location to more than one field name, the field values remain synchronized.

The %ADDR Function

The %ADDR function accepts one argument, a field name, array, table, data structure, or multiple occurrence data structure. It returns the memory location of the argument.

The Example

The example module begins with the definition of fields used. The definitions include two character fields named FIELD1 and NAME, a pointer variable named PTR, and a standalone array called *character*. The array has three elements. The standalone array definition is based on the pointer PTR using the BASED keyword. Figure 2.1 shows the definitions.

```
DCharacter              S           1     Dim(3)  Based(Ptr)
 *
DPtr              S                 *
 *
DField1           S                 3     Inz('123')
D*
DName             S                26     Inz('ABCDEFGHIJKLMNOPQRSTUVWXYZ')
```

Figure 2.1: The definitions for the example module.

The example logic begins by employing the %ADDR function to set the pointer to the address of the field FIELD1. Because the array is based on the pointer, it is automatically loaded with the data of FIELD1. Data is not actually moved; rather, the two fields are simply addressing the same location in memory. The DSPLY op code displays the contents of the second array element to prove the results, as shown in Figure 2.2.

```
C                     Eval       Ptr = %Addr(Field1)
C                     Dsply                 Character(2)
```

Figure 2.2: Addressing the pointer automatically loads the data structure.

When the logic changes the value of FIELD1 to '999', the array CHARACTER is also changed, as shown in Figure 2.3.

```
 *------------------------------------------------------------------
 * After value of Field1 is changed array Character contains '999'.
 * The array is linked to the field because they share the same
 * address.  Character(2) is now '9'.
 *------------------------------------------------------------------
C                     Eval       Field1 = '999'
C                     Dsply                 Character(2)
```

Figure 2.3: Changing the addressed field also changes the data structure.

The module concludes by resetting the pointer to the address of the NAME field. Adding 12 to the pointer changes the address to the 12th byte of the field. As the DSPLY shows in Figure 2.4, the value of the array CHARACTER now contains the 12th to 14th bytes of the CHARACTER field.

```
*--------------------------------------------------
* After pointer is set, array Character contains 'MNO' because
* pointer is set to the beginning of the field plus 12.
* Character(2) is now 'N'.
*--------------------------------------------------
C                    Eval      Ptr = %Addr(Name) + 12
C                    Dsply                  Character(2)
*
```

Figure 2.4: The pointer is reset to the 12th byte of the NAME field.

EXAMPLE

Using the %CHAR Function

This example employs the Convert to Character Data (%CHAR) built-in function to convert noncharacter data to character data.

WHAT THE EXAMPLE DOES

The example source member BIF003R converts a date field, a time field, and a packed numeric field to character fields for concatenation with message text. After each field is converted, it is concatenated with message text and displayed. The example also uses a particularly handy technique of initializing the date and time fields with the special value *SYS. This loads the fields with the current system date and time. The special value *JOB is also available for easy access to the job date and time. Listing 2.3 shows the source member.

Listing 2.3: ILE RPG member BIF003R uses the %CHAR function.

```
*
D@MsgCon1       C                     'Today is '
D@MsgCon2       C                     'The time is '
D@MsgCon3       C                     'The Dollar Amount is '
DMsg            S             50A
*
DDollarAmt      S              7  2 Inz(11237.52)
*
DToday          S              D   Inz(*Sys) DatFmt(*USA)
DNow            S              T   Inz(*Sys)
*
*--------------------------------------------------
* Date field Today is converted to character and
```

Listing 2.3: ILE RPG member
BIF003R uses the %CHAR function (continued).

```
*    concatenated with message.
*_____
C                        Eval       Msg = @MsgCon1 + %Char(Today)
C                        Dsply                 Msg
*
*_____
*   Time field Now is converted to character and
*   concatenated with message.
*_____
C                        Eval       Msg = @MsgCon2 + %Char(Now)
C                        Dsply                 Msg
*
*_____
*   Numeric field DollarAmt is converted to character and
*   concatenated with message.
*_____
C                        Eval       Msg = @MsgCon3 + %Char(DollarAmt)
C                        Dsply                 Msg
*
C                        Return
```

HOW THE EXAMPLE WORKS

The %CHAR function accepts one argument, a numeric, graphic, UCS-2, date, time, or timestamp expression, and returns the expression in character format. Date, time, and timestamp data are returned with their appropriate separators.

EXAMPLE

Using the %DEC and %DECH Functions

This example employs the Convert to Packed Decimal Format (%DEC) and Convert to Packed Decimal Format with Half Adjust (%DECH) built-in functions to set the precision and decimal places of numeric fields used in division calculations.

WHAT THE EXAMPLE DOES

The example source member BIF004R demonstrates the effect of the %DEC and %DECH functions when used to set the precision and decimal places of four numeric fields used in division calculations. As demonstrated and displayed, the functions impact the results of the calculations. Listing 2.4 shows the source member.

**Listing 2.4: ILE RPG member
BIF004R uses the %DEC and %DECH functions.**

```
*
DNumber1         S              11  5 Inz(257937.52687)
DNumber2         S               7  5 Inz(41.12409)
*
DResult          S              15  9
DResult2         S                    Like(Result)
DResult3         S                    Like(Result)
*
*_____
*  Division:  Result = 6272.175916111
*_____
C                    Eval      Result = Number1 / Number2
C                    Dsply                 Result
*
*_____
*          Result2 = 6272.175000000
*_____
C                    Eval      Result2 = %Dec(Result:15:3)
C                    Dsply                 Result2
*
*_____
*          Result2 = 6272.176000000
*_____
C                    Eval      Result2 = %Dech(Result:15:3)
C                    Dsply                 Result2
*
*_____
*          Result3 = 6272.000000000
*_____
C                    Eval      Result3 = %Dec(Result:6:0)
C                    Dsply                 Result3
*
*_____
*          Result3 = 6272.000000000
*_____
C                    Eval      Result3 = %Dech(Result:6:0)
C                    Dsply                 Result3
*
C                    Return
```

HOW THE EXAMPLE WORKS

The %DEC and %DECH functions accept up to three arguments: a numeric expression and, optionally, a precision and number of decimal positions. The numeric expression is the value to be converted to packed decimal. The precision argument allows you to set the length of the value returned. The decimal places argument determines the number of decimal places in the return value.

The %DEC and %DECH functions work identically except for how they handle the digits from the numeric expression that go beyond the returned precision. The %DEC function truncates any extra digits, while %DECH half adjusts.

EXAMPLE

Using the %DECPOS Function

This example employs the Get Number of Decimal Positions (%DECPOS) built-in function to return the number of decimal positions in numeric expressions.

WHAT THE EXAMPLE DOES

The example source member BIF005R demonstrates the use of the %DECPOS function to determine the number of decimal places in a numeric expression. Listing 2.5 shows the source member.

Listing 2.5: ILE RPG member BIF005R uses the %DECPOS function.

```
 *
DNumber1        S             11  5 Inz(257937.52687)
DNumber2        S              7  0 Inz(12409)
DNumber3        S             15  9
 *
DResult         S              5I 0
DEqual          S              5A   Inz('Equal')
DNotEqual       S              9A   Inz('Not Equal')
 *_____
 *   Result = 5
 *_____
C                   Eval      Result = %Decpos(Number1)
C                   Dsply                 Result
 *
 *_____
 *   Result = 5
 *_____
C                   Eval      Result = %Decpos(Number1 * Number2)
C                   Dsply                 Result
 *
```

Listing 2.5: ILE RPG member BIF005R
uses the %DECPOS function (continued).

```
 *_____
 *               Not Equal
 *_____
 C                      If          %Decpos(Number3) = %Decpos(Number2)
 C                      Dsply                    Equal
 C                      Else
 C                      Dsply                   NotEqual
 C                      Endif
   *
 C                      Return
```

HOW THE EXAMPLE WORKS

The %DECPOS function accepts one argument, a numeric expression. It returns a constant value that reflects the number of defined decimal positions in the expression.

It must be understood that the number returned is the number of decimal positions defined, rather than a reflection of the value of the expression. For example, if a numeric field is defined as a five-digit field with two decimal positions and contains a value of 10, the %DECPOS function returns a value of two.

EXAMPLE

Using the %DIV and %REM Functions

This example employs the Return Integer Portion of Quotient (%DIV) and Return Integer Remainder (%REM) built-in functions to perform a division calculation on numeric operands and return the whole integer quotient and the remaining portions of the calculation.

WHAT THE EXAMPLE DOES

The example source member BIF006R demonstrates use of the %DIV and %REM functions to isolate and return the whole integer and the remaining portions of division calculations. Listing 2.6 shows the source member.

Listing 2.6: ILE RPG member BIF006R uses the %DIV and %REM functions.

```
 *
DNumber1        S            11  0 Inz(257937)
DNumber2        S             7  0 Inz(12409)
DNumber3        S             5I 0 Inz(5)
DNumber4        S             5I 0 Inz(2)
 *
DResult1        S             5I 0
DResult2        S                  Like(Result1)
 *_____
 *  Result1 = 20   Result2 = 9757
 *_____
C                   Eval      Result1 = %Div(Number1:Number2)
C                   Eval      Result2 = %Rem(Number1:Number2)
C                   Dsply                 Result1
C                   Dsply                 Result2
 *
 *_____
 *  Result1 = 2   Result2 = 1
 *_____
C                   Eval      Result1 = %Div(Number3:Number4)
C                   Eval      Result2 = %Rem(Number3:Number4)
C                   Dsply                 Result1
C                   Dsply                 Result2
 *
C                   Return
```

HOW THE EXAMPLE WORKS

The %DIV Function. The %DIV function accepts two arguments: a numeric dividend and a numeric divisor. Both operands must be numeric fields with zero decimal positions. It divides the first argument by the second and returns the whole integer result of the calculation.

The %REM Function. Like the %DIV function, the %REM function accepts two arguments: a numeric dividend and a numeric divisor. Both operands must be numeric fields with zero decimal positions. It divides the first argument by the second and returns the remaining portion of the calculation as a whole integer.

EXAMPLE

Using the %EDITC, %EDITFLT, and %EDITW Functions

This example employs the three built-in edit functions Edit Value Using Edit Code (%EDITC), Convert to Float External Representation (%EDITFLT), and Edit Value Using an Edit Word (%EDITW) to convert noncharacter data to character data with edited values.

WHAT THE EXAMPLE DOES

The example source member BIF007R demonstrates use of the %EDITC, %EDITFLT, and %EDITW functions to convert numeric and date fields to edited character values. Listing 2.7 shows the source member.

Listing 2.7: ILE RPG member BIF007R uses the %EDITC, %EDITFLT, and %EDITW functions.

```
     *
     D@Con1          C                        'The Social Security Number is '
     D@Con2          C                        'The Phone Number is '
     D@Con3          C                        'The Dollar Amount is '
     D@Con4          C                        'The Number is '
     D@Con5          C                        'The Float is '
     D@Edit1         C                        '0  -  -  '
     D@Edit2         C                        '$  ,  *&Dollars&  &Cents'
     D@Edit3         C                        '0(  )&  -  '
     DMsg            S              50A
     *
     DDollarAmt      S               7  2 Inz(11237.52)
     DSSN            S               9  0 Inz(123456789)
     DPhone          S              10  0 Inz(1125551212)
     DNum1           S               9  2 Inz(1237.00)
     DNum2           S               9  2 Inz(-41004.21)
     DNum3           S               8F   Inz(1237.5567)
     *
     *_____
     *   Displays: The Social Security Number is 123-45-6789
     *_____
     C                   Eval      Msg = @Con1 + %Editw(SSN:@Edit1)
     C                   Dsply               Msg
     *
     *_____
     *   Displays: The Dollar Amount is $11,237 Dollars 52 Cents
     *_____
     C                   Eval      Msg = @Con3 + %Editw(DollarAmt:@Edit2)
     C                   Dsply               Msg
     *
     *_____
     *   Displays: The Phone Number is  (112) 555-1212
     *_____
     C                   Eval      Msg = @Con2 + %Editw(Phone:@Edit3)
     C                   Dsply               Msg
     *
     *_____
     *   Displays: The Number is    1,237.00
     *_____
     C                   Eval      Msg = @Con4 + %Editc(Num1:'1')
```

Listing 2.7: ILE RPG member BIF007R uses the %EDITC, %EDITFLT, and %EDITW functions (continued).

```
C                       Dsply               Msg
 *
 *_____
 *  Displays: The Number is    $1,237.00
 *_____
C                       Eval      Msg = @Con4 + %Editc(Num1:'1':*CURSYM)
C                       Dsply               Msg
 *
 *_____
 *  Displays: The Number is ***41,004.21CR
 *_____
C                       Eval      Msg = @Con4 + %Editc(Num2:'B':*ASTFILL)
C                       Dsply               Msg
 *
 *_____
 *  Displays: The Float is +1.237556700000000E+003
 *_____
C                       Eval      Msg = @Con5 + %Editflt(Num3)
C                       Dsply               Msg
 *
C                       Return
```

HOW THE EXAMPLE WORKS

The %EDITC Function. The %EDITC function accepts three arguments: a required numeric expression, a required edit code, and an optional filler value. The numeric value is edited using the supplied edit code the way a numeric field is edited for output specifications when creating spool. The filler indicator can be *ASTFILL to replace all leading zeros with all asterisks; *CURSYM to precede the number with a floating currency symbol; or a literal currency symbol value to use as a preceding float character.

The supported edit codes include 'A'-'D', 'J'-'Q', 'X'-'Z' and '1'-'9'. They must be supplied using either a literal value or a constant name.

The %EDITFLT Function. The %EDITFLT function accepts one argument: a required numeric expression. The numeric value is returned as a character representation of a floating-point number. As you may recall, a floating-point field is comprised of two parts: a mantissa and an exponent.

The %EDITW Function. The %EDITW function accepts two arguments: a required numeric expression and a required edit word picture. The numeric value is edited using the supplied edit word the way a numeric field is edited for output specifications when creating spool. The edit word must be defined as a character constant.

EXAMPLE

Using the %ELEM Function

This example employs the Get Number of Elements (%ELEM) built-in function to return the number of elements in a table, array, or multiple occurrence data structure.

WHAT THE EXAMPLE DOES

The example source member BIF008R demonstrates use of the %ELEM function to determine the number of defined elements in an array, table, and multiple occurrence data structure. Listing 2.8 shows the source member.

Listing 2.8: ILE RPG member BIF008R uses the %ELEM function.

```
 *
DTable1         S              1    Dim(24) CTData
 *
DArray1         S              1    Dim(10)
DArray2         S              1    Dim(%Elem(Array1))
 *
DMultDS         DS                  Occurs(%Elem(Table1))
D  Field1                      1
 *
DResult         S              3 0
 *
 *_____
 *   Result = 10
 *_____
C                   Eval      Result = %Elem(Array2)
C                   Dsply                Result
 *
 *_____
 *   Result = 24
 *_____
C                   Eval      Result = %Elem(Table1)
C                   Dsply                Result
 *
 *_____
 *   Result = 24
 *_____
C                   Eval      Result = %Elem(MultDS)
```

Listing 2.8: ILE RPG member
BIF008R uses the %ELEM function (continued).

```
     C                   Dsply                   Result
       *
     C                   Return
**CTData Table1
ABCDEFGHIJKLMNOPQRSTUVWXYZ
```

HOW THE EXAMPLE WORKS

The %ELEM function accepts one argument: the name of an array, table, or multiple occurrence data structure. The function returns the number of defined elements in the
named argument. The result can be used as an initialization to the definition of a second
array, table, or data structure.

EXAMPLE

Using the %EOF Function

This example employs the Return End or Beginning of File Condition (%EOF) built-in
function to determine when the end-of-file condition occurs while processing file records.

WHAT THE EXAMPLE DOES

The example source member BIF009R demonstrates use of the %EOF function to determine
when an end-of-file condition occurs. A Do-While construct reads a customer file until all
records have been processed. This technique is a powerful and flexible alternative to using a
resulting indicator on the READ op code. Listing 2.9 shows the source member.

Listing 2.9: ILE RPG member BIF009R uses the %EOF function.

```
     *
     FCustomer  IF   E           Disk
       *
       *_____
       *  Read all customer file records until EOF
       *_____
     C                   Read      Custr
       *
     C                   DoW       Not %EOF(Customer)
     C                   Dsply                   Customer#
```
⟶

Listing 2.9: ILE RPG member BIF009R uses the %EOF function (continued).

```
C                    Read      Custr
C                    Enddo
 *
C                    Return
```

HOW THE EXAMPLE WORKS

The %EOF function optionally accepts one argument: the name of a file. The function re-turns a '1' when the last read operation resulted in an end-of-file or beginning-of-file con-dition. It returns a '0' if neither condition occurred.

The %EOF function returns the value set by previous READ, READC, READE, READP, and READPE file operations, and by the WRITE operation used on subfiles.

If a file name is not specified, the return value reflects the status of the most recently per-formed file operation.

EXAMPLE

Using the %EQUAL Function

This example employs the Return Exact Match Condition (%EQUAL) built-in function to determine when an exact match condition occurs on specific file and table or array operations.

WHAT THE EXAMPLE DOES

The example source member BIF010R demonstrates use of the %EQUAL function to deter-mine when an exact match on a Set Lower Limit (SETLL) or Lookup occurs. This tech-nique is a powerful and flexible alternative to testing the value of resulting indicators. Listing 2.10 shows the source member.

Listing 2.10: ILE RPG member BIF010R uses the %EQUAL function.

```
 *
FCustomer  IF   E           K Disk
 *
DTable1         S             1    Dim(24) CTData
```

Listing 2.10: ILE RPG member
BIF010R uses the %EQUAL function (continued).

```
DCust#             S           10    Inz('0000000001')
D@Found            C                 'Found it'
D@NotFound         C                 'Not There'
 *
 *_____
 *  If you get an exact match by key, %Equal is True
 *_____
C      Cust#       Setll     Custr
 *
C                  If        %Equal
C      @Found      Dsply
C                  Else
C      @NotFound   Dsply
C                  Endif
 *
C      'A'         Lookup    Table1                            99
 *
C                  If        %Equal
C      @Found      Dsply
C                  Else
C      @NotFound   Dsply
C                  Endif
 *
C                  Return
**CTData Table1
ABCDEFGHIJKLMNOPQRSTUVWXYZ
```

Note: The last two lines of code are intentionally shifted five spaces to the right of where they begin.

HOW THE EXAMPLE WORKS

The %EQUAL function optionally accepts one argument: the name of a file. The function returns a '1' when the last SETLL file operation or table or array lookup operation resulted in an exact match. It returns a '0' if an exact match was not detected.

If a file name is not specified, the return value reflects the status of the most recently performed file operation.

EXAMPLE

Using the %ERROR and %STATUS Functions

This example employs the Return Error Condition (%ERROR) and Return File or Program Status (%STATUS) built-in functions to detect a file error, receive the error code, and display an appropriate error message.

WHAT THE EXAMPLE DOES

The example source member BIF011R demonstrates use of the %ERROR function to detect and trap an error condition and the%STATUS function to return the associated error code. Listing 2.11 shows the source member.

Listing 2.11: ILE RPG member BIF011R uses the %ERROR and %STATUS functions.

```
      *
     FCustomer   UF A E          K Disk
      *
     DCust#           S              10     Inz('0000000001')
     DErrorCode       S               5 0
     DErrorMsg        S              50
     D@DupKey         C                     'Duplicate Key Error'
     D@Unknown        C                     'Unspecified File Error'
      *
      *_____
      *  If Write gets an error, send appropriate message
      *_____
     C                   Write(E)  Custr
      *
     C                   If        %Error
     C                   Eval      ErrorCode = %Status
      *
     C                   Select
     C                   When      ErrorCode = 1021
     C                   Eval      ErrorMsg = @DupKey
      *
     C                   Other
     C                   Eval      ErrorMsg = @Unknown
      *
     C                   Endsl
      *
     C                   Dsply               ErrorMsg
     C                   Endif
      *
     C                   Return
```

HOW THE EXAMPLE WORKS

The %ERROR Function. The %ERROR function returns a '1' when the last qualifying operation resulted in an error condition. The %ERROR function may be used to detect errors occurring on operations that have been coded with the error code extender (E). This example uses the extender to detect errors on the WRITE operation. A current list of op codes that support the error code extender appears in Table 2.1.

The error code extender is a replacement for the traditional use of error resulting indicators. When an extender is used, the %ERROR function evaluates as True. It is good practice to immediately follow an op code using the error extender with an evaluation containing the %ERROR function. The %ERROR condition is reset before each operation having an error code extender.

The %STATUS Function. The %STATUS function returns the most recent file or program status. The status is usually changed only when an error occurs. The function accepts one optional argument: a file name whose status is to be returned. If not specified, the file or program status most recently changed is returned.

Table 2.1: RPG Op Codes Supporting the Error Code Extender (E).		
ACQ	ADDDUR	ALLOC
CALL	CALLB	CALLP
CHAIN	CHECK	CHECKR
CLOSE	COMMIT	DEALLOC
DELETE	DSPLY	EXFMT
EXTRCT	FEOD	IN
NEXT	OCCUR	OPEN
OUT	POST	READ
READC	READE	READP
READPE	REALLOC	REL
RESET	ROLBK	SCAN
SETGT	SETLL	SUBDUR
SUBST	TEST	UNLOCK
UPDATE	WRITE	XLATE

The %STATUS is commonly used in concert with the %ERROR function, but can also be used with resulting error indicators or within a program status subroutine. The value of the code returned is reset immediately preceding operations containing an error code extender.

Evaluating the returned status code allows your program to determine the appropriate action. Complete listings of all possible file and program status codes can be found in the *ILE RPG Reference Manual*.

The Example

The example module employs the error code extender on a WRITE operation to detect file errors. Because the extender is coded, the %ERROR function evaluates as True when an error occurs. Because the example customer file is defined with a unique key constraint, a record written with a duplicate key value returns 01021 to the %STATUS function. When this condition is detected, the example displays an appropriate message to the user. This logic is shown in Figure 2.5.

```
     *_____
     *  If Write gets an error, send appropriate message
     *_____
     C                    Write(E)  Custr
     *
     C                    If        %Error
     C                    Eval      ErrorCode = %Status
     *
     C                    Select
     C                    When      ErrorCode = 1021
     C                    Eval      ErrorMsg = @DupKey
     *
     C                    Other
     C                    Eval      ErrorMsg = @Unknown
     *
     C                    Endsl
     *
     C                    Dsply                ErrorMsg
     C                    Endif
```

Figure 2.5: The %ERROR and %STATUS functions work together to detect error conditions.

EXAMPLE

Using the %FOUND Function

This example employs the Return Found Condition (%FOUND) built-in function to determine when a supported operation has successfully located a record, string, or element.

WHAT THE EXAMPLE DOES

The example source member BIF012R demonstrates use of the %FOUND function to detect the success of specific file, string, and search operations. Listing 2.12 shows the source member.

Listing 2.12: ILE RPG member BIF012R uses the %FOUND function.

```
     *
    FCustomer   IF   E        K Disk
     *
    DTable1         S           1    Dim(24) CTData
     *
    DCust#          S          10    Inz('0000000001')
    D@Found         C                'Found it'
    D@NotFound      C                'Not There'
     *
     *_____
     * If you get a match by key, %Found is True
     *_____
    C      Cust#       Setll     Custr
     *
    C                  If        %Found
    C      @Found      Dsply
    C                  Else
    C      @NotFound   Dsply
    C                  Endif
     *_____
     * If you get a match by key, %Found is True
     *_____
    C      Cust#       Chain     Customer
     *
    C                  If        %Found(Customer)
    C      @Found      Dsply
    C                  Else
    C      @NotFound   Dsply
    C                  Endif
     *
     *_____
     * If lookup value is found, %Found is True.
     *_____
    C      'a'         Lookup    Table1                       99    *
    C                  If        %Found
    C      @Found      Dsply
    C                  Else
    C      @NotFound   Dsply
    C                  Endif
     *
    C                  Return
    **CTData Table1
    ABCDEFGHIJKLMNOPQRSTUVWXYZ
```

HOW THE EXAMPLE WORKS

The %FOUND function returns a '1' when the last qualifying operation resulted in a successful match. It optionally accepts one argument: the name of a file. The function returns a '1' when the last supported operation successfully locates an item. It returns a '0' if a match was not detected.

If a file name is not specified, the return value reflects the status of the most recently performed supported operation.

This example uses the extender to detect successful record location on a SETLL operation, successful record retrieval on a CHAIN, and successful lookup on a table. A current list of op codes that set the value returned by the %FOUND function appears in Table 2.2.

Table 2.2: RPG Op Codes Supporting the %FOUND Function.			
CHAIN	DELETE	SETGT	SETLL
CHECK	CHECKR	SCAN	LOOKUP

The Example

The example module employs the %FOUND function to determine the success of file and table operations. This technique is an excellent alternative to testing the value of resulting indicators.

EXAMPLE

Using the %INT and %INTH Functions

This example employs the Convert to Integer Format (%INT) and Convert to Integer Format with Half Adjust (%INTH) built-in functions to convert numeric fields to integer values used in division calculations, either truncating or half-adjusting the decimal positions.

WHAT THE EXAMPLE DOES

The example source member BIF013R demonstrates the effect of the %INT and %INTH functions when used to convert packed decimal numbers used in division calculations to integers. As demonstrated and displayed, the functions impact the results of the calculations. Listing 2.13 shows the source member.

Listing 2.13: ILE RPG member BIF013R uses the %INT and %INTH functions.

```
 *
DNumber1        S              11  5 Inz(257937.52687)
DNumber2        S               7  5 Inz(41.12409)
 *
DResult         S              15  9
 *
 *_____
 *  Division:  Result = 6272.175916111
 *_____
```

47

Listing 2.13: ILE RPG member BIF013R
uses the %INT and %INTH functions (continued).

```
C                    Eval      Result = Number1 / Number2
C                    Dsply               Result
 *
 *_____
 *         Result = 6272.000000000
 *_____
C                    Eval      Result = %Int(Number1 / Number2)
C                    Dsply               Result
 *
 *_____
 *         Result = 6272.187421046
 *_____
C                    Eval      Result = %Inth(Number1) / Number2
C                    Dsply               Result
 *
C                    Return
```

HOW THE EXAMPLE WORKS

The %INT and %INTH functions accept one argument: a numeric expression to be converted to integer format. They work identically except for how they handle the decimal positions being eliminated. The %INT function truncates any decimal positions, while %INTH half adjusts.

EXAMPLE

Using the %LEN and %SIZE Functions

This example demonstrates and contrasts the functionality performed by the Get or Set Length (%LEN) and Get Size in Bytes (%SIZE) built-in functions.

WHAT THE EXAMPLE DOES

The example source member BIF014R demonstrates use of the %LEN function to both return and set field lengths and the %SIZE function to return the number of bytes occupied by a field. Listing 2.14 shows the source member.

Listing 2.14: ILE RPG member BIF014R uses the %LEN and %SIZE functions.

```
     *
DFirstName1       S              15A    Inz('D Anna')
DLastName1        S              15A    Inz('McCall')
DNumber1          S              10I 0
DFirstName2       S              15A    Varying Inz('D Anna')
DLastName2        S              15A    Varying Inz('McCall')
     *
DArray1           S              10A    Dim(10)
     *
DResult           S              15  9
     *
     *_____
     *  Result = 15 because trailing blanks are included in Len
     *_____
C                     Eval      Result = %Len(FirstName1)
C                     Dsply               Result
     *
     *_____
     *  Result = 15 because the field occupies 15 bytes
     *_____
C                     Eval      Result = %Size(FirstName1)
C                     Dsply               Result
     *
     *_____
     *  Result = 10 because field is a 10 digit integer
     *_____
C                     Eval      Result = %Len(Number1)
C                     Dsply               Result
     *
     *_____
     *  Result = 4 because a 10 digit integer occupies 4 bytes
     *_____
C                     Eval      Result = %Size(Number1)
C                     Dsply               Result
     *
     *_____
     *  Result = 6 because the contents of variable length field
     *          is only 6 bytes.
     *_____
C                     Eval      Result = %Len(FirstName2)
C                     Dsply               Result
     *
     *_____
     *  Result = 17 because the variable length field occupies 17
     *  bytes.  Variable len fields take up 2 extra bytes that
     *  contain the length of the contents.
     *_____
C                     Eval      Result = %Size(FirstName2)
```

Listing 2.14: ILE RPG member BIF014R
uses the %LEN and %SIZE functions (continued).

```
C                       Dsply                   Result
 *
 *_____
 *   Result = 13 because the resulting concatenated value
 *            has a variable length.
 *_____
C                       Eval      Result = %Len(%Trim(FirstName1) +
C                                           ' ' +
C                                           %Trim(LastName1))
C                       Dsply                   Result
 *
 *_____
 *   Result = 10 because each element of array occupies 10 bytes
 *_____
C                       Eval      Result = %Size(Array1)
C                       Dsply                   Result
 *
 *_____
 *   Result = 100 because entire array occupies 100 bytes
 *_____
C                       Eval      Result = %Size(Array1:*All)
C                       Dsply                   Result
 *
 *_____
 *   LastName2 = Mc Because variable field length reduced to
 *               a length of 2.
 *_____
C                       Eval      %Len(LastName2) = 2
C                       Dsply                   LastName2
 *
C                       Return
```

HOW THE EXAMPLE WORKS

The %LEN function accepts one argument: a variable expression whose length is to be returned. It is capable of either returning the length of a variable expression or setting the length of a variable length field. For fixed-length fields, the returned value is the defined size of the field, not the length of the field's contents. For variable-length fields, it returns the length of the contents of the field.

The %SIZE function accepts one argument: a variable whose size is to be returned. The function returns the size that the field or constant occupies in bytes. For elemental structures such as arrays, tables, and multiple occurrence data structures, the function can return the size of either a single element or the entire structure.

Unlike the %LEN function, the %SIZE function returns the full size of variable-length fields. The returned size is always the defined maximum size of the field plus two bytes used to store the length of the field contents.

The Example

Because the %LEN and %SIZE functions are so similar, it is important to understand the key differences. The example member contrasts the differing results of the two functions.

The example module begins with the definition of fields used. The definitions include fixed- and variable-length character fields, a packed decimal field, a binary integer field, and a character array. Figure 2.6 shows the definitions.

```
     *
     DFirstName1        S              15A    Inz('D Anna')
     DLastName1         S              15A    Inz('McCall')
     DNumber1           S              10I 0
     DFirstName2        S              15A    Varying Inz('D Anna')
     DLastName2         S              15A    Varying Inz('McCall')
     *
     DArray1            S              10A    Dim(10)
     *
     DResult            S              15  9
```

Figure 2.6: The definitions for the example module.

The example logic begins by using both the %LEN and %SIZE functions on a fixed-length character field. The results of both functions are identical. The DSPLY op code displays the returned values to prove the results, as shown in Figure 2.7.

```
     *_____
     *  Result = 15 because trailing blanks are included in Len
     *_____
     C                   Eval      Result = %Len(FirstName1)
     C                   Dsply                 Result
     *
     *_____
     *  Result = 15 because the field occupies 15 bytes
     *_____
     C                   Eval      Result = %Size(FirstName1)
     C                   Dsply                 Result
```

Figure 2.7: The %LEN and %SIZE functions perform the same over fixed-length character fields.

When the functions are employed against a binary integer field defined as 10 digits in length, the functions return different values. The %LEN function returns a value of 10 because the field has 10 digits. The %SIZE function returns a value of 4 because a 10-digit integer occupies only 4 bytes of space when stored. These results are shown in Figure 2.8.

```
 *_____
 *  Result = 10 because field is a 10 digit integer
 *_____
C                        Eval      Result = %Len(Number1)
C                        Dsply              Result
 *
 *_____
 *  Result = 4 because a 10 digit integer occupies 4 bytes
 *_____
C                        Eval      Result = %Size(Number1)
C                        Dsply              Result
```

Figure 2.8: The %LEN and %SIZE functions perform differently over integer fields.

When the functions are employed against a variable-length character field defined with a maximum size of 15 characters, the functions return different values. The%LEN function returns a value of 6 because the field is initialized with a value that is 6 characters long. The %SIZE function returns a value of 17, which is the maximum field size of 15 plus the 2 bytes that store the content length. These results are shown in Figure 2.9.

```
 *_____
 *  Result = 6 because the contents of variable length field
 *           is only 6 bytes.
 *_____
C                        Eval      Result = %Len(FirstName2)
C                        Dsply              Result
 *
 *_____
 *  Result = 17 because the variable length field occupies 17
 *  bytes.  Variable len fields take up 2 extra bytes that
 *  contain the length of the contents.
 *_____
C                        Eval      Result = %Size(FirstName2)
C                        Dsply              Result
```

Figure 2.9: The %LEN and %SIZE functions perform differently over variable-length fields.

The %LEN function can be employed to return the variable length of an expression. The example shown in Figure 2.10 demonstrates this capability to determine the length of a concatenated string value. The %SIZE function cannot be used over expressions.

```
     *
     *_____
     *   Result = 13 because the resulting concatenated value
     *            has a variable length.
     *_____
     C                    Eval      Result = %Len(%Trim(FirstName1) +
     C                                        ' ' +
     C                                        %Trim(LastName1))
     C                    Dsply     Result
```

Figure 2.10: The %LEN function returns the length of a concatenated expression.

The %SIZE function can be employed to return the size of a single array element or an entire array. The example shown in Figure 2.11 demonstrates this capability to determine the size of a single element and of an entire array.

```
     *
     *_____
     *   Result = 10 because each element of array occupies 10 bytes
     *_____
     C                    Eval      Result = %Size(Array1)
     C                    Dsply     Result
     *
     *_____
     *   Result = 100 because entire array occupies 100 bytes
     *_____
     C                    Eval      Result = %Size(Array1:*All)
     C                    Dsply     Result
```

Figure 2.11: The %SIZE function returns the length of both a single element and an entire array.

The example concludes by using the %LEN function to set the length of a variable-length field. The field was originally loaded with a six-character value. By resetting the length to two, the contents of the field are truncated from six to two bytes. Figure 2.12 demonstrates this capability.

```
     *_____
     *   LastName2 = Mc Because variable field length reduced to
     *              a length of 2.
     *_____
     C                    Eval      %Len(LastName2) = 2
     C                    Dsply               LastName2
```

Figure 2.12: The %LEN function is used to change the size of a variable-length field.

EXAMPLE

Using the %OPEN Function

This example employs the Return File Open Condition (%OPEN) built-in function to determine whether a specified file is open or closed.

WHAT THE EXAMPLE DOES

The example source member BIF015R demonstrates use of the %OPEN function to detect the open status of a specific file. If the file is closed, the example opens it. Listing 2.15 shows the source member.

Listing 2.15: ILE RPG member BIF015R uses the %OPEN function.

```
 *
FCustomer  IF   E           K Disk     UsrOpn
 *
 *_____
 *  If file is closed, open it.
 *_____
C                    If         Not %Open(Customer)
C                    Open       Customer
C                    Endif
 *
C                    Return
```

HOW THE EXAMPLE WORKS

The %OPEN function returns a '1' if the specified file is open. If closed, it returns a '0'.

EXAMPLE

Using the %PARMS Function

This example employs the Return Number of Parameters (%PARMS) function within a defined subprocedure to determine the number of parameters that were passed to it.

WHAT THE EXAMPLE DOES

The example source member BIF016R demonstrates use of the %PARMS function to determine the number of parameters passed to a day-of-week subprocedure. The subprocedure accepts two parameters: the first a required date and the second an optional format indicator. The subprocedure uses the %PARMS function to determine if the second optional parameter was passed. Listing 2.16 shows the source member.

Listing 2.16: ILE RPG member BIF016R uses the %PARMS function.

```
DDateInput        S              8A
DDay              S             10A
DDayOfWeek        PR            10A
D   #DateIn                      8     Value
D   #LorS                        1     Value Options(*NoPass)
 *
C                 Move          *Date        DateInput
 *
C                 Eval          Day = DayOfWeek(DateInput)
C                 Dsply                      Day
 *
C                 Eval          Day = DayOfWeek(DateInput:'S')
C                 Dsply                      Day
C                 Return
 *================================================================
PDayOfWeek        B
DDayOfWeek        PI            10
D   DateIn                       8     Value
D   LorS                         1     Value Options(*NoPass)
 *_____
 *   Local Variables
 *_____
DLillianOut       S             10I 0
DDateFmt          S              8A
DOutFmt           S             10A
DWeekDay          S             10A
 *
C                 Move          'MMDDYYYY'      DateFmt
C                 Callb(D)      'CEEDAYS'
C                 Parm                          DateIn
C                 Parm                          DateFmt
C                 Parm                          LillianOut
C                 Parm                          *Omit
C*
C                 If            %Parms = 1
C                 Eval          OutFmt = 'Wwwwwwwwwz'
C                 Else
C                 Select
C                 When          LorS = 'S'
```

Listing 2.16: ILE RPG member BIF016R uses the %PARMS function (continued).

```
C               Eval      OutFmt = 'Www'
C               When      LorS = 'L'
C               Eval      OutFmt = 'Wwwwwwwwwz'
C               Other
C               Eval      OutFmt = 'Wwwwwwwwwz'
C               Endsl
C               EndIf
 *
C               Callb(D)  'CEEDATE'
C               Parm                   LillianOut
C               Parm                   OutFmt
C               Parm                   WeekDay
C               Parm                   *Omit
C               Return    WeekDay
P             E
```

HOW THE EXAMPLE WORKS

The %PARMS function returns the number of parameters that were passed to the procedure in which it is used. It is only useful when one or more parameters of the procedure are defined as optional.

The Example

The example module consists of a main procedure and a DAYOFWEEK subprocedure. Because the procedure prototype defines the second parameter as optional, the subprocedure uses the %PARMS function to determine whether it was passed. For more information about procedure prototypes, see the examples in chapter 1.

The optional subprocedure parameter is used to determine whether the day of the week is to be returned as a long value such as Sunday or as a short value such as Sun. If %PARMS returns a value of 1, the subprocedure knows the parameter was not passed. It then uses a default value of returning the long format. If the %PARMS value is not 1, the procedure knows both parameters were passed and uses the appropriate value.

EXAMPLE

Using the %SCAN and %REPLACE Functions

This example employs two commonly used string functions, Scan for Characters String (%SCAN) and Replace Character String (%REPLACE), to locate and replace embedded characters within a string variable.

WHAT THE EXAMPLE DOES

The example source member BIF017R demonstrates use of the %SCAN function to find characters within a string and the %REPLACE function to replace the value of characters within the string with a different value. Listing 2.17 shows the source member.

Listing 2.17: ILE RPG member BIF017R
uses the %SCAN and %REPLACE functions.

```
     *
DName1              S              50A    Varying Inz('Andrew McCall')
DName2              S               5A    Inz('Kevin')
DResult1            S              50A    Varying
DResult2            S               5I 0
     *
     *_____
     *  Result1 = Kevinw McCall
     *_____
C                    Eval          Result1 = %Replace(Name2:Name1)
C                    Dsply                   Result1
     *
     *_____
     *  Result1 = Andrew Kevinl
     *_____
C                    Eval          Result1 = %Replace(Name2:Name1:8)
C                    Dsply                   Result1
     *
     *_____
     *  Result1 = Kevin & Andrew McCall
     *_____
C                    Eval          Result1 = %Replace(Name2 + ' & ':
C                                            Name1:
C                                            1:
C                                            0)
C                    Dsply                   Result1
     *
     *_____
     *  Result2 = 4
     *_____
C                    Eval          Result2 = %Scan('rew':Name1)
C                    Dsply                   Result2
     *
     *_____
     *  Result2 = 0
     *_____
C                    Eval          Result2 = %Scan('rew':Name1:7)
C                    Dsply                   Result2
     *
```

➡

Listing 2.17: ILE RPG member BIF017R
uses the %SCAN and %REPLACE functions (continued).

```
 *_____
 *  Result1 = Andy McCall
 *_____
C                    Eval      Result1 = %Replace('y':
C                                        Name1:
C                                        %Scan('rew':Name1):
C                                        3)
C                    Dsply               Result1
 *
C                    Return
```

HOW THE EXAMPLE WORKS

The %SCAN function accepts up to three arguments: a search argument, a string name to be searched, and, optionally, a starting position for the search. The function returns an integer value that represents the position within the string in which the search argument was found. If not found, the function returns zero. Unlike the SCAN op code, the %FOUND function cannot be used to determine the success of the %SCAN function.

The %REPLACE function accepts up to four arguments: a replacement string, a source string name, an optional replacement starting position, and an optional replacement length. The function does not change the contents of the original source string; rather, it returns a new character string that reflects the replacement performed on the source string.

The Example

The example module begins with the definition of fields used. The definitions include fixed- and variable-length character fields and a binary integer field. Figure 2.13 shows the definitions.

```
DName1          S              50A    Varying Inz('Andrew McCall')
DName2          S               5A    Inz('Kevin')
DResult1        S              50A    Varying
DResult2        S               5I 0
```

Figure 2.13: The definitions for the example module.

The example logic begins by using the %REPLACE function to replace a portion of one string with the value of a second string. Because a starting position is not specified, the replacement begins in position 1. The DSPLY op code displays the returned value to prove the results, as shown in Figure 2.14.

```
     *_____
     *  Result1 = Kevinw McCall
     *_____
     C                    Eval         Result1 = %Replace(Name2:Name1)
     C                    Dsply                  Result1
```

Figure 2.14: The %REPLACE function replaces the first five characters of NAME1 with NAME2.

The example again uses the %REPLACE function to replace a portion of one string with the value of a second string. This time, a starting position of 8 is specified. The DSPLY op code displays the returned value to prove the results, as shown in Figure 2.15.

```
     *_____
     *  Result1 = Andrew Kevinl
     *_____
     C                    Eval         Result1 = %Replace(Name2:Name1:8)
     C                    Dsply                  Result1
```

Figure 2.15: The %REPLACE function replaces the 8th through 12th characters of NAME1 with NAME2.

The example again uses the %REPLACE function to replace a portion of one string with the value of a second string. The replacement value is a concatenated expression. The starting position specified is 1 with a replacement length of zero. Specifying a length of zero causes the string to be inserted rather than replace characters. The DSPLY op code displays the returned value to prove the results, as shown in Figure 2.16.

```
     *_____
     *  Result1 = Kevin & Andrew McCall
     *_____
     C                    Eval         Result1 = %Replace(Name2 + ' & ':
     C                                            Name1:
     C                                            1:
     C                                            0)
     C                    Dsply                  Result1
```

Figure 2.16: The %REPLACE function inserts a concatenated string before NAME1.

The example again uses the %REPLACE function to replace a portion of one string with the value of a second string. The replacement value is a concatenated expression. The starting position specified is 1 with a replacement length of zero. Specifying a length of zero causes the string to be inserted rather than replace characters. The DSPLY op code displays the returned value to prove the results, as shown in Figure 2.17.

```
 *_____
 *   Result1 = Kevin & Andrew McCall
 *_____
 C                    Eval      Result1 = %Replace(Name2 + ' & ':
 C                                        Name1:
 C                                        1:
 C                                        0)
 C                    Dsply                Result1
```

Figure 2.17: The %REPLACE function inserts a concatenated string before NAME1.

The example uses the %SCAN function to search the string contents of NAME1 for the literal value 'rew'. Because this value appears in positions 4 through 6, the function returns a value of 4. The second %SCAN operation performs the same search again, this time beginning in position 7. The function returns a value of zero because the literal is not found in positions 7 through 13. The DSPLY op code displays the returned value to prove the results, as shown in Figure 2.18.

```
 *_____
 *   Result2 = 4
 *_____
 C                    Eval      Result2 = %Scan('rew':Name1)
 C                    Dsply                Result2
 *
 *_____
 *   Result2 = 0
 *_____
 C                    Eval      Result2 = %Scan('rew':Name1:7)
 C                    Dsply                Result2
```

Figure 2.18: The %SCAN function searches for a literal value.

The final example uses the %REPLACE function and %SCAn function together to perform a single search-and-replace operation. Because %SCAN returns an integer value, its results are used as the starting location for the %REPLACE function. The example searches for the value 'rew' in the name Andrew and replaces it with a 'Y' when it's found. The result changes Andrew to Andy. The DSPLY op code displays the returned value to prove the results, as shown in Figure 2.19.

```
*_____
*   Result1 = Andy McCall
*_____
C                   Eval      Result1 = %Replace('y':
C                                       Name1:
C                                       %Scan('rew':Name1):
C                                       3)
C                   Dsply                Result1
*
```

Figure 2.19: The %SCAN and %REPLACE functions can work together.

EXAMPLE

Using the %SUBST Function

This example employs the Get Substring (%SUBST) function to retrieve a portion of a string.

WHAT THE EXAMPLE DOES

The example source member BIF018R demonstrates use of the %SUBST function to isolate and return an embedded portion of a string. Listing 2.18 shows the source member.

Listing 2.18: ILE RPG member BIF018R uses the %SUBST function.

```
*
DName1            S              50A   Varying Inz('Kevin McCall')
DName2            S               6A   Inz('Andrew')
DResult1          S              50A   Varying
*
*_____
*   Result1 = Kev
*_____
C                   Eval      Result1 = %Subst(Name1:1:3)
C                   Dsply                Result1
*
*_____
*   Result1 = drew
*_____
C                   Eval      Result1 = %Subst(Name2:3)
C                   Dsply                Result1
```

Listing 2.18: ILE RPG member
BIF018R uses the %SUBST function (continued).

```
 *_____
 *   Displays True
 *_____
 C                        If        %Subst(Name1:7) = 'McCall'
 C          'True'        Dsply
 C                        Else
 C          'False'       Dsply
 C                        Endif
  *
 C                        Return
```

HOW THE EXAMPLE WORKS

The %SUBST function accepts up to three arguments: a source string, a starting location, and, optionally, a length of the substring to return. The function returns a string that is derived from the source string. The function can also be used to set or test an embedded value within a source string.

EXAMPLE

Using the %TRIM, %TRIML, and %TRIMR Functions

This example employs three very handy string functions, Trim Blanks at Edges (%TRIM), Trim Leading Blanks (%TRIML), and Trim Trailing Blanks (%TRIMR), to eliminate blanks from string variables.

WHAT THE EXAMPLE DOES

The example source member BIF019R demonstrates use of the three trim functions to remove leading and trailing blanks from a number of string variables. Listing 2.19 shows the source member.

Listing 2.19: ILE RPG member BIF019R uses the %TRIM functions.

```
 DName1          S            50A    Inz('Betty')
 DName2          S            50A    Inz('     Thompson    ')
 DCity           S            15A    Inz('Spokane')
 DState          S             2A    Inz('WA')
 DZip            S             5A    Inz('99208')
```

**Listing 2.19: ILE RPG member
BIF019R uses the %TRIM functions (continued).**

```
DResult1            S              50A    Varying
    *
    *_____
    *   Result1 = 'Thompson'
    *_____
C                   Eval        Result1 = %Trim(Name2)
C                   Dsply                 Result1
    *
    *_____
    *   Result1 = 'Spokane        WA 99208'
    *_____
C                   Eval        Result1 = City + State + ' ' + Zip
C                   Dsply                 Result1
    *
    *_____
    *   Result1 = 'Spokane, WA 99208'
    *_____
C                   Eval        Result1 = %Trimr(City) +
C                                         ', ' +
C                                         State +
C                                         ' ' +
C                                         Zip
C                   Dsply                 Result1
    *
    *_____
    *   Result1 = 'Betty Thompson'
    *_____
C                   Eval        Result1 = %Trimr(Name1) +
C                                         ' ' +
C                                         %Triml(Name2)
C                   Dsply                 Result1
    *
C                   Return
```

HOW THE EXAMPLE WORKS

The %TRIM function accepts a string argument and returns the string with both leading and trailing blanks removed.

The %TRIML function accepts a string argument and returns the string with leading blanks removed. Any trailing blanks remain.

The %TRIMR function accepts a string argument and returns the string with trailing blanks removed. Any leading blanks remain.

EXAMPLE

Using the %UNS and %UNSH Functions

This example employs the Convert to Unsigned Format (%UNS) and Convert to Un-signed Format with Half Adjust (%UNSH) built-in functions to convert numeric fields to unsigned integer values used in division calculations, either truncating or half adjusting the decimal positions.

WHAT THE EXAMPLE DOES

The example source member BIF020R demonstrates the effect of the %UNS and %UNSH functions when used to convert packed decimal numbers used in division calculations to unsigned integers. As demonstrated and displayed, the functions impact the results of the calculations. Listing 2.20 shows the source member.

Listing 2.20: ILE RPG member
BIF020R uses the %UNS and %UNSH functions.

```
*
DNumber1        S              11  5 Inz(35)
DNumber2        S               7  5 Inz(7.60)
 *
DResult         S              15  5
 *
*_____
 *  Division:  Result = 4.60526
 *_____
C                   Eval      Result = Number1 / Number2
C                   Dsply                 Result
 *
*_____
 *        Result = 7
 *_____
C                   Eval      Result = %Uns(Number2)
C                   Dsply                 Result
 *
*_____
 *        Result = 5
 *_____
C                   Eval      Result = Number1 / %Uns(Number2)
C                   Dsply                 Result
 *
*_____
 *        Result = 4.375
 *_____
```

Listing 2.20: ILE RPG member
BIF020R uses the %UNS and %UNSH functions (continued).

```
C                    Eval      Result = Number1 / %Unsh(Number2)
C                    Dsply              Result
  *
C                    Return
```

HOW THE EXAMPLE WORKS

The %UNS and %UNSH functions accept one argument: a numeric expression to be converted to unsigned integer format. The %UNS and %UNSH functions work identically except for how they handle the decimal positions being eliminated. The %UNS function truncates any decimal positions, while %UNSH half adjusts. Attempting to use the functions on a negative number results in an error.

EXAMPLE

Using the %XFOOT Function

This example employs the Sum Array Expression Elements (%XFOOT) built-in function to sum the elements of numeric arrays.

WHAT THE EXAMPLE DOES

The example source member BIF021R demonstrates the capability of the %XFOOT function to summarize all of the elements of numeric arrays. Listing 2.21 shows the source member.

Listing 2.21: ILE RPG member BIF021R uses the %XFOOT function.

```
  *
DArray1          S              3  0 Dim(3)
DArray2          S              3  0 Dim(3)
  *
DResult          S              4  0
C*
C                    Eval      Array1(1) = 100
C                    Eval      Array1(2) = 100
C                    Eval      Array1(3) = 100
C*
C                    Eval      Array2(1) = 50
C                    Eval      Array2(2) = 50
C                    Eval      Array2(3) = 50
```

Listing 2.21: ILE RPG member
BIF021R uses the %XFOOT function (continued).

```
*
*_____
*  Result = 300
*_____
C                     Eval      Result = %XFoot(Array1)
C                     Dsply              Result
*
*_____
*  Result = 150
*_____
C                     Eval      Result = %XFoot(Array2)
C                     Dsply              Result
*
*_____
*  Result = 450
*_____
C                     Eval      Result = %XFoot(Array1 + Array2)
C                     Dsply              Result
C                     Return
```

HOW THE EXAMPLE WORKS

If you are familiar with the XFOOT op code in RPG, the %XFOOT function does the same thing. It accepts one argument, an array or array expression, and returns the sum of the elements. The %XFOOT function can sum amounts up to 30 digits in length.

EXAMPLE

Using the %FLOAT Function

This example employs the Convert to Floating Format (%FLOAT) built-in function to convert numeric fields to floating point values used in division calculations.

WHAT THE EXAMPLE DOES

The example source member BIF022R demonstrates use of the %FLOAT function to convert packed decimal numbers used in division calculations to floating point format. Listing 2.22 shows the source member.

Listing 2.22: ILE RPG member BIF022R uses the %FLOAT function.

```
 *
DNumber1          S              11  0 Inz(35)
DNumber2          S               7  5 Inz(7.55)
 *
DResult           S              15  9
 *
 *_____
 *  Division:  Result = 4.35761589
 *_____
C                 Eval      Result = Number1 / Number2
C                 Dsply               Result
 *
 *_____
 *         Result = 4.35761589
 *_____
C                 Eval      Result = %Float(Number1 / Number2)
C                 Dsply               Result
 *
 *_____
 *         Result = 4.35761589
 *_____
C                 Eval      Result = Number1 / %Float(Number2)
C                 Dsply               Result
 *
C                 Return
```

HOW THE EXAMPLE WORKS

The %FLOAT function accepts one argument: a numeric expression to be converted to floating point format.

EXAMPLE

Using the %PADDR Function

This example employs the Get Procedure Address (%PADDR) built-in function to call, using their addresses, two bound procedures.

WHAT THE EXAMPLE DOES

The example source member BIF023R calls the bound procedures PROCEDURE1 and PROCEDURE2, using their addresses to demonstrate use of the %PADDR function. Listing

2.23 shows the source member BIF023R. Source members PROCEDURE1 and PROCEDURE2 are shown in Listings 2.24 and 2.25 respectively.

Listing 2.23: ILE RPG member BIF023R uses %PADDR function.

```
DPtr1              S                *    ProcPtr Inz(*Null)
 *
C                  Eval        Ptr1 = %Paddr('PROCEDURE1')
 *
C                  Callb       Ptr1
 *
C                  Eval        Ptr1 = %Paddr('PROCEDURE2')
 *
C                  Callb       Ptr1
 *
C                  Return
```

Listing 2.24: ILE RPG member PROCEDURE1 is called by address.

```
DMsg               S                50A   Inz('Hello from Procedure1')
 *
C                  Dsply                  Msg
C                  Return
```

Listing 2.25: ILE RPG member PROCEDURE2 is called by address.

```
DMsg               S                50A   Inz('Hello from Procedure2')
 *
C                  Dsply                  Msg
C                  Return
```

HOW THE EXAMPLE WORKS

If you have not used pointers in an RPG program before, they are simply a way to address a specific storage location in memory. A pointer is just another data type—like a character, packed numeric, or date field. Instead of holding text or a number, pointer fields hold an address location. The memory address of a procedure entry point is loaded into a pointer variable using the %PADDR function.

The %PADDR function accepts one argument: a string representing the name of a procedure. The procedure must be resolved at program binding time, meaning it must be a valid entry point available when the program is bound. The name of the procedure is case sensitive.

The Example

The example module begins with the definition of the procedure pointer PTR1. Figure 2.20 shows the definition.

```
DPtr1             S              *    ProcPtr Inz(*Null)
```

Figure 2.20: The procedure pointer definition.

The example logic begins by employing the %PADDR function to set the pointer to the address of PROCEDURE1. Once the address has been retrieved, the procedure is called, using the pointer as a parameter to the bound call operation (CALLB). Figure 2.21 shows this logic. The DSPLY op code within PROCEDURE1 displays a hello message to verify it was called. This is shown in Figure 2.22.

```
C                 Eval      Ptr1 = %Paddr('PROCEDURE1')
 *
C                 Callb     Ptr1
```

Figure 2.21: Addressing the pointer allows you to call the procedure using the pointer.

```
DMsg              S              50A   Inz('Hello from Procedure1')
 *
C                 Dsply               Msg
C                 Return
```

Figure 2.22: PROCEDURE1 sends a hello message.

The module concludes by resetting the pointer to the value of PROCEDURE2. Another CALLB operation using the pointer name results in calling PROCEDURE2.

Creating the Example Objects

Because the address returned by %PADDR must refer to an entry point, the procedure specified cannot be a subprocedure. The exception to this rule is that a subprocedure can be called by address if it resides in the same module as the calling procedure. The example objects were first created as ILE RPG modules with the following statements:

```
CRTRPGMOD MODULE(BIF023R) SRCFILE(SRCLIB/SRCFILE) SRCMBR(*MODULE)
CRTRPGMOD MODULE(PROCEDURE1) SRCFILE(SRCLIB/SRCFILE) SRCMBR(*MODULE)
CRTRPGMOD MODULE(PROCEDURE2) SRCFILE(SRCLIB/SRCFILE) SRCMBR(*MODULE)
```

After the modules were created, they were compiled and bound using the Create Program (CRTPGM) command as follows:

```
CRTPGM PGM(BIF023R) MODULE(*LIBL/BIF023R *LIBL/PROCEDURE1 *LIBL/PROCEDURE2)
       ENTMOD(*FIRST) ACTGRP(*CALLER)
```

EXAMPLE

Using the %NULLIND Function

This example employs the Get or Set Null Indicator (%NULLIND) built-in function to test a null-capable field input from a database file for a null status.

WHAT THE EXAMPLE DOES

The example source member BIF024R demonstrates use of the %NULLIND function to determine and set the null status of null-capable file fields. Listing 2.26 shows the source member.

Listing 2.26: ILE RPG member BIF024R uses the %NULLIND function.

```
HAlwNull(*UsrCtl)
FNullFile  IF   E           Disk
 *
DMsg1            S           50A    Inz('Date1 is null.')
DMsg2            S           50A    Inz('Date1 was set to null.')
 *
 *_____
 *  If file field Date1 is Null, displays Date1 is null.
 *  If not Null, changes field to Null.
 *_____
C                    Read    FileRec
 *
C                    DoW     Not %EOF(NullFile)
 *
```

Listing 2.26: ILE RPG member
BIF024R uses the %NULLIND function (continued).

```
C                     If        %NullInd(Date1)
C                     Dsply                Msg1
C                     Else
C                     Eval      %NullInd(Date1) = *On
C                     Dsply                Msg2
C                     Endif
  *
C                     Read      FileRec
  *
C                     Enddo
  *
C                     Return
```

HOW THE EXAMPLE WORKS

The %NULLIND function accepts one argument: the name of a null-capable field. The function returns a '1' if the field's null indicator is set to *ON. Otherwise, it returns a '0'. Because there is currently no way to define a null-capable field within RPG, the field you are testing must be input from a file containing null-capable fields. You can change the null indicator of a field by using the %NULLIND to set the value to *ON or *OFF.

To use null-capable fields in an RPG Module, the ALWNULL(*USRCTL) keyword must be specified on a control specification or as a parameter of the Create RPG Module (CRTRPGMOD) or Create Bound RPG Program (CRTBNDRPG) commands.

3

Exit Programs

In today's open environments, maintaining a safe and secure system is a daunting challenge. The first line of defense in maintaining a secure AS/400 is a sound object-level security scheme. Object-level security allows you to define the data, application, and system functions available to each individual user. It is highly customizable to allow control over what system users may do and see. Is a strategy based entirely on object-level security enough to keep your data safe and secure? Many systems have security exposures not adequately addressed by object-level security. Luckily, the AS/400 provides capabilities necessary to creating a second line of defense against improper system activities.

What Are User Exit Programs?

Typically, when a system function is performed, execution of the function takes place without user interaction or involvement. The system performs a requested function, then returns the result to the user. Exit programs are simply programs you write that allow you to intervene in system processes that are ordinarily transparent. The operating system provides several preset points, called exit points, that allow you to attach a user-written program to designated system functions. An exit point is simply a step within the execution of a system function when control is handed to a user-written exit program. Each exit point has a set of unique parameters that are passed by the system to your exit program. Some exit points allow your program to intervene in the process by rejecting the system function, while others merely allow you to monitor the activity.

THE REGISTRATION FACILITY

Exit programs are attached to system exit points using the AS/400 Registration Facility, which is accessed using the Work with Registration Information (WRKREGINF) command. Figure 3.1 shows the Registration Facility. The WRKREGINF command displays a list of all defined system exit points. From this display, you can work with exit programs associated with each exit point.

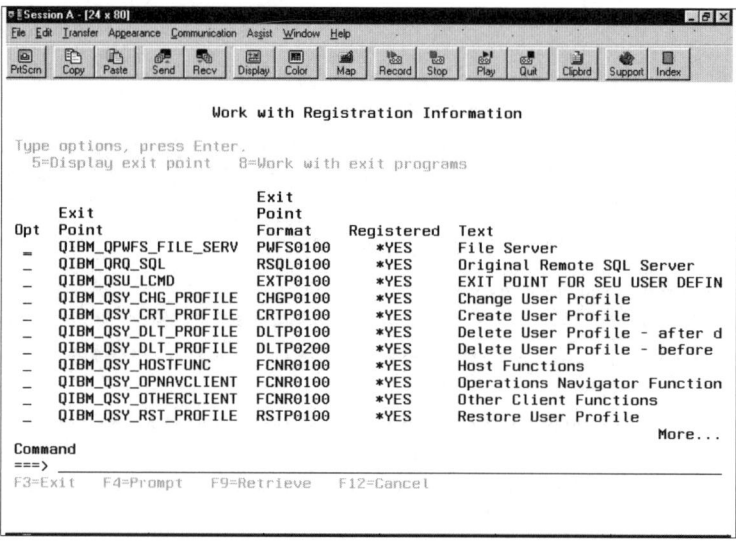

Figure 3.1: The Work with Registration Information display.

COMMON USES FOR EXIT PROGRAMS

In the past few years, the AS400 has evolved from a closed, proprietary system to a system that works well with other platforms. This open system approach has bolstered the value of the AS/400, but it has also left the system more vulnerable to questionable activity. This is where exit programs can help provide an extra level of security. This chapter presents example exit programs that can be adapted to control and monitor specific system functions.

Remote Data Access

Technologies that enable users to easily port data to their desktops are prevalent in to-day's networking environments. It can be difficult to control or monitor such activities using only object-level security. For example, it may be necessary for all users to have authority to use a sensitive file in an application. This doesn't mean it is appropriate for them to download the file to their PCs for indiscriminant use. Such a download is easily accomplished using common database tools such as ODBC or the Client Access file transfer function. If an individual has authority to use the file, he or she also has authority to download the file. User exit programs can be used to limit or monitor the movement of data from or to the AS/400.

System Security Functions

When making changes to your database, keep in mind that there are a number of tools available to assist you with enforcing your unique database rules. Mechanisms such as constraints and trigger programs (both covered in part 2 of this book) allow you to inte-grate the rules of your business into your database. But what about your user profile administration?

Chances are, you also have a unique set of business rules when it comes to your user pro-file schemes. Unfortunately, there aren't nearly as many tools available to assist with the enforcement of your user profile rules.

Because object-level authority is such an integral part of an effective security strategy, it is important to monitor the administration of user profiles. Exit programs can be a valu-able tool to enforce your unique user profile rules. The exit points available for user pro-file monitoring do not allow you to intervene in the process, but they do allow you to automatically interrogate what was done and send an alert message if necessary.

A Tool with Many Uses

Exit points allow you to tap into a number of system functions. Their use should be closely monitored because they are so closely tied with system functions. If not properly controlled, they can pose a security exposure. At a minimum, your exit programs should reside in a secure library and allow only public access of *USE. It is also good practice to explicitly qualify each exit program call with the library name to avoid unwanted manip-ulation using the library list.

These examples focus on security, but exit programs also have applications in systems administration and networking. They can be used to accomplish a number of tasks, from conducting anonymous FTPs to distributing user profile information across systems. Exit programs can be valuable tools when used properly.

EXAMPLE

Using an Exit Program to Monitor User Profile Creation

The system provides a set of exit points that allows you to attach an exit program that is called whenever a user profile is created, changed, deleted, or restored. Unfortunately, these exit points do not allow the exit program to actively participate in the event. In other words, the exit program call is strictly informational. It cannot reject undesirable activity or alter the contents of the user profile in any way. However, the ability to monitor user profile activity allows you to keep track of what is going on and alert others if undesirable activity occurs.

WHAT THE EXAMPLE DOES

The example consists of one exit program source member. When attached to the Create User Profile exit point QIBM_QSY_CRT_PROFILE, member EXT001R tests the values of the created user profile and sends messages to the QSYSOPR message queue if any rules are violated. Listing 3.1 shows the ILE RPG module EXT001R.

Listing 3.1: ILE RPG member EXT001R monitors new user profiles.

```
     *_____
     *  Retrieve User Information API Parameters
     *_____
    DReceiverLen      S              10I 0 Inz(%Size(RcvQSYRUSRI))
    DFormat           S               8A   Inz('USRI0300')
    DUser             S              10A
     *
     *_____
     *  API Receiver Structure
     *_____
    DRcvQSYRUSRI       DS
    D  BytesReturn                   10I 0
    D  BytesAvail                    10I 0
    D  Profile                       10A
    D  PrevSgnon                     13A
    D  Reserved1                      1A
    D  InvAttempts                   10I 0
    D  Status                        10A
```

Listing 3.1: ILE RPG member
EXT001R monitors new user profiles (continued).

```
     D   PwdChgDate               8A
     D   NoPwd                    1A
     D   Reserved2                1A
     D   PwdExpInt               10I 0
     D   PwdExpDate               8A
     D   PwdExpDays              10I 0
     D   PwdExpire                1A
     D   UserClass               10A
     D   SplAuth                 15A
     D    AllObj                  1A   Overlay(SplAuth:1)
     D    SecAdm                  1A   Overlay(SplAuth:2)
     D    JobCtl                  1A   Overlay(SplAuth:3)
     D    SavSys                  1A   Overlay(SplAuth:4)
     D    Service                 1A   Overlay(SplAuth:5)
     D    Audit                   1A   Overlay(SplAuth:6)
     D    IOSysCfg                1A   Overlay(SplAuth:7)
     D   GroupProf               10A
     D   Owner                   10A
     D   GroupAuth               10A
     D   AssistLevel             10A
     D   CurLib                  10A
     D   InlMnu                  10A
     D   InlMnuLib               10A
     D   InlPgm                  10A
     D   InlPgmLib               10A
     D   LimitCap                10A
     D   TextDesc                50A
      *_____
      * Send Message API Declarations
      *_____
     DSMMsgId         S           7
     DSMMsgFile       S          20
     DSMMsgTxt        S         100
     DSMMsgLen        S          10I 0 Inz(%Size(SMMsgTxt))
     DSMMsgType       S          10   Inz('*INFO')
     DSMMsgQ          S          20   Inz('QSYSOPR   *LIBL      ')
     DSMMsgQ#         S          10I 0 Inz(1)
     DSMReplyQ        S          20
     DSMMsgKey        S           4
      *
      *
      *_____
      *  Common API Error Structure
      *_____
     DAPIErrorDS      DS
     D   APIBytes                10I 0 Inz(%Size(APIErrorDS))
     D   APIBytesOut             10I 0
     D   APIErrID                 7A
     D   APIReserved              1A
     D   APIErInDta             256A
```

Listing 3.1: ILE RPG member
EXT001R monitors new user profiles (continued).

```
         *
DCrtUsrPrf        DS            38
D  ExitPnt                      20
D  ExitFmt                       8
D  UserPrf                      10
         *
D@Msg1            C                         'User Profile Created with -
D                                           USRCLS *USER and LMT CAPABILITY -
D                                           *NO:'
D@Msg2            C                         'User Profile Created with -
D                                           Special Authority *ALLOBJ: '
D@Msg3            C                         'User Profile Created with -
D                                           Special Authority *SECADM: '
         *
C      *Entry     PList
C                 Parm                      CrtUsrPrf
   *
C                 Eval      User = UserPrf
   *

   *_____
   *  Call API QSYRUSRI to Get User Information
   *_____
C                 Call      'QSYRUSRI'
C                 Parm                      RcvQSYRUSRI
C                 Parm                      ReceiverLen
C                 Parm                      Format
C                 Parm                      User
C                 Parm                      APIErrorDS
   *

   *_____
   *  Enforce user profile rules. Send message to QSYSOPR
   *  when rules violated.
   *_____
C
C                 If        UserClass = '*USER     ' And
C                           LimitCap =  '*NO       '
C                 Eval      SMMsgTxt = @Msg1 + User
C                 Exsr      SendAlert
C                 Endif
   *
C                 If        AllObj = 'Y'
C                 Eval      SMMsgTxt = @Msg2 + User
C                 Exsr      SendAlert
C                 Endif
   *
C                 If        SecAdm = 'Y'
C                 Eval      SMMsgTxt = @Msg3 + User
C                 Exsr      SendAlert
C                 Endif
   *
```

Listing 3.1: ILE RPG member
EXT001R monitors new user profiles (continued).

```
C                   Return
*
C       SendAlert   Begsr
*
C                   Call      'QMHSNDM'
C                   Parm                    SMMsgId
C                   Parm                    SMMsgFile
C                   Parm                    SMMsgTxt
C                   Parm                    SMMsgLen
C                   Parm                    SMMsgType
C                   Parm                    SMMsgQ
C                   Parm                    SMMsgQ#
C                   Parm                    SMReplyQ
C                   Parm                    SMMsgKey
C                   Parm                    APIErrorDS
C*
C                   Endsr
```

HOW THE EXAMPLE WORKS

The AS/400 provides exit point QIBM_QSY_CRT_PROFILE, which allows your user-written program to be called whenever a new user profile is created. The exit program is called after the new user profile is created. Each system exit point has at least one *format name* associated with it. A format name either identifies the format of the information that is returned to your program or distinguishes the timing of when the exit point is called. The QIBM_QSY_CRT_PROFILE exit point provides one format, CRTP0100.

When your exit program is called as the result of a new user profile being created, it receives one parameter: a structure that defines three subfields. The parameter subfields are shown in Table 3.1.

Table 3.1: CRTP0100 Format Parameter List.

Sequence	Parameter	I/O	Type
1	Exit Point Name	Output	Char(20)
2	Format Name	Output	Char(8)
3	User Profile	Output	Char(10)

The ILE Example

The example member EXT001R employs a system API to retrieve detailed information about the created user profile. The values are then tested against criteria to ensure compliance with shop standards and policies. The example triggers an alert if the user class is defined as *USER but the limit capabilities parameter is set to *NO. It also triggers an alert if the special authority is set to *SECADM or *ALLOBJ. An alert is triggered by sending a formatted message to the QSYSOPR message queue. System API QMHSNDM is used to send a message from within an RPG module. For more detailed information about using system APIs, please see chapter 4.

Adding the Exit Program

Once compiled, the exit program is added to the exit point using either the WRKREGINF command or the Add Exit Program (ADDEXITPGM) CL command. The ADDEXITPGM display is shown in Figure 3.2.

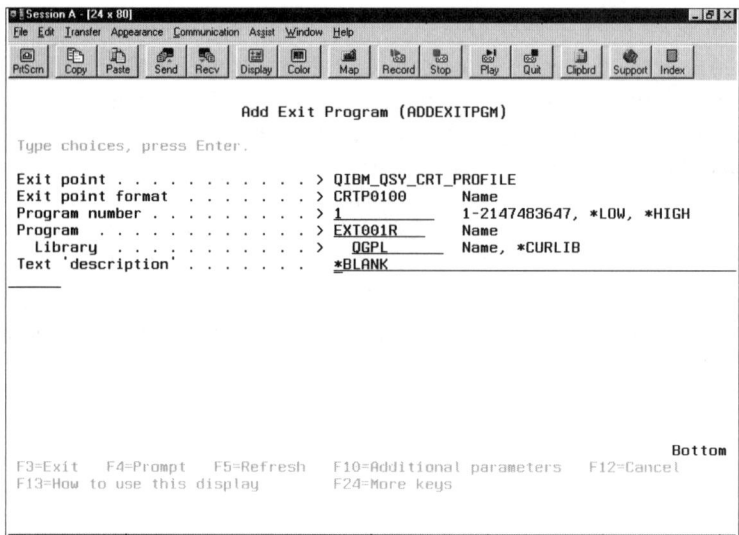

Figure 3.2: The ADDEXITPGM display.

EXAMPLE
Using an Exit Program to Monitor User Profile Changes

The system provides a set of exit points that allows you to attach an exit program that is called whenever a user profile is created, changed, deleted, or restored. Unfortunately, these exit points do not allow the exit program to actively participate in the event. In other words, the exit program call is strictly informational. It cannot reject undesirable activity or alter the contents of the user profile in any way. However, the ability to monitor user profile activity allows you to keep track of what is going on and alert others if undesirable activity occurs.

WHAT THE EXAMPLE DOES

The example consists of one exit program source member. When attached to the Change User Profile exit point QIBM_QSY_CHG_PROFILE, member EXT002R tests the current values of a user profile that was changed and sends messages to the QSYSOPR message queue if any rules are violated. Listing 3.2 shows the ILE RPG module EXT002R.

Listing 3.2: ILE RPG member EXT002R monitors user profile changes.

```
     *_____
     *   Retrieve User Information API Parameters
     *_____
    DReceiverLen       S              10I 0 Inz(%Size(RcvQSYRUSRI))
    DFormat            S               8A   Inz('USRI0300')
    DUser              S              10A
     *
     *_____
     *   API Receiver Structure
     *_____
    DRcvQSYRUSRI       DS
    D  BytesReturn                    10I 0
    D  BytesAvail                     10I 0
    D  Profile                        10A
    D  PrevSgnon                      13A
    D  Reserved1                       1A
    D  InvAttempts                    10I 0
    D  Status                         10A
    D  PwdChgDate                      8A
    D  NoPwd                           1A
    D  Reserved2                       1A
    D  PwdExpInt                      10I 0
    D  PwdExpDate                      8A
    D  PwdExpDays                     10I 0
    D  PwdExpire                       1A
```

Listing 3.2: ILE RPG member EXT002R monitors user profile changes (continued).

```
D   UserClass                      10A
D   SplAuth                        15A
D     AllObj                        1A    Overlay(SplAuth:1)
D     SecAdm                        1A    Overlay(SplAuth:2)
D     JobCtl                        1A    Overlay(SplAuth:3)
D     SavSys                        1A    Overlay(SplAuth:4)
D     Service                       1A    Overlay(SplAuth:5)
D     Audit                         1A    Overlay(SplAuth:6)
D     IOSysCfg                      1A    Overlay(SplAuth:7)
D   GroupProf                      10A
D   Owner                          10A
D   GroupAuth                      10A
D   AssistLevel                    10A
D   CurLib                         10A
D   InlMnu                         10A
D   InlMnuLib                      10A
D   InlPgm                         10A
D   InlPgmLib                      10A
D   LimitCap                       10A
D   TextDesc                       50A
   *_____
   * Send Message API Declarations
   *_____
D SMMsgId          S               7
D SMMsgFile        S              20
D SMMsgTxt         S             100
D SMMsgLen         S              10I 0 Inz(%Size(SMMsgTxt))
D SMMsgType        S              10    Inz('*INFO')
D SMMsgQ           S              20    Inz('QSYSOPR    *LIBL      ')
D SMMsgQ#          S              10I 0 Inz(1)
D SMReplyQ         S              20
D SMMsgKey         S               4
   *
   *
   *_____
   *  Common API Error Structure
   *_____
D APIErrorDS       DS
D   APIBytes                      10I 0 Inz(%Size(APIErrorDS))
D   APIBytesOut                   10I 0
D   APIErrID                       7A
D   APIReserved                    1A
D   APIErInDta                   256A
   *
D ChgUsrPrf        DS              38
D   ExitPnt                       20
D   ExitFmt                        8
D   UserPrf                       10
   *
D @Msg1            C                     'User Profile Changed having -
```

Listing 3.2: ILE RPG member EXT002R monitors user profile changes (continued).

```
D                                              USRCLS *USER and LMT CAPABILITY-
D                                              *NO: '
D@Msg2          C                              'User Profile Changed having -
D                                              Special Authority *ALLOBJ: '
D@Msg3          C                              'User Profile Changed having -
D                                              Special Authority *SECADM: '
*
C    *Entry      PList
C                Parm                ChgUsrPrf
*
C                Eval      User = UserPrf
*

*_____
*   Call API QSYRUSRI to Get User Information
*_____
C                Call      'QSYRUSRI'
C                Parm                RcvQSYRUSRI
C                Parm                ReceiverLen
C                Parm                Format
C                Parm                User
C                Parm                APIErrorDS
*

*_____
*   Enforce user profile rules. Send message to QSYSOPR
*   when rules violated.
*_____
C
C                If        UserClass = '*USER     ' And
C                          LimitCap = '*NO       '
C                Eval      SMMsgTxt = @Msg1 + User
C                Exsr      SendAlert
C                Endif
*
C                If        AllObj = 'Y'
C                Eval      SMMsgTxt = @Msg2 + User
C                Exsr      SendAlert
C                Endif
*
C                If        SecAdm = 'Y'
C                Eval      SMMsgTxt = @Msg3 + User
C                Exsr      SendAlert
C                Endif
*
C                Return
*
C    SendAlert   Begsr
*
C                Call      'QMHSNDM'
C                Parm                SMMsgId
C                Parm                SMMsgFile
```

Listing 3.2: ILE RPG member EXT002R monitors user profile changes (continued).

```
C                 Parm                    SMMsgTxt
C                 Parm                    SMMsgLen
C                 Parm                    SMMsgType
C                 Parm                    SMMsgQ
C                 Parm                    SMMsgQ#
C                 Parm                    SMReplyQ
C                 Parm                    SMMsgKey
C                 Parm                    APIErrorDS
C*
C                 Endsr
```

HOW THE EXAMPLE WORKS

The AS/400 provides exit point QIBM_QSY_CHG_PROFILE, which allows your user-written program to be called whenever a user profile is changed. The exit program is called after the change has been made. Each system exit point has at least one format name associated with it. A format name either identifies the format of the information that is returned to your program or distinguishes the timing of when the exit point is called. The QIBM_QSY_CHG_PROFILE exit point provides one format, CHGP0100.

When your exit program is called as the result of a user profile being changed, it receives one parameter: a structure that defines three subfields. The parameter subfields are shown in Table 3.2.

Table 3.2: CHGP0100 Format Parameter List.

Sequence	Parameter	I/O	Type
1	Exit Point Name	Output	Char(20)
2	Format Name	Output	Char(8)
3	User Profile	Output	Char(10)

The ILE Example

The example member EXT002R employs a system API to retrieve detailed information about the user profile that was changed. Unfortunately, the only information available is the user profile parameter values after the change was made. The values are then tested against criteria to ensure compliance with shop standards and policies. The example triggers an alert if the user class is defined as *USER but the limit capabilities parameter is set to *NO. It also triggers an alert if the special authority is set to *SECADM or *ALLOBJ. An alert is triggered by sending a formatted message to the QSYSOPR message queue. System API QMHSNDM is used to send a message from within an RPG module.

Adding the Exit Program

Once compiled, the exit program is added to the exit point using either the WRKREGINF command or the ADDEXITPGM CL command. The ADDEXITPGM display is shown in Figure 3.3.

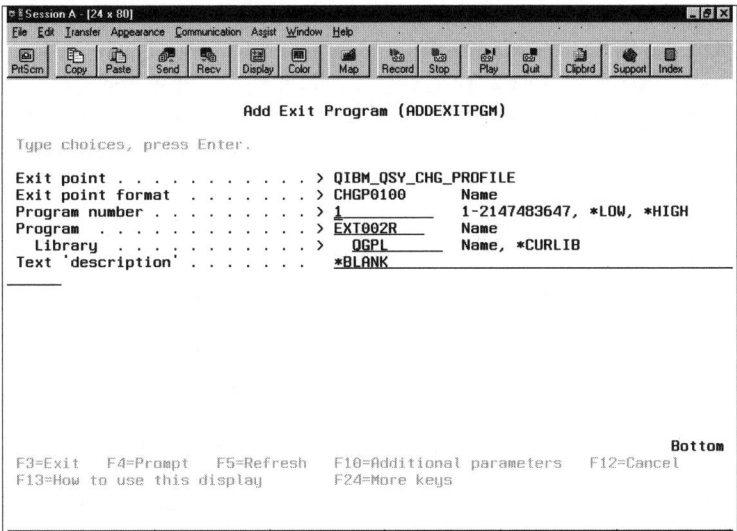

Figure 3.3: The ADDEXITPGM display.

EXAMPLE

Using an Exit Program to Monitor User Profile Deletion

The system provides a set of exit points that allows you to attach an exit program that is called whenever a user profile is created, changed, deleted, or restored. Unfortunately, these exit points do not allow the exit program to actively participate in the event. In other words, the exit program call is strictly informational. It cannot reject undesirable activity or alter the contents of the user profile in any way. However, the ability to monitor user profile activity allows you to keep track of what is going on and alert others if undesirable activity occurs.

WHAT THE EXAMPLE DOES

Unlike the Create and Change User Profile exit points, the Delete User Profile exit point offers more than one format. It has two defined exit point formats that determine the timing of when the exit program is called. When attached to exit point format DLTP0200, the exit program is called immediately before the user profile is deleted. Format DLTP0100 calls the exit program after the user profile is deleted.

The example consists of two exit program source members. When attached to the Delete User Profile exit point QIBM_QSY_DLT_PROFILE format DLTP0200, member EXT003R is called before a user profile is deleted and sends a notification message to the QSYSOPR message queue. Listing 3.3 shows the ILE RPG module EXT003R. Member EXT004R is attached to format DLTP0100 and is called after a user profile is deleted. It also sends a notification message to the QSYSOPR message queue, as shown in Listing 3.4.

Listing 3.3: ILE RPG member EXT003R is called before user profile deletion.

```
     *_____
     * Send Message API Declarations
     *_____
DSMMsgId          S              7
DSMMsgFile        S              20
DSMMsgTxt         S              100
DSMMsgLen         S              10I 0 Inz(%Size(SMMsgTxt))
DSMMsgType        S              10    Inz('*INFO')
DSMMsgQ           S              20    Inz('QSYSOPR   *LIBL     ')
DSMMsgQ#          S              10I 0 Inz(1)
DSMReplyQ         S              20
DSMMsgKey         S              4
     *
DDltUsrPrf        DS             38
D  ExitPnt                       20
D  ExitFmt                        8
D  UserPrf                       10
     *
     *_____
     *  Common API Error Structure
     *_____
DAPIErrorDS       DS
D  APIBytes                      10I 0 Inz(%Size(APIErrorDS))
D  APIBytesOut                   10I 0
```

Listing 3.3: ILE RPG member EXT003R is called before user profile deletion (continued).

```
D   APIErrID                     7A
D   APIReserved                  1A
D   APIErInDta                   256A
    *
D@Msg1              C                      'User Profile is being -
D                                          deleted: '
    *
C       *Entry      PList
C                   Parm                        DltUsrPrf
    *
C                   Eval        SMMsgTxt = @Msg1 + UserPrf
    *
C                   Call        'QMHSNDM'
C                   Parm                        SMMsgId
C                   Parm                        SMMsgFile
C                   Parm                        SMMsgTxt
C                   Parm                        SMMsgLen
C                   Parm                        SMMsgType
C                   Parm                        SMMsgQ
C                   Parm                        SMMsgQ#
C                   Parm                        SMReplyQ
C                   Parm                        SMMsgKey
C                   Parm                        APIErrorDS
    *
C                   Return
```

Listing 3.4: ILE RPG member EXT004R is called after user profile deletion.

```
*------------------------------------------------------------
* Send Message API Declarations
*------------------------------------------------------------
DSMMsgId        S             7
DSMMsgFile      S            20
DSMMsgTxt       S           100
DSMMsgLen       S            10I 0 Inz(%Size(SMMsgTxt))
DSMMsgType      S            10   Inz('*INFO')
DSMMsgQ         S            20   Inz('QSYSOPR    *LIBL        ')
DSMMsgQ#        S            10I 0 Inz(1)
DSMReplyQ       S            20
DSMMsgKey       S             4
    *
DDltUsrPrf      DS           38
D   ExitPnt                  20
D   ExitFmt                   8
```

**Listing 3.4: ILE RPG member EXT004R
is called after user profile deletion (continued).**

```
D  UserPrf                     10
 *
 *_____
 *  Common API Error Structure
 *_____
DAPIErrorDS        DS
D  APIBytes                    10I 0 Inz(%Size(APIErrorDS))
D  APIBytesOut                 10I 0
D  APIErrID                     7A
D  APIReserved                  1A
D  APIErInDta                 256A
 *
D@Msg1             C                   'User Profile has been -
D                                      deleted: '
 *
C      *Entry      PList
C                  Parm                        DltUsrPrf
 *
C                  Eval      SMMsgTxt = @Msg1 + UserPrf
 *
C                  Call      'QMHSNDM'
C                  Parm                        SMMsgId
C                  Parm                        SMMsgFile
C                  Parm                        SMMsgTxt
C                  Parm                        SMMsgLen
C                  Parm                        SMMsgType
C                  Parm                        SMMsgQ
C                  Parm                        SMMsgQ#
C                  Parm                        SMReplyQ
C                  Parm                        SMMsgKey
C                  Parm                        APIErrorDS
 *
C                  Return
```

HOW THE EXAMPLE WORKS

The AS/400 provides exit point QIBM_QSY_DLT_PROFILE, which allows your user-written program to be called whenever a user profile is deleted. Depending on which of the two available formats are used, the exit program is called either before or after the profile is deleted.

When your exit program is called as the result of a user profile being deleted, it receives one parameter: a structure that defines three subfields. The parameter subfields are shown in Table 3.3.

	Table 3.3: DLTP0100 and DLTP0200 Format Parameter List.		
Sequence	Parameter	I/O	Type
1	Exit Point Name	Output	Char(20)
2	Format Name	Output	Char(8)
3	User Profile	Output	Char(10)

The ILE Example

The example members EXT003R and EXT004R employ system API QMHSNDM to send a message from within the RPG modules. An alert is triggered by sending a formatted message to the QSYSOPR message queue.

Adding the Exit Programs

Once compiled, the exit programs are added to the exit point using either the WRKREGINF or ADDEXITPGM command. The ADDEXITPGM display is shown in Figures 3.4 and 3.5.

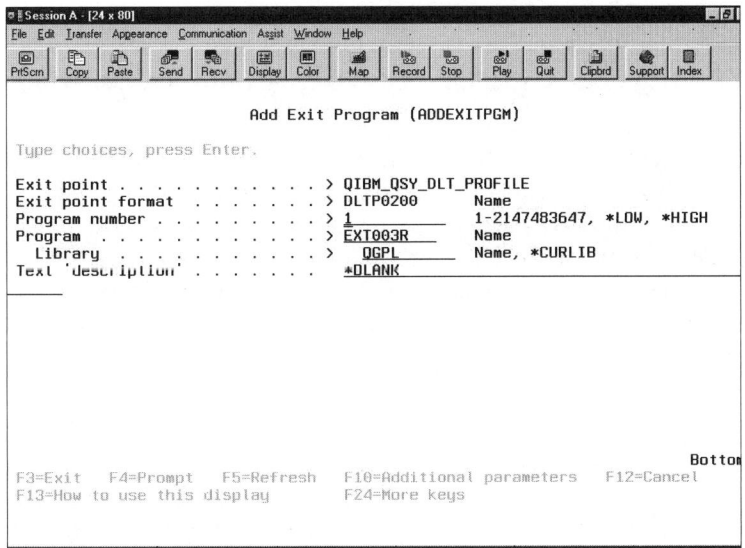

Figure 3.4: The ADDEXITPGM display.

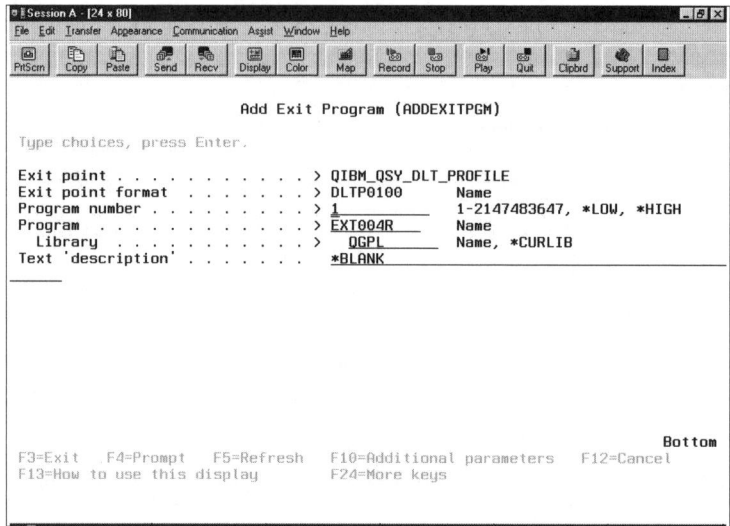

Figure 3.5: The ADDEXITPGM display.

EXAMPLE

Using an Exit Program to Monitor User Profile Restoration

The system provides a set of exit points that allows you to attach an exit program that is called whenever a user profile is created, changed, deleted, or restored. Unfortunately, these exit points do not allow the exit program to actively participate in the event. In other words, the exit program call is strictly informational. It cannot reject undesirable activity or alter the contents of the user profile in any way. However, the ability to monitor user profile activity allows you to keep track of what is going on and alert others if undesirable activity occurs.

WHAT THE EXAMPLE DOES

The example consists of one exit program source member. When attached to the Restore User Profile exit point QIBM_QSY_RST_PROFILE format RSTP0100, member EXT005R is called after a user profile is restored from backup medium and sends a notification message to the QSYSOPR message queue. Listing 3.5 shows the ILE RPG module EXT005R.

Listing 3.5: ILE RPG member EXT005R monitors user profile restoration.

```
      *_____
      * Send Message API Declarations
      *_____
     DSMMsgId        S              7
     DSMMsgFile      S             20
     DSMMsgTxt       S            100
     DSMMsgLen       S             10I 0 Inz(%Size(SMMsgTxt))
     DSMMsgType      S             10    Inz('*INFO')
     DSMMsgQ         S             20    Inz('QSYSOPR    *LIBL     ')
     DSMMsgQ#        S             10I 0 Inz(1)
     DSMReplyQ       S             20
     DSMMsgKey       S              4
      *
     DRstUsrPrf      DS            38
     D ExitPnt                     20
     D ExitFmt                      8
     D UserPrf                     10
      *

      *_____
      *   Common API Error Structure
      *_____
     DAPIErrorDS     DS
     D  APIBytes                   10I 0 Inz(%Size(APIErrorDS))
     D  APIBytesOut                10I 0
     D  APIErrID                    7A
     D  APIReserved                 1A
     D  APIErInDta                256A
      *
     D@Msg1          C                   'User Profile was restored: '
      *
     C     *Entry      PList
     C                 Parm                      RstUsrPrf
      *
     C                 Eval      SMMsgTxt = @Msg1 + UserPrf
      *
     C                 Call      'QMHSNDM'
     C                 Parm                      SMMsgId
     C                 Parm                      SMMsgFile
     C                 Parm                      SMMsgTxt
     C                 Parm                      SMMsgLen
     C                 Parm                      SMMsgType
     C                 Parm                      SMMsgQ
     C                 Parm                      SMMsgQ#
     C                 Parm                      SMReplyQ
     C                 Parm                      SMMsgKey
     C                 Parm                      APIErrorDS
      *
     C                 Return
```

HOW THE EXAMPLE WORKS

The AS/400 provides exit point QIBM_QSY_RST_PROFILE, which allows your user-written program to be called whenever a user profile is restored. The exit program is called after the restore occurs. Each system exit point has at least one format name associated with it. A format name either identifies the format of the information that is returned to your program or distinguishes the timing of when the exit point is called. The QIBM_QSY_RST_ PROFILE exit point provides one format, RSTP0100.

When your exit program is called as the result of a user profile being restored, it receives one parameter: a structure that defines three subfields. The parameter subfields are shown in Table 3.4.

Table 3.4: RSTP0100 Format Parameter List.

Sequence	Parameter	I/O	Type
1	Exit Point Name	Output	Char(20)
2	Format Name	Output	Char(8)
3	User Profile	Output	Char(10)

The ILE Example

The example member EXT005R employs system API QMHSNDM to send a message from within an RPG module. An alert is triggered by sending a formatted message to the QSYSOPR message queue.

Adding the Exit Program

Once compiled, the exit program is added to the exit point using either the WRKREGINF command or the ADDEXITPGM CL command. The ADDEXITPGM display is shown in Figure 3.6.

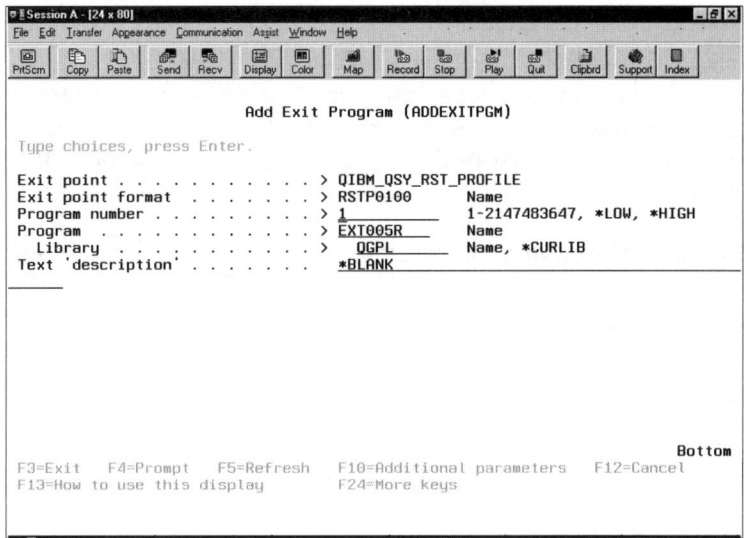

Figure 3.6: The ADDEXITPGM display.

EXAMPLE

Using an Exit Program to Monitor Database Server Access

The system database server provides database-related services to remote users transferring data from or to the AS/400. If you employ database tools such as IBM's ODBC driver or the Client Access File Transfer Function, the movement of data is serviced by the database server. The database server provides a set of exit points that allows you to attach exit programs that are called whenever a user initiates a database server request and when specific functions of the server are initiated. Fortunately, these exit points allow the exit program to actively participate in the event. The exit program logic can be employed to interrogate each request and reject it if deemed inappropriate.

It is important to understand that most third-party tools and drivers do not use IBM's database server exit points. In this case, adding an exit program to these points will not provide any additional security. If you strictly use IBM's standard offerings, the exit points will be in effect.

WHAT THE EXAMPLE DOES

The example consists of one exit program source member. When attached to the database server initiation exit point QIBM_QZDA_INIT format ZDAI0100, member EXT006R is called when a user first initiates a function of the remote database server. The example sends a notification message to the QSYSOPR message queue. Listing 3.6 shows the ILE RPG module EXT006R.

Listing 3.6: ILE RPG member EXT006R monitors database server startup.

```
     *_____
     * Send Message API Declarations
     *_____
DSMMsgId         S              7
DSMMsgFile       S             20
DSMMsgTxt        S            100
DSMMsgLen        S             10I 0 Inz(%Size(SMMsgTxt))
DSMMsgType       S             10    Inz('*INFO')
DSMMsgQ          S             20    Inz('QSYSOPR    *LIBL      ')
DSMMsgQ#         S             10I 0 Inz(1)
DSMReplyQ        S             20
DSMMsgKey        S              4
     *_____
     *   Common API Error Structure
     *_____
     DAPIErrorDS      DS
     D  APIBytes                 10I 0 Inz(%Size(APIErrorDS))
     D  APIBytesOut              10I 0
     D  APIErrID                  7A
     D  APIReserved               1A
     D  APIErInDta              256A
     *
D@Msg1           C                    'Remote Database Server Job -
D                                     started by user: '
     *
DReturnCode      S              1A
     *
DFmtZDAI0100     DS
D  User                         10A
D  ServerId                     10A
D  Format                        8A
D  Function                     10I 0
     *
C       *Entry     PList
C                  Parm                      ReturnCode
C                  Parm                      FmtZDAI0100
     *
C                  Eval      SMMsgTxt = @Msg1 + User
     *
C                  Call      'QMHSNDM'
C                  Parm                      SMMsgId
C                  Parm                      SMMsgFile
```

Listing 3.6: RPG member EXT006R
monitors database server startup (continued).

```
C                       Parm                        SMMsgTxt
C                       Parm                        SMMsgLen
C                       Parm                        SMMsgType
C                       Parm                        SMMsgQ
C                       Parm                        SMMsgQ#
C                       Parm                        SMReplyQ
C                       Parm                        SMMsgKey
C                       Parm                        APIErrorDS
 *
C                       Eval       ReturnCode = '1'
 *
C                       Return
```

HOW THE EXAMPLE WORKS

The AS/400 provides exit point QIBM_QZDA_INIT, which allows your user-written program to be called whenever a user first requests a service provided by the database server. The exit program is called before the request is processed and has the capability to reject it.

Each system exit point has at least one format name associated with it. A format name either identifies the format of the information that is returned to your program or distinguishes the timing of when the exit point is called. The QIBM_ZDA_INIT exit point provides one format, ZDAI0100.

When your exit program is called as the result of a database request, it receives two parameters: a return code and a structure that defines four subfields. The parameters are shown in Table 3.5.

Table 3.5: Exit Point QIBM_QZDA_INIT Parameter List.

Sequence	Parameter	I/O	Type
1	Return Code	I/O	Char(1)
2	Format Structure ZDAI0100	Output	Char(32)
Format Structure ZDAI0100 Subfields.			
Sequence	Parameter	I/O	Type
1	User Profile making request	Output	Char(10)
2	Server ID	Output	Char(10)
3	Format Name	Output	Char(8)
4	Requested Function	Output	Binary(4)

The ILE Example

The example member EXT005R employs system API QMHSNDM to send a message from within an RPG module. An alert is triggered by sending a formatted message to the QSYSOPR message queue when a user first requests a database server function. If you want the program to reject the request, the program will change the value of the return code parameter to '0'. If the exit program ends with a return code value of '1', the request is allowed.

Adding the Exit Program

Once compiled, the exit program is added to the exit point using either the WRKREGINF or ADDEXITPGM command. The ADDEXITPGM display is shown in Figure 3.7.

Great care should be used when adding exit programs to system functions. They should be added during off-hours, allowing you to perform an IPL if necessary. At a minimum, you will need to end and restart the QSERVER subsystem. When exit programs are added to the database server, all functions of the server may be rejected until after an IPL reinitializes the proper system server jobs.

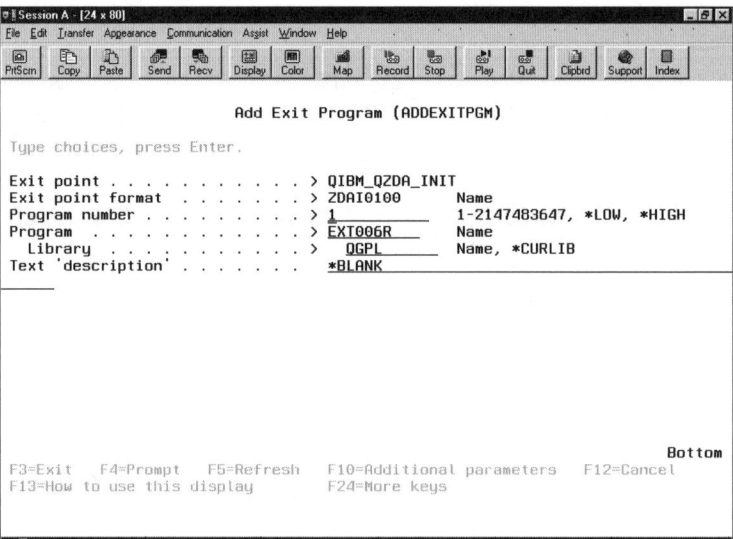

Figure 3.7: The ADDEXITPGM display.

EXAMPLE
Using an Exit Program to Log Database Server Requests

The system database server provides database-related services to remote users transferring data from or to the AS/400. If you employ database tools such as IBM's ODBC driver or the Client Access File Transfer Function, the movement of data is serviced by the database server. The database server provides a set of exit points that allows you to attach exit programs that are called whenever a user initiates a database server request and when specific functions of the server are initiated. Fortunately, these exit points allow the exit program to actively participate in the event. The exit program logic can be employed to interrogate each request and reject it if deemed inappropriate.

It is important to understand that most third-party tools and drivers do not use IBM's database server exit points. In this case, adding an exit program to these points will not provide any additional security. If you strictly use IBM's standard offerings, the exit points will be in effect.

WHAT THE EXAMPLE DOES
The example consists of one exit program source member. When attached to the database server SQL request exit point QIBM_QZDA_SQL1 format ZDAQ0100, member EXT007R is called when a user requests a specific SQL function of the remote database server. SQL functions are used to support database requests such as file transfers and statements executed through the IBM ODBC driver. The example logs each detail request by user, writing the details to a log file. Requests are written to an externally defined file whose layout matches the layout of the parameter data received by the exit program. Listing 3.7 shows the ILE RPG module EXT007R, and Listing 3.8 shows the DDS source for the externally defined log file.

Listing 3.7: ILE RPG member EXT007R logs database server SQL requests.

```
*
FZDAQ0100   O   C           Disk
*
DReturnCode     S           1A
*
DFmtZDAQ0100    E DS             ExtName(ZDAQ0100)
*
C     *Entry    PList
C               Parm                ReturnCode
C               Parm                FmtZDAQ0100
```

Listing 3.7: ILE RPG member EXT007R logs database server SQL requests (continued).

```
C                    Write      SQL1
 *
C                    Eval       ReturnCode = '1'
 *
C                    Return
```

Listing 3.8: DDS source member ZDAQ0100 is the log file for SQL requests.

```
A          R SQL1
A            USER        10
A            SERVERID    10
A            FORMAT       8
A            FUNCTION     9B 0
A            STATEMENT   18
A            CURSOR      18
A            PREPAREOP    2
A            OPENATTR     2
A            PACKAGENM   10
A            PACKAGELB   10
A            DRDAIND      4B 0
A            COMMITLVL    1
A            SQLSTMT    512
```

HOW THE EXAMPLE WORKS

The AS/400 provides exit point QIBM_QZDA_SQL1, which allows your user-written program to be called whenever a user requests a detailed SQL service provided by the database server. The exit program is called before the request is processed and has the capability to reject it.

Each system exit point has at least one format name associated with it. A format name either identifies the format of the information that is returned to your program or distinguishes the timing of when the exit point is called. The QIBM_ZDA_SQL1 exit point provides one format, ZDAQ0100.

When your exit program is called as the result of a database request, it receives two parameters: a return code and a structure that defines 13 subfields. The parameters are shown in Table 3.6.

Sequence	Parameter	I/O	Type
Table 3.6: Exit Point QIBM_QZDA_SQL1 Parameter List.			
1	Return Code	I/O	Char(1)
2	Format Structure ZDAQ0100	Output	Char(607)
Format Structure ZDAI0100 Subfields			
Sequence	Parameter	I/O	Type
1	User Profile making request	Output	Char(10)
2	Server ID	Output	Char(10)
3	Format Name	Output	Char(8)
4	Requested Function	Output	Binary(4)
5	Statement Name	Output	Char(18)
6	Cursor Name	Output	Char(18)
7	Prepare Option	Output	Char(2)
8	Open Attributes	Output	Char(2)
9	Extended Dynamic Package Name	Output	Char(10)
10	Package Library Name	Output	Char(10)
11	DRDA Indicator	Output	Char(1)
12	Commit Control Level	Output	Char(1)
13	First 512 Bytes of SQL Statement	Output	Char(512)

Requested Function

The Requested Function returned by the exit point provides a code that identifies the type of SQL operation being requested. Table 3.7 shows the possible values and their meanings.

The ILE Example

The example member EXT007R receives detailed information about the database request when called by the system exit point. The information is written to file ADAQ0100, where it can be used as a source of information to be monitored. This program could be modified to interrogate the content of the SQL statement, and reject or accept certain types of requests. If you want the program to reject the request, it must change the value of the return code parameter to '0'. If the exit program ends with a return code value of '1', the request is allowed.

Adding the Exit Program

Once compiled, the exit program is added to the exit point using either the WRKREGINF or ADDEXITPGM command. The physical file that is to receive the log entries must also be created and placed in a library that is assured to be on the library list of the database server jobs. This is controlled via system value. The ADDEXITPGM display is shown in Figure 3.8.

Great care should be used when adding exit programs to system functions. They should be added during off-hours, allowing you to perform an IPL if necessary. At a minimum, you will need to end and restart the QSERVER subsystem. When exit programs are added to the database server, all functions of the server may be rejected until after an IPL reinitializes the proper system server jobs.

Table 3.7: Function Values.	
Requested Function	Description
6144	Prepare
6147	Prepare and Describe
6148	Open and Describe
6149	Execute
6150	Execute Immediate
6153	Connect
6156	Stream Fetch
6157	Prepare and Execute
6158	Open and Fetch
6159	Create Package
6160	Clear Package
6161	Delete Package
6162	Execute or Open

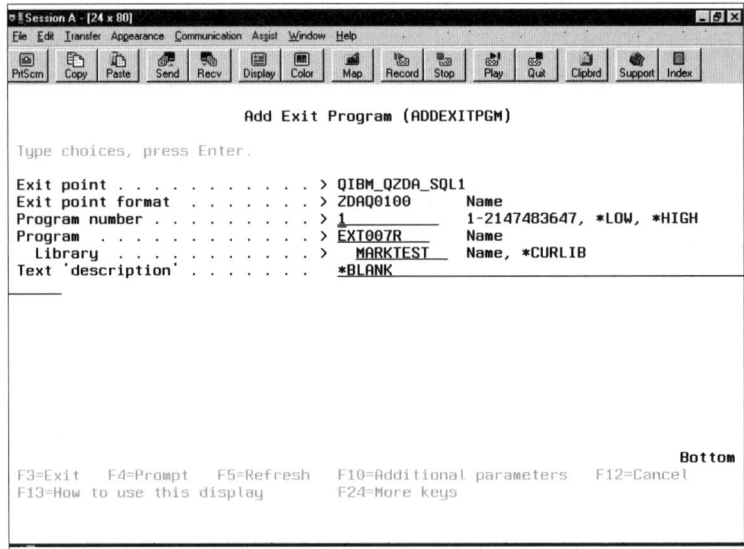

Figure 3.8: The ADDEXITPGM display.

EXAMPLE

Using the Job Notification Exit Point

The AS/400 provides an exit point QIBM_QWT_JOBNOTIFY that is triggered whenever a job is placed on a job queue, whenever a job starts, or whenever a job ends. The exit point allows you to monitor the activity for a specific subsystem description or for all subsystems.

However, unlike other previously discussed exit points, the job notification exit point does not call an exit program. Instead, the event causes an entry to be written to a data queue, allowing you to read the queue and monitor job activity. Job notification can be extremely handy for applications where a process is dependent upon the successful completion of other jobs.

WHAT THE EXAMPLE DOES

The example consists of one data queue object called JOBNOTIFY and an ILE RPG source member that reads entries from the data queue. When attached to the job notification exit point QIBM_QWT_JOBNOTIFY format NTFY0100, the data queue receives entries based on criteria supplied to the exit point as exit program data. Member EXT008R is called when it is desired to process the job notification entries on the data queue. It reads all the job start, job end, and jobs on queue entries and prints them. Figure 3.9 shows the statement used to create the data queue, and Listing 3.9 shows the ILE RPG module EXT008R.

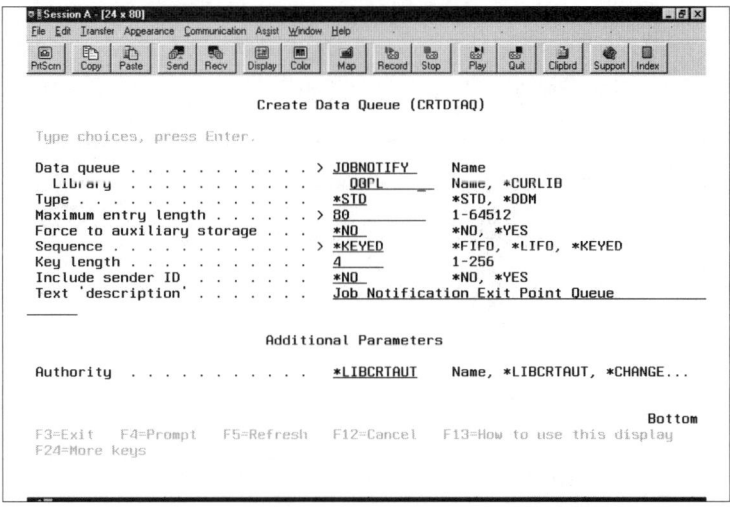

Figure 3.9: The job notification data queue is created as a keyed data queue.

Listing 3.9: ILE RPG member EXT008R reads job notification entries.

```
FQPRINT     O    F  132         Printer OFLIND(*InOF)
 *
DJob             S          26
 *
DDQData          DS         80
D  MessageID               10
D  MessageFm                2
D  JobID                   16
D  FullJobID               26
D    JobNm                 10      Overlay(FullJobID:1)
D    JobUsr                10      Overlay(FullJobID:11)
D    JobNbr                 6      Overlay(FullJobID:21)
D  Reserved                20
 *_____
 * Data Queue API Parameters
 *_____
DDataQueue       S          10      inz('JOBNOTIFY ')
DDQLib           S          10      inz('*LIBL      ')
DDQWait          S          5p 0 inz(0)
DDQDtaLen        S          5p 0
DDQKeyLen        S          3p 0 inz(4)
DDQKeyOrd        S           2      inz('EQ')
DDQSendLen       S          3P 0 inz(0)
DDQSendDta       S          10
DDQKeyData       S           4
 *
D@JobStart       C                   '0001'
D@JobEnd         C                   '0002'
D@JobOnQueue     C                   '0004'
 *
C                  Except    Header1
 *
 *_____
 * Read all Job Start Entries from Queue
 *_____
C                  Eval      DQKeyData = @JobStart
 *
C                  DoU       DQDtaLen = 0
 *
C                  CALL      'QRCVDTAQ'
C                  PARM                  DataQueue
C                  PARM                  DQLib
C                  PARM                  DQDtaLen
C                  PARM                  DQData
C                  PARM                  DQWait
C                  PARM                  DQKeyOrd
C                  PARM                  DQKeyLen
C                  PARM                  DQKeyData
C                  PARM                  DQSendLen
C                  PARM                  DQSendDta
 *
C                  If        DQDtaLen > 0
```

Listing 3.9: ILE RPG member EXT008R
reads job notification entries (continued).

```
C                        Eval      Job = %Trimr(JobNm) +
C                                    '/' +
C                                    %Trimr(JobUsr) +
C                                    '/' +
C                                    JobNbr
C    *
C                        Except    JobSDtl
C                        EndIf
C                        EndDo
     *
     *_____
     * Read all Job Ending Entries from Queue
     *_____
C                        Eval      DQKeyData = @JobEnd
C    *
C                        DoU       DQDtaLen = 0
C    *
C                        CALL      'QRCVDTAQ'
C                        PARM                    DataQueue
C                        PARM                    DQLib
C                        PARM                    DQDtaLen
C                        PARM                    DQData
C                        PARM                    DQWait
C                        PARM                    DQKeyOrd
C                        PARM                    DQKeyLen
C                        PARM                    DQKeyData
C                        PARM                    DQSendLen
C                        PARM                    DQSendDta
C    *
C                        If        DQDtaLen > 0
C                        Eval      Job = %Trimr(JobNm) +
C                                    '/' +
C                                    %Trimr(JobUsr) +
C                                    '/' +
C                                    JobNbr
C    *
C                        Except    JobEDtl
C                        EndIf
C                        EndDo
     *
     *_____
     * Read all Job on Job Queue Entries from Data Queue
     *_____
C                        Eval      DQKeyData = @JobOnQueue
C    *
C                        DoU       DQDtaLen = 0
C    *
C                        CALL      'QRCVDTAQ'
C                        PARM                    DataQueue
C                        PARM                    DQLib
C                        PARM                    DQDtaLen
```

Listing 3.9: ILE RPG member EXT008R reads job notification entries (continued).

```
C                        PARM                           DQData
C                        PARM                           DQWait
C                        PARM                           DQKeyOrd
C                        PARM                           DQKeyLen
C                        PARM                           DQKeyData
C                        PARM                           DQSendLen
C                        PARM                           DQSendDta
 *
C                        If         DQDtaLen > 0
 *
C                        Eval       Job = %Trimr(JobNm) +
C                                       '/' +
C                                       %Trimr(JobUsr) +
C                                       '/' +
C                                       JobNbr
 *
C                        Except     JobQDtl
C                        EndIf
C                        EndDo
 *
C                        Return
 *_____
OQPRINT    E             Header1          2 01
O                                                  54 'Monitored Job Acti'
O                                                  58 'vity'
O                                                  70 'Page:'
O                        Page1            z        76
O          E             Header1        1 1
O                                                   6 'Job'
O                                                  54 'Activity'
O          E             JobSDtl          1
O                        Job                        30
O                                                  57 'Job Started'
O          E             JobEDtl          1
O                        Job                        30
O                                                  57 'Job Ended   '
O          E             JobQDtl          1
O                        Job                        30
O                                                  58 'Job On Queue'
```

HOW THE EXAMPLE WORKS

The AS/400 provides exit point QIBM_QWT_JOBNOTIFY, which allows job activity to be logged to a data queue. You can then supply a user-written program to read and process each entry from the queue as your needs dictate.

Each system exit point has at least one format name associated with it. A format name either identifies the format of the information that is returned to your program or distinguishes the timing of when the exit point is called. The QIBM_QWT_JOBNOTIFY exit point provides one format, NTFY0100. When the exit point places entries on the data queue, it receives a string comprising five data subfields, as shown in Table 3.8.

Table 3.8: Job Notification Data Queue Entry Subfields.			
Sequence	Field	I/O	Type
1	Message Identifier	Output	Char(10)
2	Message Format	Output	Char(2)
3	Internal Job Identifier	Output	Char(16)
4	Qualified Job Name	Output	Char(26)
5	Reserved	Output	Char(20)

The ILE Example

The example member EXT008R employs system API QRCVDTAQ to receive entries from the job notification data queue. Looping control structures read entries from the queue by key, first by reading all of the type-0001 (job start) entries and completing by reading all of the type-0004 (job placed on job queue) keyed entries. Each entry received is printed on a list for review.

Registering the Data Queue

Once created, the data queue JOBNOTIFY is added to the exit point using either the WRKREGINF or ADDEXITPGM command. The ADDEXITPGM command accepts an Exit Program Data parameter that allows you to specify the notification type of entries to be logged, the subsystem name to monitor, and the subsystem library. The permissible Exit Program Data values are shown as follows:

Notification Type

The first data value identifies to the exit point the types of entries that are to be written to the data queue. The valid values are:

0001	Job start notifications are sent to the data queue.
0002	Job end notifications are sent to the data queue.
0003	Job start and job end notifications are sent to the data queue.
0004	Job queue notifications are sent to the data queue.
0005	Job start and job queue notifications are sent to the data queue.
0006	Job end and job queue notifications are sent to the data queue.
0007	Job start, job end, and job queue notifications are sent to the data queue.

Subsystem Description

The second data value identifies to the exit point the subsystem whose activity is to be written to the data queue. In addition to allowing a specific subsystem description name, the following special value is also permissible:

*ANY	The data queue is used for all subsystems.

Subsystem Description Library

The final data value identifies to the exit point the library of the subsystem whose activity is to be written to the data queue. In addition to allowing a specific library name, the following special value is also permissible:

*ANY	The named subsystem is monitored, regardless of the library in which it resides.

The ADDEXITPGM command to monitor job start and job ending notifications for subsystem QSYS/QBATCH is shown in Figure 3.10 and continues in Figure 3.11.

Great care should be used when registering system exit points. They should be added during off-hours, allowing you to perform an IPL if necessary. Remember to thoroughly test the results in a controlled situation.

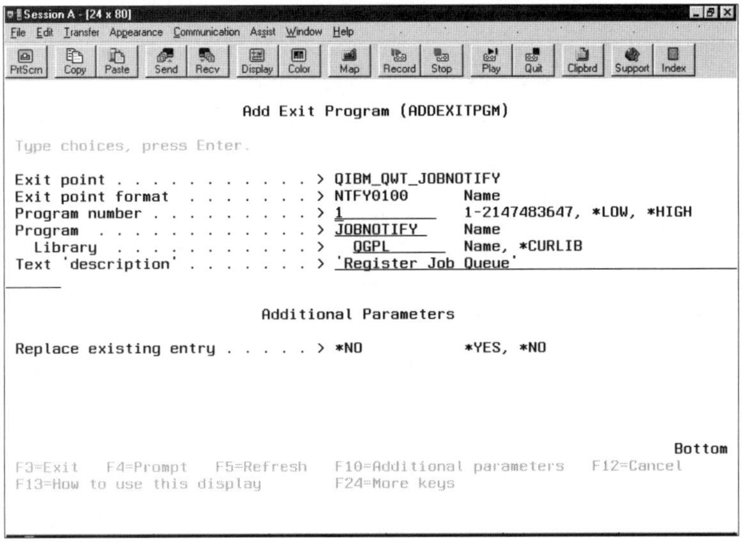

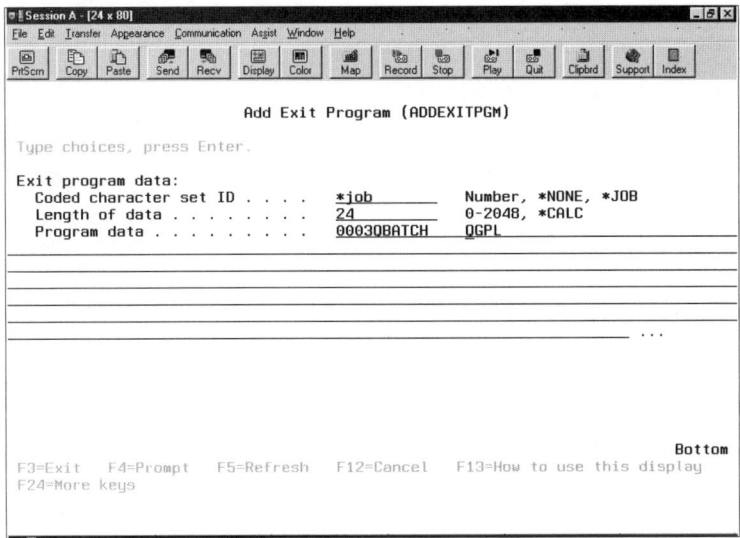

Figure 3.10: The ADDEXITPGM display.

Figure 3.11: Continuation of the ADDEXITPGM command display.

4

APPLICATION PROGRAMMING INTERFACES

E veryone knows the easiest way to perform system functions from a command line is to execute CL commands. However, the choice is not as clear when system functions are to be performed from within your RPG source code. Many programmers elect to code CL statements into a separate CL module or program, then call it from their RPG code. This approach is severely hampered for all but the simplest applications by the limitations of CL. Because many commands do not provide output to a file, retrieval of large amounts of information is limited.

Luckily, there is a better, more powerful way to programatically perform system functions. IBM provides a set of system APIs that allows you to perform hundreds of system functions. Although APIs are frequently enhanced with new release levels, IBM has assured reliability of the code you write by maintaining backward compatibility with previous releases. What this means to you is that if you write a program using an API, IBM implements changes to the API in a way that assures your call to the API will run correctly without modification.

Many programmers have dismissed APIs as too difficult and complicated to use. Unfortunately, the IBM *System API Reference Manual* doesn't do much to dispel this belief.

APIs were clearly developed by IBM to interface with the C programming language. The concept of using such data types as binary, floating point, and variable-length character fields is common to C programmers, but unfamiliar to most RPG developers. With the increased power and flexibility of ILE RPG over traditional RPG/400, these APIs are now much more accessible.

THE CATEGORIES OF APIS

APIs are available to perform many hundreds of diverse system functions, and there is a high degree of consistency among them. Most system APIs fall into one of four basic categories:

- Execution APIs
- Conversion APIs
- Retrieval APIs
- List APIs

Execution APIs

The simplest form of APIs, Execution APIs, are used to perform specific system actions. These APIs generally accept one or more input parameters used to direct the system function and may return feedback to confirm the status of API completion.

An example of an Execution API is the Command Execution (QCMDEXC) API. This commonly used API accepts two parameters: a character string containing a CL command to execute and a numeric field containing the length of the command string. When called, the API passes the command string to the AS/400 command processor for execution. Other examples of Execution APIs include QMHSNDBM, which sends a break message to a user, and QSYCHGPW, which is used to change a user password.

Conversion APIs

Conversion APIs are used to alter the type or format of data. These APIs commonly accept one or more input parameters, change the contents to an alternate form, and then return the results.

Examples of Conversion APIs include CEEDATE, which converts an input date to a variety of character formats, QLGCNVCS, which converts a string between upper and lowercase, and QDCXLATE, which converts data using a defined translation table.

Retrieval APIs

Retrieval APIs are used to retrieve finite amounts of information from the system. These APIs commonly accept one or more input parameters defining the type of information requested, then return one or more fields of information satisfying the request. Retrieval APIs commonly allow you to select from one or more predefined formats of information to retrieve. For example, many APIs offer a format that returns only basic-level information about the object or item. Alternate formats provide more detailed or obscure information. By selecting the desired format, you specify the information you want to retrieve.

Examples of Retrieval APIs include QDBRTVFD, which retrieves a file description, QWCRJBST, which retrieves the current status of a specific job, and CEERAN0, which generate a pseudo-random number.

List APIs

List APIs are used to retrieve information from the system when the volume of information varies. These APIs commonly accept one or more input parameters defining the type of information requested, then return multiple sets of one or more fields of information satisfying the request. While Retrieval APIs return information about a specific object or item found on the system, List APIs return information about multiple objects or items. For example, when retrieving information about currently executing user jobs, there may be only one or there may be hundreds of active user jobs. List APIs provide a mechanism flexible and powerful enough to accommodate both scenarios.

Like Retrieval APIs, List APIs commonly allow you to select from one or more predefined formats identifying the content to be retrieved. Many APIs offer a format that returns only basic-level information about the object or item. Alternate formats provide more detailed or obscure information. By selecting the desired format, you specify the information you want to retrieve.

Examples of List APIs include QWCLSCDE, which retrieves a list of jobs entered into the system job scheduler; QUSLJOB, which retrieves a list of jobs; and QUSLSPL, which lists spool files.

AS/400 SYSTEM API REFERENCE MANUAL

To effectively use APIs, you must have a complete and thorough reference. This chapter provides example uses of many APIs, but it is simply not possible within this text to cover all of the hundreds that are available. The goal of this chapter is to teach you how to use any API with confidence. To locate and work with an API not covered in this chapter, you will need to access the *System API Reference Manual*.

Manual Structure

The *System API Reference Manual* for V4R4 organizes APIs into 36 categories. These categories broadly identify the system area to which the API pertains. To locate information about a specific API, you must know under which category it appears. This can at times be a frustrating process if it is not obvious how an API is categorized. The following is a list of AS/400 system API categories:

- Backup and Recovery APIs
- Client Management Support APIs
- Cluster APIs
- Communications APIs
- Configuration APIs
- Debugger APIs
- Directory Services APIs
- Dynamic Screen Manager APIs
- Edit Function APIs
- File APIs
- Hardware Resource APIs
- Hierarchical File System APIs
- High-Level Language APIs
- Integrated Language Environment (ILE) CEE APIs
- Journal and Commit APIs
- Message Handling APIs
- Miscellaneous APIs
- National Language Support APIs
- Network Management APIs
- Object APIs
- Office APIs
- Operational Assistant APIs
- Performance Collector APIs
- Print APIs
- Problem Management APIs
- Program and CL Command APIs
- Registration Facility APIs

- Remote Procedure Call APIs

- Security APIs

- Server Support APIs

- Software Product APIs

- UNIX-Type APIs

- User Interface APIs

- Virtual Terminal APIs

- Work Management APIs

- Work Station Support APIs

When you locate the desired API, the manual follows a basic structure in presenting the information about most APIs. First, the API parameters are listed. The parameters are grouped by those that are required, often followed by one or more sets of optional parameters. The manual lists the sequence and name of each parameter, whether the parameter is input, output, or both, and the data type and length of the parameter. Table 4.1 shows an example of an API parameter list.

Table 4.1: Example API Parameter List.			
Sequence	Parameter	I/O	Type
1	Receiver Variable	Output	Char(*)
2	Length of Receiver Variable	Input	Binary(4)
3	Input Number	Input	INT4
4	Output Number	Output	FLOAT8
5	Error Code	I/O	Char(*)

Understanding API Data Types

When using system APIs, you will be presented with data types that may be unfamiliar to you. As Table 4.1 exemplifies, APIs require you to handle such types as binary, integer, floating point, and variable-length character fields. Defining these types in RPG can result in some gotchas that, unless you understand a few basic rules, will cause a great deal of frustration.

Variable-Length Character Fields

API parameters defined as type CHAR(*) generally are interpreted in one of two ways: either as a structure that contains multiple subfields or as a single field whose length varies depending on the request. When you encounter a parameter defined in this way in the system documentation, you will usually find a further subdefinition later in the section. If the parameter calls for a structure of subfields, you will define the parameter as a data structure with each of the established subfields. The following is an example of a CHAR(*) parameter definition:

```
DName+++++++++++ETDsFrom+++To/L+++IDc.Keywords++++++++++++++++++++++++
DAPIParameter     DS
D  CmdType                        10I 0
D  DBCSData                       1
D  Prompter                       1
D  CmdSyntax                      1
D  MsgKey                         4
D  Reserved9                      9
```

Binary Fields

The area of greatest confusion to most AS/400 programmers attempting to use APIs is caused by the definition of binary fields. System APIs extensively use binary fields for parameters when numeric data is being passed. Defining binary data in RPG can be a confusing proposition. To demonstrate this fact, look at the following two RPG definitions of binary data fields:

```
DName+++++++++++ETDsFrom+++To/L+++IDc.Keywords++++++++++++++++++++++++
Dbinary4          S              4B 0
and
DName+++++++++++ETDsFrom+++To/L+++IDc.Keywords++++++++++++++++++++++++
D                 DS
Dbinary4                      1    4B 0
```

The first definition of field BINARY4 defines a four-digit binary field as standalone for a length of four. The second definition of the field uses positional notation in a data structure to define the field as binary beginning in position 1 and ending in position 4. These two definitions are the same, right?

Wrong. If you happened to be defining character fields instead of binary fields, these two definitions would be the same. Binary data definitions work differently. The first definition of BINARY4 that specifies a length of four is actually two bytes long. This is because binary fields defined in RPG using an explicit length are actually being defined for a specific precision instead of a specific length. That is, the first definition is actually creating a four-digit binary field, which only occupies two bytes of storage. Therefore, defining a binary field with an explicit length of four digits does not result in a four-byte field. It defines a two-byte field. Because the second definition uses a data structure to allow positional definition from position 1 to position 4, the result is a four-byte binary field.

So, if an API calls for a parameter of type Binary(4), the permissible definitions are any of the following, because all result in a four-byte binary integer, as shown below:

```
DName++++++++++++ETDsFrom+++To/L+++IDc.Keywords++++++++++++++++++++++++
Dbinary4#1       S                5B 0
Dbinary4#2       S                6B 0
Dbinary4#3       S                7B 0
Dbinary4#4       S                8B 0
Dbinary4#5       S                9B 0
D                DS
Dbinary4#6              1         4B 0
Dbinary4#7       S               10I 0
```

It may seem hard to believe, but all seven fields defined result in the creation of four-byte binary fields. Fields having a precision of five to nine digits all occupy four bytes of storage.

The final definition, field BINARY4#7, does not even use the binary data type. Relatively new to RPG, the integer data type is an excellent substitute for the binary data type.

Integer Fields

According to a source within IBM's RPG Compiler Development Team, RPG handles the integer data type more reliably and more efficiently than it handles the binary data type. The integer data type is similar to the binary data type with the following exceptions:

- The integer data type allows a full range of binary values

- An integer data type must always have zero decimal positions

Like binary fields, integer fields are also explicitly defined by their number of digits, or precision, rather than by the number of bytes they occupy. An integer field can be defined in RPG as 3, 5, 10, or 20 digits in length. An integer defined as three digits long results in the creation of a one-byte field. Five-digit integers are two bytes long, 10-digit integers are four bytes long, and 20-digit integers are eight bytes in length. Therefore, APIs that call for a four-byte binary parameter are best defined as a 10-digit integer.

Some APIs define parameters as integer types and list a length. For example, the type INT4 is a four-byte integer field. As you will recall, a four-byte integer is defined not with a length of 4, but with a length of 10.

Floating Point Fields

Certain APIs require parameters to be passed as floating point data type fields. You will see a notation such as FLOAT8, meaning an eight-byte floating point field. RPG supports floating point fields for applications using a data-type F in the field definition specification. The number of decimal positions in the definition specification is always left blank when defining floating point fields. An example definition of a FLOAT8 field is as follows:

```
DName++++++++++ETDsFrom+++To/L+++IDc.Keywords+++++++++++++++++++++++
DFloat8              S              8F
```

EXAMPLE

Using the Command Execution API

One of the simplest APIs, the Command Execution (QCMDEXC) API, executes a CL command. Use of this API is a good alternative to calling a separate CL program to execute a command from within an RPG program or module.

WHAT THE EXAMPLE DOES

The example ILE RPG module API001R employs the QCMDEXC API to execute two CL commands. The first command executed displays the output queue QPRINT. The second command uses the command prompter to display a prompted Add Library List Entry (ADDLIBLE) command. Listing 4.1 shows the source member.

Listing 4.1: ILE RPG member API001R employs the QCMDEXC API.

```
DWrkOutq            C                      'WRKOUTQ QPRINT'
DAddLibLE           C                      '?ADDLIBLE MARKTEST *FIRST'
 *
DCmdString          S              100
DCmdLength          S               15   5
 *
C                        Eval      CmdString = WrkOutq
```
→

Listing 4.1: ILE RPG member API001R
employs the QCMDEXC API (continued).

```
C                     Eval      CmdLength = %Size(WrkOutq)
 *
C                     Call      'QCMDEXC'
C                     Parm                  CmdString
C                     Parm                  CmdLength
 *
C                     Eval      CmdString = AddLibLE
C                     Eval      CmdLength = %Size(AddLibLE)
 *
C                     Call      'QCMDEXC'
C                     Parm                  CmdString
C                     Parm                  CmdLength
 *
C                     Return
```

HOW THE EXAMPLE WORKS

The QCMDEXC API runs a single CL command from within a high-level language program.

The API receives two required parameters and one optional parameter, as shown in Table 4.2.

Table 4.2: QCMDEXC API Parameter List.
Required Parameters

Sequence	Parameter	I/O	Type
1	Command String	Input	Char(*)
2	Length of Command String	Input	Packed (15, 5)

Optional Parameters

Sequence	Parameter	I/O	Type
3	IGC Process Control	Input	Char(3)

The first parameter is a character input field that contains the command that is to be executed when the API is called. The length of the character field may vary as appropriate to accommodate the command string to be processed. The maximum allowable size of the command string field is 32,702 bytes.

The second parameter is a 15-digit packed decimal field with five decimal positions that contains the length of the field used to pass the command string parameter.

The third parameter, not used in this example, is used to instruct the system to accept double-byte data. To use this feature, you will simply define a three-byte character field initialized with the value 'IGC'. Passing the field as the third API parameter will instruct the system to accept DBCS data.

API Characteristics

When called, the API passes the supplied command string parameter to the AS/400 command processor for execution. When command execution completes, control is returned to the program that called the API and continues execution with the next sequential statement.

One of the main limitations of the QCMDEXC API is its lack of a controlled error feedback. If the command executed by the API fails, the API returns a generic hard program error. The only way to get feedback about the error is to handle the error in the calling program via the Program Status Data Structure.

The ILE RPG Example

The example source member API001R executes two CL commands using the QCMDEXC API. The first command performed is a Display Output Queue (DSPOUTQ) command. The command string size field is initialized using a soft-coding technique. The %SIZE built-in function loads the field CMDLENGTH with the size of the command string field without hard coding the field length. This technique enhances the maintainability of the code by reducing the steps necessary to changing the size of the command string field. When the API is called, the command executes, displaying the QPRINT output queue.

The example then executes the ADDLIBLE command. The command string is preceded with the common command prompt character '?', which displays the command in a prompted state. The library name supplied in the command string, in this case MARKTEST, serves as a default value to the prompted command. The user can hit Enter to accept the default library name or key in a new value as desired. If the ADDLIBLE command fails or if the user cancels the prompted command by pressing F3 or F12, a hard API call failure error is triggered in the calling program.

EXAMPLE

Using the Command Processor API

Similar to the QCMDEXC API, the Command Processor (QCAPCMD) API executes a CL command and provides additional functionality. Use of this API is a good alternative to calling a separate CL program to execute a command from within an RPG program or module. In addition to executing a command, the Command Processor API also allows you to:

- Test a command's syntax without running it

- Prompt a command and receive the user's changes to the command

- Monitor a command's execution for errors

WHAT THE EXAMPLE DOES

The example ILE RPG module API002R employs the QCAPCMD API to execute two CL commands. The first command executed displays the output queue QPRINT2. The second command uses the API command prompter parameter to display a prompted WRKOUTQ command. Listing 4.2 shows the source member.

Listing 4.2: ILE RPG member API002R employs the QCAPCMD API.

```
 *
D@WrkOutq1        C                         'WRKOUTQ QPRINT2'
D@WrkOutq2        C                         'WRKOUTQ OUTQ(QPRINT)'
 *
 *_____
 * API Parameters
 *_____
DCmdString        S             100
DCmdLen           S              10I 0
DCBLen            S              10I 0 Inz(%Size(FmtCPOP0100))
DCBFormat         S               8    Inz('CPOP0100')
DNewCmd           S             100
DNewLenIn         S              10I 0 Inz(%Size(NewCmd))
DNewLenOut        S              10I 0
 *
 *_____
 * API Control Block
 *_____
DFmtCPOP0100      DS
D  CmdType                       10I 0
D  DBCSData                       1
```

Listing 4.2: ILE RPG member API002R employs the QCAPCMD API (continued).

```
D  Prompter                      1
D  CmdSyntax                     1
D  MsgKey                        4
D  Reserved9                     9
   *
   *_____
   *  Common API Error Structure
   *_____
DAPIErrorDS      DS
D  APIBytes                     10I 0 Inz(%Size(APIErrorDS))
D  APIBytesOut                  10I 0
D  APIErrID                      7A
D  APIReserved                   1A
D  APIErInDta                  256A
   *
C                 Eval      CmdString = @WrkOutq1
C                 Eval      CmdLen    = %Size(@WrkOutq1)
   *
C                 Eval      CmdType   = 0
C                 Eval      DBCSData  = '0'
C                 Eval      Prompter  = '0'
C                 Eval      CmdSyntax = '0'
C                 Eval      MsgKey    = *Blanks
C                 Eval      Reserved9 = *Loval
   *
C                 Call      'QCAPCMD'
C                 Parm                  CmdString
C                 Parm                  CmdLen
C                 Parm                  FmtCPOP0100
C                 Parm                  CBLen
C                 Parm                  CBFormat
C                 Parm                  NewCmd
C                 Parm                  NewLenIn
C                 Parm                  NewLenOut
C                 Parm                  APIErrorDS
   *
C                 Eval      CmdString = @WrkOutq2
C                 Eval      CmdLen    = %Size(@WrkOutq2)
C                 Eval      Prompter  = '1'
   *
C                 Call      'QCAPCMD'
C                 Parm                  CmdString
C                 Parm                  CmdLen
C                 Parm                  FmtCPOP0100
C                 Parm                  CBLen
C                 Parm                  CBFormat
C                 Parm                  NewCmd
```

Listing 4.2: ILE RPG member *API002R* employs the QCAPCMD API (continued).

```
C                    Parm                    NewLenIn
C                    Parm                    NewLenOut
C                    Parm                    APIErrorDS
C    *
C                    Return
```

HOW THE EXAMPLE WORKS

The QCAPCMD API runs a single CL command from within a high-level language program. Unlike the QCMDEXC API, the QCAPCMD API returns an error feedback buffer, allowing you to monitor the successful completion of the command. If the command prompter is used to prompt the command, the final executing command string is returned from the API, allowing your program to interrogate the parameters selected by the user.

QCAPCMD Parameters

The API receives nine required parameters, as listed in Table 4.3.

Table 4.3: QCAPCMD API Parameter List. Required Parameters			
Sequence	Parameter	I/O	Type
1	Command String	Input	Char(*)
2	Length of Command String	Input	Binary(4)
3	Options Control Block	Input	Char(*)
4	Options Control Block Length	Input	Binary(4)
5	Options Control Block Format	Input	Char(8)
6	Changed Command String	Output	Char(*)
7	Length Available for Changed Command	Input	Binary(4)
8	Length of Changed Command String	Output	Binary(4)
9	Error Code	I/O	Char(*)

Command String Parameter

The first parameter is a character input field that contains the command that is to be executed when the API is called. The length of the character field may vary as appropriate to accommodate the command string to be processed. The maximum allowable size of the command string field is 32,702 bytes.

Length of Command String Parameter

The second parameter is a four-byte binary field that contains the length of the field used to pass the command string parameter. As discussed in detail earlier in this chapter, the most desirable way to define a four-byte binary parameter is to declare the field as a 10-digit integer. As you will recall, a 10-digit integer occupies four bytes of space.

Options Control Block Parameter

The third parameter is a structure containing the options that control how the command string is to be handled. In an RPG program, the Options Control Block parameter is defined as a data structure having multiple defined subfields. The name of the Options Control Block parameter format is CPOP0100. Table 4.4 shows the subfields that comprise the Options Control Block format.

Table 4.4: Options Control Block Parameter Subfields.

Sequence	Parameter	I/O	Type
1	Type of Command Processing	Input	Binary(4)
2	DBCS Data Handling	Input	Char(1)
3	Prompter Action	Input	Char(1)
4	Command String Syntax	Input	Char(1)
5	Message Retrieve Key	Input	Char(4)`
6	Reserved	Input	Char(9)

Type of Command Processing

The Type of Command Processing option determines the action that is to be performed with the command string. The permissible options are:

122

0 Run the command.

1 Check the syntax of the command string.

2 Run the command with the following features:
- Perform limited user checking
- Prompt the command for any missing required parameters
- Run the command in System/36 environment if the command is a System/36 command

3 Check the syntax of the command with the following features:
- Perform limited user checking
- Prompt the command for any missing required parameters

4 Check the syntax of the command as a CL program statement:
- Checks syntax as using same rules as SEU entry in a CL program
- Prompt the command for missing parameters using SEU options

5 Check the syntax of the command using CL batch job rules.

6 Check the syntax of the string using rules of command definition.

7 Check the syntax of the string using rules of binder definition.

8 Run the command string as a user-defined option.
- This is similar to running a user-defined option in PDM

9 Check the syntax of the command as an ILE CL statement:
- Checks syntax as using the same rules as SEU in a CLLE module
- Prompt the command for missing parameters using SEU options

DBCS Data Handling

The DBCS Data Handling option is used to instruct the system to accept double-byte data. The permissible options are:

0 Ignore DBCS Data.

1 Handle DBCS Data.

Prompter Action

The Prompter Action defines how the system command prompter is to be used. The permissible options are:

0 Do not prompt the command.

1 Always prompt the command.

2 Prompt the command only if the prompting character (?) is found.

3 Show the Help display for the command.

Command String Syntax

The Command String Syntax option allows you to direct the system to use System/38 syntax. The permissible options are:

---

0   Use AS/400 command syntax.

1   Use System/38 command syntax.

Message Retrieve Key

The Message Retrieve Key identifies a request message and allows you to locate the request in the job log. If initialized to blanks or hexadecimal zeros, no request message is updated.

Reserved

The remainder of the structure is filled with nine characters of reserved space. Note: This field must be initialized with hexadecimal zeros. This is easily accomplished by moving *LOVAL to the field.

Options Control Block Length Parameter

The fourth parameter of the API is a four-byte binary field that contains the length of the Options Control Block parameter. As discussed in detail earlier in this chapter, the most desirable way to define a four-byte binary parameter is to declare the field as a 10-digit integer. As you will recall, a 10-digit integer occupies four bytes of space.

Options Control Block Format Parameter

The fifth parameter is an eight-byte character field that contains the name of the Options Control Block Format. This is defined by IBM to be CPOP0100.

Changed Command String Parameter

The sixth parameter is an output parameter returned by the API. The field varies in length depending on the length of the updated command string. When returned, the parameter contains the actual command string that was processed. This reflects any changes made by the user when the command is prompted. You should size the parameter field large enough to handle any potential changes that might be made when the command is prompted.

Length Available for Changed Command Parameter

The seventh parameter is a four-byte binary field containing the length of the field used for the Changed Command String parameter. Use of the %SIZE function in RPG assures the field is initialized with the correct value. As you will recall, defining a 10-digit integer results in the creation of a field that occupies four bytes of space.

Length of Changed Command Parameter

The eighth parameter is an output parameter returned by the API. It is a four-byte binary field containing the length of the Changed Command String returned. As you will recall, defining a 10-digit integer results in the creation of a field that occupies four bytes of space.

Error Code Parameter

The ninth and final parameter is a standard parameter used by many APIs. It is a variable-length structure containing a number of error-related subfields. In an RPG program, the Error Code parameter is defined as a data structure having multiple defined subfields.

Table 4.5 shows the subfields that comprise the standard Error Code parameter structure.

Table 4.5: Standard Error Code Parameter Subfields.

Sequence	Parameter	I/O	Type
1	Bytes Provided	Input	Binary(4)
2	Bytes Available	Output	Binary(4)
3	Exception ID	Output	Char(7)
4	Reserved	Output	Char(1)
5	Exception Data	Output	Char(*)

Bytes Provided

The Bytes Provided subfield is a four-byte binary input field identifying the total size of the error code structure. A 10-digit integer is used to define the four-byte field.

Bytes Available

The Bytes Available subfield is a four-byte binary output field containing the number of bytes of error information returned to the API. This field is commonly used by the calling program to determine if the API encountered an error. If the field value is zero, the API did not end in error. A 10-digit integer is used to define the four-byte field.

Exception ID

The Exception ID subfield is a seven-character output field containing the message identifier for the error encountered by the API. If the API did not encounter an error, the Exception ID is blank.

Reserved

The Reserved subfield is a one-character field reserved for future use.

Exception Data

The Exception Data subfield is a character field used to return the data associated with the returned error. Inclusion of this field is optional. If used, it can be a field of any size you desire. It is good practice to make the field large enough to hold return data that could be expected from most errors.

Defining the Common Error Code Structure

The Common API Error Code structure is used by numerous APIs. The RPG definition in Figure 4.1 shows the commonly used structure layout.

```
     *_____
     *   Common API Error Structure
     *_____
     DAPIErrorDS       DS
     D  APIBytes                    10I 0 Inz(%Size(APIErrorDS))
     D  APIBytesOut                 10I 0
     D  APIErrID                     7A
     D  APIReserved                  1A
     D  APIErInDta                 256A
```

Figure 4.1: This is the Common API Error Code structure.

API Characteristics

When called, the API passes the supplied command string parameter to the AS/400 command processor for execution or validation. When the API execution completes, control is returned to the program that called the API and continues execution with the next sequential statement.

One of the main strengths of the QCAPCMD API is its ability to provide meaningful error control information.

The ILE RPG Example

The example source member API002R executes two CL commands using the QCAPCMD API. The first command performed is a WRKOUTQ command. Because the control block field CMDTYPE is set to zero, the command is executed. The prompter option is also set to zero, meaning the command is to execute without prompting.

The example then executes the second WRKOUTQ command. The prompter option is set to '2', forcing the command to be displayed in a prompted state.

EXAMPLE

Using the Retrieve Job Status API

The Retrieve Job Status (QWCRJBST) API returns the status for a specified job. The possible status values returned are *ACTIVE, *JOBQ, or *OUTQ.

WHAT THE EXAMPLE DOES

The example ILE RPG module API003R employs the QWCRJBST API to determine the status of a job. The fully qualified job name is accepted as a parameter and used as input to the API. The status of the job is displayed using the RPG DSPLY op code. Listing 4.3 shows the source member.

Listing 4.3: ILE RPG member API003R employs the QWCRJBST API.

```
     *
     D@ErrorMsg          C                        'An error was encountered -
     D                                             for selected job'
     D@StatusMsg          C                        'The status of the selected -
     D                                             job is: '
     DReturnMsg           S              50A
     *_____
     *   API Parameters
     *_____
     DReceiverLen         S              10I 0 Inz(%Size(RcvQWCRJBST))
     DJobIDFormat         S               8A   Inz('JOBS0300')
     DJobID               S              26A
```

Listing 4.3: ILE RPG member *API003R* employs the QWCRJBST API (continued).

```
 *
 *_____
 *  API Receiver Structure
 *_____
DRcvQWCRJBST       DS
D BytesReturn                10I 0
D BytesAvail                 10I 0
D JobStatus                  10A
D InternalJobID              16A
D QualJobName                26A
 *
 *_____
 *  Common API Error Structure
 *_____
DAPIErrorDS        DS
D APIBytes                   10I 0 Inz(%Size(APIErrorDS))
D APIBytesOut                10I 0
D APIErrID                    7A
D APIReserved                 1A
D APIErInDta                256A
 *
 *_____
 *  Module Entry Parameters
 *_____
DJobNameIn       S           10A
DJobUserIn       S           10A
DJobNumIn        S            6A
 *
C     *Entry        PList
C                   Parm                    JobNameIn
C                   Parm                    JobUserIn
C                   Parm                    JobNumIn
 *
C                   Eval      JobID = JobNameIn + JobUserIn + JobNumIn
 *
C                   Call      'QWCRJBST'
C                   Parm                    RcvQWCRJBST
C                   Parm                    ReceiverLen
C                   Parm                    JobID
C                   Parm                    JobIDFormat
C                   Parm                    APIErrorDS
 *
C                   If        JobStatus = '*ERROR    '
C                   Eval      ReturnMsg = @ErrorMsg
C                   Else
C                   Eval      ReturnMsg = @StatusMsg + JobStatus
```

Listing 4.3: ILE RPG member API003R
employs the QWCRJBST API (continued).

```
  C                       Endif
  *
  C                       Dsply                   ReturnMsg
  *
  C                       Return
```

HOW THE EXAMPLE WORKS

The QWCRJBST API is employed to determine the status of a single, specific job. The API returns a status of *ERROR if the job name passed to the API is not found.

QWCRJBST Parameters

The API receives five required parameters, and shown in Table 4.6.

Table 4.6: QWCRJBST API Parameter List. Required Parameters			
Sequence	Parameter	I/O	Type
1	Receiver Variable	Output	Char(*)
2	Length of Receiver Variable	Input	Binary(4)
3	Job Identifier	Input	Char(*)
4	Format of Job Identifier	Input	Char(8)
5	Error Code	I/O	Char(*)

Receiver Variable Parameter

The first parameter is a structure containing the output results from the API. In an RPG program, the Receiver Variable parameter is defined as a data structure having multiple defined subfields. You do not have to define all of the possible five subfields in the receiver variable. For example, if you want to receive only the first three fields, you may omit the last two fields. Table 4.7 shows the subfields that comprise the Receiver Variable parameter.

Table 4.7: Receiver Variable Parameter Subfields.			
Sequence	Parameter	I/O	Type
1	Bytes Returned	Output	Binary(4)
2	Bytes Available	Output	Binary(4)
3	Job Status	Output	Char(10)
4	Internal Job Identifier	Output	Char(16)
5	Fully Qualified Job Name	Output	Char(26)`

Bytes Returned

The Bytes Returned subfield receives the number of bytes the API returned in the Receiver Variable parameter. The subfield is a four-byte binary field that is defined in RPG as a 10-digit integer field. As you will recall, a 10-digit integer occupies four bytes of space.

Bytes Available

The Bytes Available subfield receives the number of bytes that were available to return as a result of the API execution. All available data is returned if the full 60-byte Receiver Variable structure is defined. The subfield is a four-byte binary field that is defined in RPG as a 10-digit integer field. As you will recall, a 10-digit integer occupies four bytes of space.

Job Status

The status of the specified job is returned in the Job Status subfield. The field has a length of 10 characters. The possible returned status values are:

*ACTIVE	Indicates that the job has started execution. Jobs that are held or have an error will return an *ACTIVE status.
*JOBQ	Indicates that the job is currently waiting on a job queue.
*OUTQ	Indicates that the job has completed and has output waiting to print on an output queue.
*ERROR	An error was encountered. This usually indicates that the specified job was not found.

Internal Job Identifier

The internal job identifier is an internal system representation of the job name for the specified job. Once returned, this internal identifier can be used as input to other APIs. It allows the system to locate a job quicker than it can when given a job name.

Fully Qualified Job Name

The fully qualified job name is returned from the API. This may be useful if you provided the API with a different job identifier, such as an internal job identifier. The first 10 characters contain the job name, followed by the job user name in the next 10 characters. The final six characters contain the job number.

Length of Receiver Variable Parameter

The second parameter of the API is a four-byte binary field that contains the length of the Receiver Variable parameter. If you choose to return the full structure available, the length is 60 bytes.

Job Identifier Parameter

The third parameter is a character field that contains the identifier for the job whose status you wish to retrieve. The length of the field depends on which of the three possible job identifier formats you use. You may identify a job using a 6-character job number, a 16-character internal job identifier, or a 26-character fully qualified job name.

Job Identifier Format Parameter

The fourth parameter specifies which of the three possible job identifier types you are using. The three possible choices are:

JOBS0100	Indicates that the job identifier is a six-character job number. This option is not very reliable because more than one job may have the same number. If more than one exists, the API returns the status of the first job found.
JOBS0200	Indicates that the job is identified using a 16-character internal job identifier. This may be useful if the source of your job information is another API, such as the List Job API. This API runs quickest when supplied with an internal job identifier.
JOBS0300	Indicates that the job is identified using a fully qualified job name consisting of a 10-character job name, a 10-character user name, and a 6-character job number. Unless the source of your job information is another API, this is the most commonly used format.

Error Code Parameter

The fifth and final parameter is a standard parameter used by many APIs. It is a variable-length structure containing a number of error-related subfields. In an RPG program, the Error Code parameter is defined as a data structure having multiple defined subfields. Table 4.8 shows the subfields that comprise the standard Error Code parameter structure.

Table 4.8: Standard Error Code Parameter Subfields.			
Sequence	Parameter	I/O	Type
1	Bytes Provided	Input	Binary(4)
2	Bytes Available	Output	Binary(4)
3	Exception ID	Output	Char(7)
4	Reserved	Output	Char(1)
5	Exception Data	Output	Char(*)

Bytes Provided

The Bytes Provided subfield is a four-byte binary input field identifying the total size of the error code structure. A 10-digit integer is used to define the four-byte field.

Bytes Available

The Bytes Available subfield is a four-byte binary output field containing the number of bytes of error information returned to the API. This field is commonly used by the calling program to determine if the API encountered an error. If the field value is zero, the API did not end in error. A 10-digit integer is used to define the four-byte field.

Exception ID

The Exception ID subfield is a seven-character output field containing the message identifier for the error encountered by the API. If the API did not encounter an error, the Exception ID is blank.

Reserved

The Reserved subfield is a one-character field reserved for future use.

Exception Data

The Exception Data subfield is a character field used to return the data associated with the returned error. Inclusion of this field is optional. If used, it can be a field of any size you desire. It is good practice to make the field large enough to hold return data that could be expected from most errors.

Defining the Common Error Code Structure

The Common API Error Code structure is used by numerous APIs. The RPG definition in Figure 4.2 shows the commonly used structure layout.

```
     *------------------------------------------------------
     *  Common API Error Structure
     *------------------------------------------------------
     DAPIErrorDS        DS
     D  APIBytes                      10I 0 Inz(%Size(APIErrorDS))
     D  APIBytesOut                   10I 0
     D  APIErrID                       7A
     D  APIReserved                    1A
     D  APIErInDta                   256A
```

Figure 4.2: The Common API Error Code structure .

The ILE RPG Example

The example source member API003R accepts three input parameters. The parameters comprise all three components of a fully qualified job name. The input parameters are used as input to the QWCRJBST API. If a return status of *ERROR is received, an error message is displayed. If a valid status is returned, the program formats the status into a message and displays it for the user.

EXAMPLE

Using the List Job Schedule Entries API

To this point, all of the APIs presented have either executed a single command or re-trieved a single value. Use of the List Job Schedule Entries (QWCLSCDE) API takes these examples up a notch by demonstrating the power of List APIs. List APIs allow you to re-trieve information about a list of objects or items of undetermined length. The QWCLSCDE API returns a list of entries entered into the system job scheduler.

WHAT THE EXAMPLE DOES

The example ILE RPG module API004R employs the QWCLSCDE API to retrieve a list of entries entered into the system job scheduler. For simplicity, the example displays each job name retrieved by the API. Listing 4.4 shows the source member.

Listing 4.4: ILE RPG member API004R employs the QWCLSCDE API.

```
     *
     *_____
     *   Create User Space API Parameters
     *_____
    DSpaceName      S             20A    Inz('USERSPC    QTEMP     ')
    DSpaceAttrib    S             10A
    DSpaceSize      S             10I 0 Inz(1024)
    DSpaceInit      S              1A
    DSpaceAuth      S             10A    Inz('*CHANGE')
    DSpaceText      S             50A
    DSpaceReplace   S             10A    Inz('*YES')
     *
     *_____
     *   Change User Space Attribute API Parameters
     *_____
    DSpaceLibOut    S             10A
    DSpaceChgAtt    DS
    D  NbrAttrib                  10I 0 Inz(1)
    D  KeyAttrib                  10I 0 Inz(3)
    D  SizeAttrib                 10I 0 Inz(%Size(DataAttrib))
    D  DataAttrib                  1A    Inz('1')
     *_____
     *   List Job Schedule Entries API Parameters
     *_____
    DJobSFormat     S              8A    Inz('SCDL0100')
    DJobSEntry      S             10A    Inz('*ALL')
    DJobSContinue   S             16A
     *_____
     *   Common List API Header
     *_____
    DAPIHeader0100  DS                   Based(SpacePtr)
    D  HdrUserArea                64A
    D  HdrSize                    10I 0
    D  HdrRelease                  4A
    D  HdrFormat                   8A
    D  HdrAPIName                 10A
    D  HdrDateTime                13A
    D  HdrInfoSts                  1A
    D  HdrUsrSpcSize              10I 0
    D  HdrOffInp                  10I 0
    D  HdrSizeInput               10I 0
    D  HdrOffHdr                  10I 0
    D  HdrSizeHdr                 10I 0
    D  HdrOffList                 10I 0
    D  HdrSizeList                10I 0
```

**Listing 4.4: ILE RPG member *API004R*
employs the *QWCLSCDE* API (continued).**

```
D  HdrList#                        10I 0
D  HdrListSize                     10I 0
D  HdrCCSID                        10I 0
D  HdrCountry                       2A
D  HdrLanguage                      3A
D  HdrSubset                        1A
D  HdrReserved                     42A
 *_____
 *  List Job Schedule Entries API Header
 *_____
DSCHeader        DS
D  SCEntryName                     10A
D  SCContinue                      16A
 *
 *_____
 *  API Format SCDL0100 Structure
 *_____
DFmtSCDL0100     DS                       Based(ListPtr)
D  SCInfoSts                        1A
D  SCJobName                       10A
D  SCEntry#                        10A
D  SCSchedDate                     10A
D  SCSchedDays                     70A
D  SCSchedTime                      6A
D  SCFrequency                     10A
D  SCDayOfMon                      10A     Dim(5)
D  SCRecovery                      10A
D  SCNextDate                      10A
D  SCStatus                        10A
D  SCJobQueue                      10A
D  SCJobQueueLib                   10A
D  SCEntryUser                     10A
D  SCLastDate                      10A
D  SCLastTime                       6A
D  SCText                          50A
D  SCReserved                      23A
 *
 *_____
 *  Common API Error Structure
 *_____
DAPIErrorDS      DS
D  APIBytes                        10I 0 Inz(%Size(APIErrorDS))
D  APIBytesOut                     10I 0
D  APIErrID                         7A
D  APIReserved                      1A
D  APIErInDta                     256A
 *
DSpacePtr        S                 *
DListPtr         S                 *
DNumList         S                 9 0
 *
 *_____
 *  Create User Space
 *_____
```

135

Listing 4.4: ILE RPG member API004R employs the QWCLSCDE API (continued).

```
C                   Call      'QUSCRTUS'
C                   Parm                    SpaceName
C                   Parm                    SpaceAttrib
C                   Parm                    SpaceSize
C                   Parm                    SpaceInit
C                   Parm                    SpaceAuth
C                   Parm                    SpaceText
C                   Parm                    SpaceReplace
C                   Parm                    APIErrorDS
 *
 *_____
 *   Change User Space to be extendible
 *_____
C                   Call      'QUSCUSAT'
C                   Parm                    SpaceLibOut
C                   Parm                    SpaceName
C                   Parm                    SpaceChgAtt
C                   Parm                    APIErrorDS
 *
 *_____
 *   List all job schedule entries to
 *   user space.
 *_____
C                   Call      'QWCLSCDE'
C                   Parm                    SpaceName
C                   Parm                    JobSFormat
C                   Parm                    JobSEntry
C                   Parm                    JobSContinue
C                   Parm                    APIErrorDS
 *
 *_____
 *   Get a pointer to the user space
 *_____
C                   Call      'QUSPTRUS'
C                   Parm                    SpaceName
C                   Parm                    SpacePtr
C                   Parm                    APIErrorDS
 *
 *_____
 *   Set position to first list entry
 *_____
 *
C                   Eval      Listptr = SpacePtr + HdrOffList
 *
 *_____
 *   Loop for each entry.  Retrieve each
 *   entry from user space.
 *_____
C                   Do        HdrList#    NumList
 *
```

***Listing 4.4: ILE RPG member API004R
employs the QWCLSCDE API (continued).***

```
 *_____
 *  Display the job name for each entry.
 *  This is where you would add your
 *  desired process for each list entry.
 *_____
C                   Dsply                   SCJobName
 *
C                   If        NumList < HdrList#
C                   Eval      Listptr = Listptr + HdrListSize
C                   Endif
C                   Enddo
 *
C                   Return
```

HOW THE EXAMPLE WORKS

List APIs allow you to retrieve multiple items from the system whose volume is undeterminable. To accomplish this, a mechanism called a *user space* is employed to contain the output contents of the List API.

The AS/400 User Space Object

APIs that produce lists of unpredictable size require a means of delivering the information to the requesting program. To accomplish this task, the AS/400 provides an object that represents space in memory to contain API results. This object, called a *user space*, is simply a buffer of contiguous, dedicated space to hold data. User space object manipulation—including creating, changing, and deleting a user space—is done using a set of user space APIs. The user space APIs used in this example are:

- Create User Space (QUSCRTUS)

- Change User Space Attributes (QUSCUSAT)

- Retrieve Pointer to User Space (QUSPTRUS)

The Create User Space API

The Create User Space (QUSCRTUS) API creates a user space object used to hold the results of List APIs. The API accepts nine parameters, six that are required and three that are optional.

The API receives six required parameters. The first optional parameter group accepts two additional parameters. A second optional parameter group accepts one additional parameter. Table 4.9 shows the QUSCRTUS API parameter groups.

Table 4.9: QUSCRTUS API Parameter List. Required Parameters			
Sequence	Parameter	I/O	Type
1	Qualified User Space Name	Input	Char(20)
2	Extended Attribute	Input	Char(10)
3	Initial Size	Input	Binary(4)
4	Initial Value	Input	Char(1)
5	Public Authority	Input	Char(10)
6	Text Description	Input	Char(50)
First Optional Parameter Group			
Sequence	Parameter	I/O	Type
7	Replace	Input	Char(10)
8	Error Code	I/O	Char(*)
Second Optional Parameter Group			
Sequence	Parameter	I/O	Type
9	Domain	Input	Char(10)

Qualified User Space Name

The first parameter is an input parameter containing the name and library name of the new user space being created. The first 10 characters are the user space name, followed by the library name in the second 10 characters. The special value *CURLIB may be used in place of a library name.

Extended Attribute

The second parameter is an input parameter containing an extended attribute for the user space. This is similar to a file object having the possible extended attributes PF, LF, or DSPF. It is of little use for user space objects and is generally left blank.

Initial Size

The third parameter is an input parameter containing the initial size of the user space. The value can range from 1 to 16,776,704 bytes. Because the parameter is a four-byte binary, the field is defined as a 10-digit integer that occupies four bytes of space.

Initial Value

The fourth parameter is an input parameter containing a character that is to be used as the initial value of the entire user space. Blanks or hexadecimal zeros (x'00') are generally good options for initial values. Initializing with x'00' will generally lead to slightly better system performance.

Public Authority

The fifth parameter is an input parameter containing a value that defines the default authority public users have when using the user space. The valid values are:

*ALL	Users can perform all operations on the user space.
Authorization List Name	The user space authority is determined by the authorization list specified.
*CHANGE	Users can read the object description and can manipulate the contents of the user space.
*EXCLUDE	Users cannot access the user space in any way.
*LIBCRTAUT	The public authority level of the library is used as the authority level of the user space.
*USE	Users can read the user space contents but not change them.

Text Description

The sixth parameter is an input parameter containing a 50-character text description for the user space object.

Replace

The first parameter in the first optional parameter group specifies whether you want to replace an existing user space if the named space already exists. The valid values are:

*NO	Do not replace an existing user space if found.
*YES	The existing user space is deleted before the new space is created (provided the user is authorized to do so).

Error Code

The second parameter in the first optional parameter group is a standard parameter used by many APIs. It is a variable-length structure containing a number of error-related subfields. In an RPG program, the Error Code parameter is defined as a data structure having multiple defined subfields. Table 4.10 lists the subfields that comprise the standard Error Code parameter structure.

	Table 4.10: Standard Error Code Parameter Subfields.		
Sequence	Parameter	I/O	Type
1	Bytes Provided	Input	Binary(4)
2	Bytes Available	Output	Binary(4)
3	Exception ID	Output	Char(7)
4	Reserved	Output	Char(1)
5	Exception Data	Output	Char(*)

Bytes Provided

The Bytes Provided subfield is a four-byte binary input field identifying the total size of the error code structure. A 10-digit integer is used to define the four-byte field.

Bytes Available

The Bytes Available subfield is a four-byte binary output field containing the number of bytes of error information returned to the API. This field is commonly used by the calling program to determine if the API encountered an error. If the field value is zero, the API did not end in error. A 10-digit integer is used to define the four-byte field.

Exception ID

The Exception ID subfield is a seven-character output field containing the message identifier for the error encountered by the API. If the API did not encounter an error, the Exception ID is blank.

Reserved

The Reserved subfield is a one-character field reserved for future use.

Exception Data

The Exception Data subfield is a character field used to return the data associated with the returned error. Inclusion of this field is optional. If used, it can be a field of any size you desire. It is good practice to make the field large enough to hold return data that could be expected from most errors.

Domain

The first parameter in the second optional parameter group specifies whether you want to create the user space in the user or system domain. In most cases, you will create all user spaces in the user domain. The valid values are:

*USER	The user space is created in the user domain.
*SYSTEM	The user space is created in the system domain.
*DEFAULT	The system decides into which domain the user space is created. If this parameter is not specified, the value of *DEFAULT is used.

The Change User Space Attributes API

The Change User Space Attributes (QUSCUSAT) API changes the attributes of an existing user space object. It is used to change the initial size or initial value of the user space. Additionally, it is used to set the user space size to be automatically extended by the system when more space is needed.

The API receives four required parameters, as shown in Table 4.11.

Table 4.11: QUSCUSAT API Parameter List. Required Parameters			
Sequence	Parameter	I/O	Type
1	Returned Library Name	Output	Char(10)
2	Qualified User Space Name	Input	Char(20)
3	Attributes to Change	Input	Char(*)
4	Error Code	I/O	Char(*)

Returned Library Name

The first parameter is an output parameter returned by the API. It contains the name of the library of the user space whose attributes were changed. This is useful when a special value of *LIBL or *CURLIB is specified in the qualified user space name parameter.

Qualified User Space Name

The second parameter is an input parameter containing the name and library name of the user space whose attributes are to be changed. The first 10 characters are the user space name, followed by the library name in the second 10 characters. The special values *CURLIB or *LIBL may be used in place of a library name.

Attributes to Change

The third parameter is an input parameter containing a variable-length structure that specifies the user space attributes to be changed. The structure consists of a four-byte binary field that specifies the number of attributes you are changing, followed by a data group of three subfields for each attribute. The format of the data group depends on the attribute being changed. The data group for the Attributes to Change parameter consists of three subfields, as shown in Table 4.12.

Table 4.12: Attribute Data Group Subfields.			
Sequence	Parameter	I/O	Type
1	Key for Attribute	Input	Binary(4)
2	Length of Attribute Data	Input	Binary(4)
3	Attribute Data Value	Input	Char(*)

Key for Attribute. The first subfield used for the Attribute to Change parameter is a key that specifies which attribute you want to change. Because the parameter is a four-byte binary, the field is defined as a 10-digit integer that occupies four bytes of space. There are three possible keys from which to select: the first to change the space size, the second to change the initial value, or the third to set the automatic extendibility.

Length of Attribute Data. The second subfield contains the size of the Attribute Data Value subfield. This length depends on which key value is selected. However, the length of the value should always maintain a four-byte boundary. For instance, if the data value is only one byte in length, you should add a three-byte filler to the end of the parameter to maintain the four-byte boundary.

Attribute Data Value. The third subfield contains the attribute data that corresponds to the selected key. The length of this subfield depends on the key being used. If a key value 1 is specified, the data value must be a four-byte binary value that specifies the new initial size of the user space. If a key value of 2 is specified, the value must be a one-character initial value. The final key value of 3 must be a one-character field that sets the automatic extendibility to on or off. A value of '0' turns automatic extendibility off, while a '1' sets it on.

Error Code

The fourth and final parameter of the QUSCUSAT API is a standard error code structure. It is a variable-length structure containing a number of error-related subfields. In an RPG program, the Error Code parameter is defined as a data structure having multiple defined subfields and is used by many APIs.

The Retrieve Pointer to User Space API

The Retrieve Pointer to User Space (QUSPTRUS) API returns a basing pointer to the contents of a user space object. A basing pointer allows you to address the contents of a user space simply by basing a data structure on the pointer.

The API receives two required parameters and one optional parameter, as shown in Table 4.13.

Table 4.13: QUSPTRUS API Parameter List. Required Parameters			
Sequence	Parameter	I/O	Type
1	Qualified User Space Name	Input	Char(20)
2	Pointer to User Space Contents	Output	Pointer
Optional Parameter			
Sequence	Parameter	I/O	Type
3	Error Code	I/O	Char(*)

Qualified User Space Name

The first parameter is an input parameter containing the name and library name of the user space whose address is to be returned as a basing pointer. The first 10 characters are the user space name, followed by the library name in the second 10 characters. The special values *CURLIB or *LIBL may be used in place of a library name.

Pointer to User Space Contents

The second parameter is an output parameter that receives a basing pointer that addresses the user space. The parameter field is defined in RPG as a pointer variable. The pointer variable is used in conjunction with a data structure having the based keyword specified. This causes the data structure subfields to be automatically loaded with the data residing in the address stored in the pointer variable.

Error Code

The third parameter is optional. It is a standard error code structure. It is a variable-length structure containing a number of error-related subfields. In an RPG program, the Error Code parameter is defined as a data structure having multiple defined subfields and is used by many APIs. List API Output

When executed, List APIs produce output that is written to and stored in a user space object. The API output follows a standardized format, allowing you to use the same basic logic to process most List APIs. The data returned by List APIs is divided into sections. Figure 4.3 shows the format of the standard List API output. The output generated by List APIs consists of the following four sections:

- Generic Header

- Input Parameter Section

- API Specific Header Section

- List Data Section

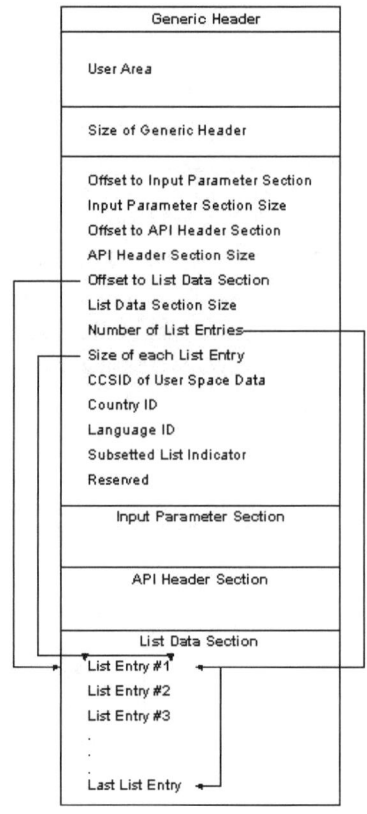

Figure 4.3: The layout of the standard List API output.

Generic Header

The Generic Header section of the user space contents provides information needed to access the data output by the list API. It provides offset values needed to access the information in all the other sections. The Generic Header section is the map that guides you to the data within the user space. The fields of most value in the Generic Header section are the offset to the List Data section, the number of list entries in the List Data section, and the size of each list entry. Figure 4.4 shows the RPG definition of the Generic Header section.

```
*-------------------------------------------------------
* Common List API Header
*-------------------------------------------------------
DAPIHeader0100      DS
D  HdrUserArea                        64A
D  HdrSize                            10I 0
D  HdrRelease                          4A
D  HdrFormat                           8A
D  HdrAPIName                         10A
D  HdrDateTime                        13A
D  HdrInfoSts                          1A
D  HdrUsrSpcSize                      10I 0
D  HdrOffInp                          10I 0
D  HdrSizeInput                       10I 0
D  HdrOffHdr                          10I 0
D  HdrSizeHdr                         10I 0
D  HdrOffList                         10I 0
D  HdrSizeList                        10I 0
D  HdrList#                           10I 0
D  HdrListSize                        10I 0
D  HdrCCSID                           10I 0
D  HdrCountry                          2A
D  HdrLanguage                         3A
D  HdrSubset                           1A
D  HdrReserved                        42A
```

Figure 4.4: An example definition of the List API generic header section.

Input Parameter Section

The Input Parameter section contains a mirror of the parameter values provided to the List API at the time of its execution.

API-Specific Header Section

Most List APIs provide a small amount of header-level information that is specific to the API.

List Data Section

The List Data section contains the resulting list entries output by the API. Each list entry appears consecutively as a string of data and is accessed using the offset and length of each entry information found in the Generic Header section.

Retrieving Data from a User Space

There are two commonly used methods to retrieve data from a user space. The first employs the Retrieve User Space API to return a portion of the user space contents when given a starting location and length. When using ILE RPG, there is an easier, better performing method. ILE RPG allows you to use basing pointers to address desired portions of the contiguous user space.

If you have not used pointers in an RPG program before, they are simply a way to address a specific storage location in memory. Pointers are used with data structures to parse the data residing in the pointer location into individual subfields. When coded on a data structure definition, the RPG BASED keyword specifies that the data structure is to be loaded with the data residing in the address provided by a pointer. Setting or changing the value of the pointer causes the contents of the data structure to automatically change.

The logic used to access List API data from a user space follows a basic flow of six steps. These steps are:

1. Run the List API to load the user space.

2. Call the QUSPTRUS API to assign a pointer to the user space.

3. Because a data structure is based on the pointer, access the Generic Header data.

4. Add the offset to the List Data section to the pointer, assigning a list pointer to the location of the first list entry.

5. Because a second data structure is based on the list pointer, access the data for the first list entry.

6. To access subsequent list entries, add the length of each entry to the list pointer, which automatically reloads the data structure with the next list entry.

The QWCLSCDE API

The List Job Schedule Entries (QWCLSCDE) API produces a list of the entries appearing in the system job scheduler. The API returns all entries or a subset based on the job schedule entry name. The output of the API is similar to the information displayed by the interactive Work with Job Schedule Entries (WRKJOBSCDE) command. Entries meeting the desired criteria are written to a user space. The output information is available in two different formats: SCDL0100 for basic job schedule entry information and SCDL0200 for more detailed information.

The API receives five required parameters, as shown in Table 4.14.

	Table 4.14: QWCLSCDE API Parameter List.		
	Required Parameters		
Sequence	Parameter	I/O	Type
1	Qualified User Space Name	Input	Char(20)
2	Format Name	Input	Char(8)
3	Job Schedule Entry Name	Input	Char(10)
4	Continuation Handle	Input	Char(16)
5	Error Code	I/O	Char(*)

Qualified User Space Name

The first parameter is an input parameter containing the name and library name of the user space that is to receive the API output. The first 10 characters are the user space name, followed by the library name in the second 10 characters. The special values *CURLIB or *LIBL may be used in place of a library name.

Format Name

The second parameter is an input parameter containing the name of the format to be used. The format name determines whether the API is to return basic job schedule information or more detailed information for each entry. The API offers two formats from which to choose: format SCDL0100 for basic information and format SCDL0200 for more detailed information.

Table 4.15 shows the layout for format SCDL0100 and Table 4.16 shows the layout for format SCDL0200.

Table 4.15: List Job Schedule Entries API (Format SCDL0100).

Sequence	Parameter	I/O	Type
1	Information Status	Output	Char(1)
2	Job Name	Output	Char(10)
3	Entry Number	Output	Char(10)
4	Scheduled Date	Output	Char(10)
5	Scheduled Days	Output	Char(70)
6	Scheduled Time	Output	Char(6)
7	Frequency	Output	Char(10)
8	Relative Day of the Month	Output	Array of 5 Char(10)
9	Recovery Action	Output	Char(10)
10	Next Submission Date	Output	Char(10)
11	Status	Output	Char(10)
12	Job Queue Name	Output	Char(10)
13	Job Queue Library Name	Output	Char(10)
14	User Profile of Entry User	Output	Char(10)
15	Last Submission Date	Output	Char(10)
16	Last Submission Time	Output	Char(6)
17	Text	Output	Char(50)
18	Reserved	Output	Char(23)

Table 4.16: List Job Schedule Entries API (Format SCDL0200).

Sequence	Parameter	I/O	Type
	Entire SCDL0100 Format	Output	
19	Job Queue Status	Output	Char(10)
20	Dates Omitted	Output	Array of 20 Char(10)
21	Job Description Name	Output	Char(10)
22	Job Description Library Name	Output	Char(10)
23	User Profile for Submitted Job	Output	Char(10)
24	Message Queue Name	Output	Char(10)
25	Message Queue Library Name	Output	Char(10)
26	Save Entry	Output	Char(10)
27	Last Submission Job Name	Output	Char(10)
28	Last Submission User Name	Output	Char(10)
29	Last Submission Job Number	Output	Char(6)
30	Last Attempted Submission Date	Output	Char(10)
31	Last Attempted Submission Time	Output	Char(6)
32	Status of Last Attempted Submission	Output	Char(10)
33	Reserved	Output	Char(2)
34	Length of Command String	Output	Binary(4)
35	Command String	Output	Char(512)

Job Schedule Entry Name

The third parameter is a 10-character input parameter that specifies the name of the job schedule entry to be retrieved by the API. Special values can be used to create a subset of job schedule entries. The following is a list of permissible special values:

*ALL	Returns all job schedule entries
generic*	Returns entries generically matching entry names
name	Returns job schedule entries having a specific name

Continuation Name

The fourth parameter is a 16-character input parameter that specifies the name of a *continuation handle*. A continuation handle is used when the API previously returned only a portion of the available entries. Passing a continuation handle on a subsequent call to the API returns the remaining output. If left blank, the API starts at the beginning of the list.

Error Code

The fourth and final parameter of the QUSCUSAT API is a standard error code structure. It is a variable-length structure containing a number of error-related subfields. In an RPG program, the Error Code parameter is defined as a data structure having multiple defined subfields and is used by many APIs.

The ILE RPG Example

As you will recall, the example ILE RPG module API004R employs the QWCLSCDE API to retrieve a list of entries entered into the system job scheduler. For simplicity, the example merely displays each job name retrieved by the API. Module API004R begins by creating the user space that is to receive the List API output. Figure 4.5 shows the call to the QUSCRTUS API and the definition of the API parameters.

The module continues with a call to the QUSCUSAT API. The API changes the user space to be automatically extendible. This means the system will automatically increase the size of the user space if the available space is exceeded. Figure 4.6 shows the call to the QUSCUSAT API and the definition of the API parameters.

150

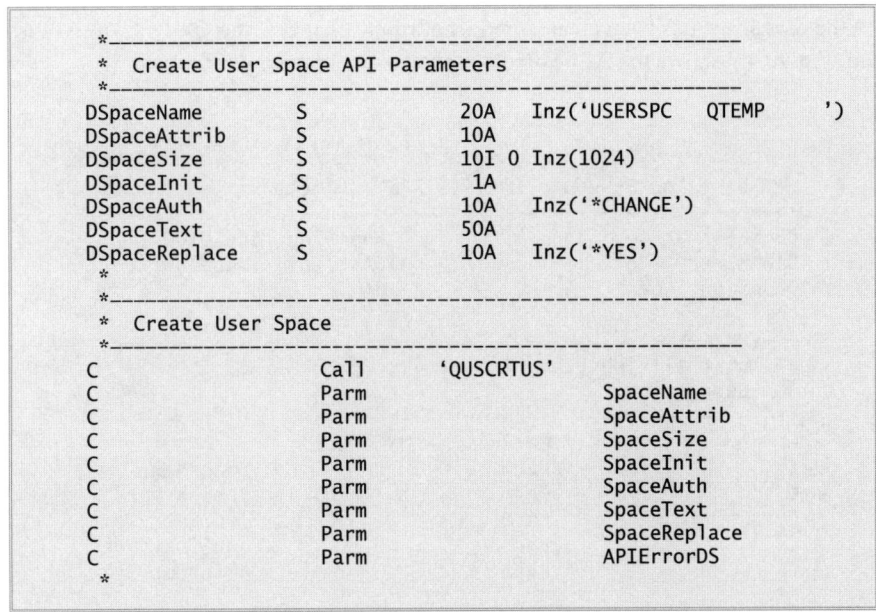

```
 *_____
 *   Create User Space API Parameters
 *_____
DSpaceName        S              20A    Inz('USERSPC    QTEMP    ')
DSpaceAttrib      S              10A
DSpaceSize        S              10I 0  Inz(1024)
DSpaceInit        S               1A
DSpaceAuth        S              10A    Inz('*CHANGE')
DSpaceText        S              50A
DSpaceReplace     S              10A    Inz('*YES')
 *
 *_____
 *   Create User Space
 *_____
C                 Call       'QUSCRTUS'
C                 Parm                    SpaceName
C                 Parm                    SpaceAttrib
C                 Parm                    SpaceSize
C                 Parm                    SpaceInit
C                 Parm                    SpaceAuth
C                 Parm                    SpaceText
C                 Parm                    SpaceReplace
C                 Parm                    APIErrorDS
 *
```

Figure 4.5: The module creates user space QTEMP/USERSPC.

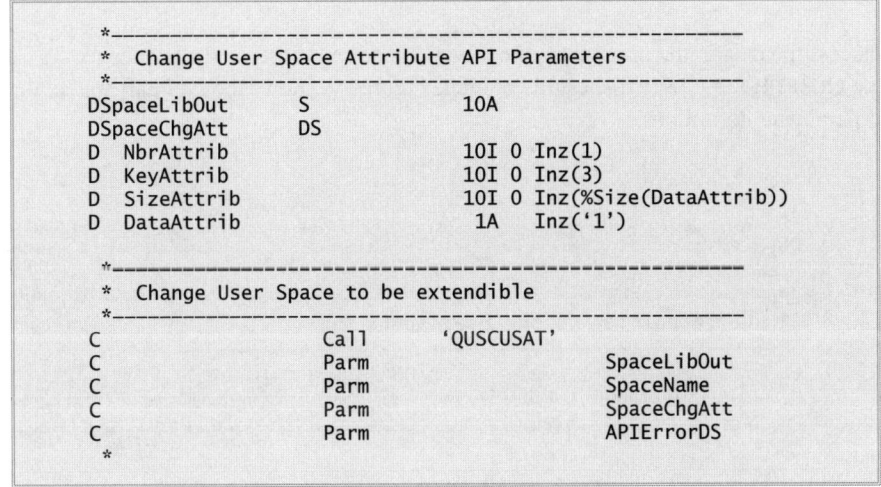

```
 *_____
 *   Change User Space Attribute API Parameters
 *_____
DSpaceLibOut      S              10A
DSpaceChgAtt      DS
D  NbrAttrib                     10I 0  Inz(1)
D  KeyAttrib                     10I 0  Inz(3)
D  SizeAttrib                    10I 0  Inz(%Size(DataAttrib))
D  DataAttrib                     1A    Inz('1')
 *
 *_____
 *   Change User Space to be extendible
 *_____
C                 Call       'QUSCUSAT'
C                 Parm                    SpaceLibOut
C                 Parm                    SpaceName
C                 Parm                    SpaceChgAtt
C                 Parm                    APIErrorDS
 *
```

Figure 4.6: The module changes the user space to be automatically extendible.

Once the user space has been created and its attribute changed, the QWCLSCDE API is called. Figure 4.7 shows the API call and associated parameter definitions.

```
 *_____
 *  List Job Schedule Entries API Parameters
 *_____
DJobSFormat      S              8A   Inz('SCDL0100')
DJobSEntry       S             10A   Inz('*ALL')
DJobSContinue    S             16A
 *
 *_____
 *  List all job schedule entries to
 *  user space.
 *_____
C                   Call      'QWCLSCDE'
C                   Parm                    SpaceName
C                   Parm                    JobSFormat
C                   Parm                    JobSEntry
C                   Parm                    JobSContinue
C                   Parm                    APIErrorDS
 *
```

Figure 4.7: The module calls the QWCLSCDE API.

To access the data in the user space, the module needs a pointer to the user space. A call to the QUSPTRUS API establishes this pointer. Figure 4.8 shows the API call and associated parameter definitions.

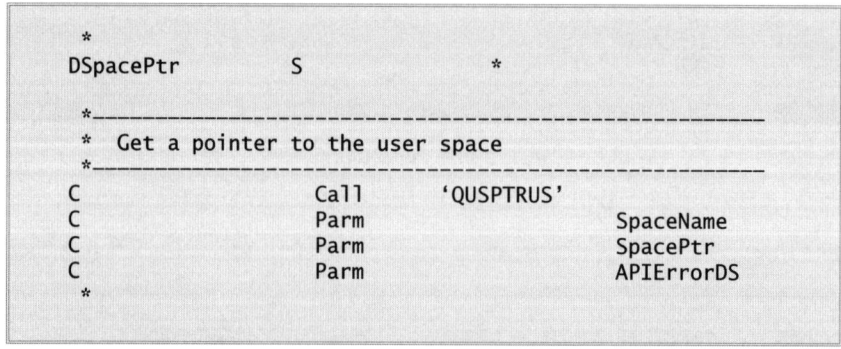

```
 *
DSpacePtr        S              *
 *
 *_____
 *  Get a pointer to the user space
 *_____
C                   Call      'QUSPTRUS'
C                   Parm                    SpaceName
C                   Parm                    SpacePtr
C                   Parm                    APIErrorDS
 *
```

Figure 4.8: A pointer to the user space is established by calling an API.

Because a data structure is defined based on the pointer, the data structure is automatically loaded when the pointer is assigned. The pointer addresses the first byte of the user space, which represents the Generic Header section of the List API output. Figure 4.9 shows the definition of the Generic Header data structure.

```
     *_____
     *   Common List API Header
     *_____
     DAPIHeader0100    DS                         Based(SpacePtr)
     D  HdrUserArea                   64A
     D  HdrSize                       10I 0
     D  HdrRelease                     4A
     D  HdrFormat                      8A
     D  HdrAPIName                    10A
     D  HdrDateTime                   13A
     D  HdrInfoSts                     1A
     D  HdrUsrSpcSize                 10I 0
     D  HdrOffInp                     10I 0
     D  HdrSizeInput                  10I 0
     D  HdrOffHdr                     10I 0
     D  HdrSizeHdr                    10I 0
     D  HdrOffList                    10I 0
     D  HdrSizeList                   10I 0
     D  HdrList#                      10I 0
     D  HdrListSize                   10I 0
     D  HdrCCSID                      10I 0
     D  HdrCountry                     2A
     D  HdrLanguage                    3A
     D  HdrSubset                      1A
     D  HdrReserved                   42A
```

Figure 4.9: When the pointer is assigned, the contents of this data structure are loaded.

Once the pointer is assigned, the module has access to the information needed to retrieve list entries from the user space using fields from the Generic Header section. A second pointer, called LISTPTR, is assigned using the value of the user space pointer plus the offset to the first list entry. This addresses the pointer to the first byte of the first list entry. A data structure, FMTSCDL0100, is based on the pointer. This loads the data structure with the data of the first list entry. The layout of the data structure subfields matches the format selected when the List API was run. Figure 4.10 shows the pointer arithmetic and the data structure based on the pointer.

```
        *─────────────────────────────────────────────────────
        *  API Format SCDL0100 Structure
        *─────────────────────────────────────────────────────
        DFmtSCDL0100        DS                      Based(ListPtr)
        D  SCInfoSts                     1A
        D  SCJobName                    10A
        D  SCEntry#                     10A
        D  SCSchedDate                  10A
        D  SCSchedDays                  70A
        D  SCSchedTime                   6A
        D  SCFrequency                  10A
        D  SCDayOfMon                   10A    Dim(5)
        D  SCRecovery                   10A
        D  SCNextDate                   10A
        D  SCStatus                     10A
        D  SCJobQueue                   10A
        D  SCJobQueueLib                10A
        D  SCEntryUser                  10A
        D  SCLastDate                   10A
        D  SCLastTime                    6A
        D  SCText                       50A
        D  SCReserved                   23A
        *
        DSpacePtr            S                      *
        DListPtr             S                      *
        *
        *─────────────────────────────────────────────────────
        *  Set position to first list entry
        *─────────────────────────────────────────────────────
        *
        C                   Eval      Listptr = SpacePtr + HdrOffList
        *
```

Figure 4.10: The offset is added to the space pointer, addressing the first list entry.

A control loop in the module executes detail logic for each list entry in the API. The field HDRLIST# from the Generic Header section tells you how many list entries were returned by the API and is the basis of the Do-Loop value. The detailed processing you desire for each job schedule entry returned by the API is performed within the Do-Loop construct. The example module simply displays the job name for the list entry using the RPG DSPLY op code.

After each entry is processed, the pointer is advanced to the next entry by adding the length of each entry to the pointer value. Figure 4.11 shows the control construct used to process each list entry. When all entries have been processed, the module ends.

```
    *_____
    *   Loop for each entry.  Retrieve each
    *   entry from user space.
    *_____
    C                       Do          HdrList#      NumList
    *
    *_____
    *   Display the job name for each entry.
    *   This is where you would add your
    *   desired process for each list entry.
    *_____
    C                       Dsply                     SCJobName
    *
    C                       If          NumList < HdrList#
    C                       Eval        Listptr = Listptr + HdrListSize
    C                       Endif
    C                       Enddo
    *
    C                       Return
```

Figure 4.11: Each list entry is processed using a Do-Loop construct.

EXAMPLE

Using the List Job API

The List Job (QUSLJOB) API is a powerful tool that allows you to interrogate the jobs on your system. The ability to specify multiple selection criteria makes the API handy for many applications. The QUSLJOB API returns a list of system jobs to a user space.

WHAT THE EXAMPLE DOES

The example ILE RPG module API005R employs the QUSLJOB API to retrieve a list of jobs on the system. Unlike the simplistic fixed-format interface of many List APIs, the QUSLJOB API allows you to specify the information you desire using key values.

All jobs having a status of *OUTQ, meaning the job has completed and has output in an output queue, are included in the list. The example processes the list and prints all entries where the job ended with a severity greater than zero. Listing 4.5 shows the source member.

Listing 4.5: ILE RPG member *API005R* employs the QUSLJOB *API.*

```
FQPRINT     O   F   132          Printer OFLIND(*InOF)
 *
 *_____
 *  Create User Space API Parameters
 *_____
DSpaceName       S            20A  Inz('USERSPC    QTEMP      ')
DSpaceAttrib     S            10A
DSpaceSize       S            10I 0 Inz(1024)
DSpaceInit       S             1A
DSpaceAuth       S            10A  Inz('*CHANGE')
DSpaceText       S            50A
DSpaceReplace    S            10A  Inz('*YES')
 *
 *_____
 *  Change User Space Attribute API Parameters
 *_____
DSpaceLibOut     S            10A
DSpaceChgAtt     DS
D  NbrAttrib                  10I 0 Inz(1)
D  KeyAttrib                  10I 0 Inz(3)
D  SizeAttrib                 10I 0 Inz(%Size(DataAttrib))
D  DataAttrib                  1A  Inz('1')
 *_____
 *  List Jobs API Parameters (REQUIRED)
 *_____
DJobLFormat      S             8A  Inz('JOBL0200')
DJobLJobName     S            26A  Inz('*ALL       *ALL       -
D                                      *ALL  ')
DJobLStatus      S            10A  Inz('*OUTQ     ')
 *_____
 *  List Jobs API Parameters (OPTIONAL GROUP 2)
 *_____
DJobLType        S             1A  Inz('*')
DJobL#Fields     S            10I 0 Inz(%Elem(JobLKeys))
DJobLKeys        S            10I 0 Dim(2)
 *_____
 *  Common List API Header
 *_____
DAPIHeader0100   DS                 Based(SpacePtr)
D  HdrUserArea                64A
D  HdrSize                    10I 0
D  HdrRelease                  4A
D  HdrFormat                   8A
D  HdrAPIName                 10A
D  HdrDateTime                13A
D  HdrInfoSts                  1A
D  HdrUsrSpcSize              10I 0
D  HdrOffInp                  10I 0
```

Listing 4.5: ILE RPG member API005R employs the QUSLJOB API (continued).

```
D  HdrSizeInput               10I 0
D  HdrOffHdr                  10I 0
D  HdrSizeHdr                 10I 0
D  HdrOffList                 10I 0
D  HdrSizeList                10I 0
D  HdrList#                   10I 0
D  HdrListSize                10I 0
D  HdrCCSID                   10I 0
D  HdrCountry                  2A
D  HdrLanguage                 3A
D  HdrSubset                   1A
D  HdrReserved                42A
 *
 *_____
 *  API Format JOBL0200 Structure
 *_____
DFmtJOBL0200     DS                          Based(ListPtr)
D  JLJobName                  10A
D  JLJobUser                  10A
D  JLJob#                      6A
D  JLIntJobID                 16A
D  JLStatus                   10A
D  JLJobType                   1A
D  JLJobSubType                1A
D  JLReserved1                 2A
D  JLJobInfoSts                1A
D  JLReserved2                 3A
D  JL#Fields                  10I 0
 *_____
 *  Variable portion of return parameters.
 *  Depends upon keys you requested.
 *_____
D  JLKey1Len                  10I 0
D  JLKey1                     10I 0
D  JLKey1Type                  1A
D  JLKey1Reserve               3A
D  JLKey1DataLen              10I 0
D  JLEndSeverity              10I 0
 *_____
 *  Second key value
 *_____
D  JLKey2Len                  10I 0
D  JLKey2                     10I 0
D  JLKey2Type                  1A
D  JLKey2Reserve               3A
D  JLKey2DataLen              10I 0
D  JLCentury                   1A
```

Listing 4.5: ILE RPG member API005R employs the QUSLJOB API (continued).

```
D  JLyymmdd                    6A
D  JLhhmmss                    6A
D  JLFiller3                   3A
   *
   *_____
   *  Common API Error Structure
   *_____
DAPIErrorDS       DS
D  APIBytes                    10I 0 Inz(%Size(APIErrorDS))
D  APIBytesOut                 10I 0
D  APIErrID                     7A
D  APIReserved                  1A
D  APIErInDta                 256A
   *
DSpacePtr        S              *
DListPtr         S              *
DNumList         S              9 0
DJobName         S             26A
   *
   *_____
   *  Create User Space
   *_____
C                    Call      'QUSCRTUS'
C                    Parm                    SpaceName
C                    Parm                    SpaceAttrib
C                    Parm                    SpaceSize
C                    Parm                    SpaceInit
C                    Parm                    SpaceAuth
C                    Parm                    SpaceText
C                    Parm                    SpaceReplace
C                    Parm                    APIErrorDS
   *
   *_____
   *  Change User Space to be extendible
   *_____
C                    Call      'QUSCUSAT'
C                    Parm                    SpaceLibOut
C                    Parm                    SpaceName
C                    Parm                    SpaceChgAtt
C                    Parm                    APIErrorDS
   *
   *_____
   *  List job information entries to
   *  user space.
   *_____
C*
C                    Eval      JobLKeys(1) = 0501
```

Listing 4.5: ILE RPG member *API005R* employs the *QUSLJOB* API (continued).

```
C                       Eval       JobLKeys(2) = 0401
C*
C                       Call       'QUSLJOB'
C                       Parm                   SpaceName
C                       Parm                   JobLFormat
C                       Parm                   JobLJobName
C                       Parm                   JobLStatus
C                       Parm                   APIErrorDS
C                       Parm                   JobLType
C                       Parm                   JobL#Fields
C                       Parm                   JobLKeys
 *
 *_____
 *  Get a pointer to the user space
 *_____
C                       Call       'QUSPTRUS'
C                       Parm                   SpaceName
C                       Parm                   SpacePtr
C                       Parm                   APIErrorDS
 *
 *_____
 *  Set position to first list entry
 *_____
 *
C                       Eval       Listptr = SpacePtr + HdrOffList
 *
C                       Except     Header1
 *
 *_____
 *  Loop for each entry.  Retrieve each
 *  entry from user space.
 *_____
C                       Do         HdrList#     NumList
 *
 *_____
 *  This is where you would add your
 *  desired process for each list entry.
 *
 *  The example test the returned Job End
 *  severity.  Prints if greater than zero.
 *_____
C                       If         JLEndSeverity  > 0
 *
C                       Eval       JobName = %Trim(JLJobName) + '/' +
C                                            %Trim(JLJobUser) + '/' +
C                                            JLJob#
 *
```

Listing 4.5: ILE RPG member APIoosR employs the QUSLJOB API (continued).

```
C                    Except    JobDtl
C                    Endif
 *
C                    If        NumList < HdrList#
C                    Eval      Listptr = Listptr + HdrListSize
C                    Endif
C                    Enddo
 *
C                    Eval      *InLR = *On
C                    Return
 *_____
OQPRINT     E                  Header1        2 01
O                                                      50 'Jobs Ending with a'
O                                                      64 'severity > 00'
O                                                      70 'Page:'
O                              Page1        z 76
O           E                  Header1      1 1
O                                                       6 'Job'
O                                                      54 'Active Date & Time'
O                                                      72 'Ending Severity'
O           E                  JobDtl       1
O                              JobName        30
O                              JLyymmdd       45
O                              JLhhmmss       54
O                              JLEndSeverity z 66
```

HOW THE EXAMPLE WORKS

List APIs allow you to retrieve multiple items from a system whose volume is undeterminable. To accomplish this, a mechanism called a user space is employed to contain the output contents of the List API.

APIs that produce lists of unpredictable size require a means of delivering the information to the requesting program. To accomplish this task, the AS/400 provides an object that represents space in memory to contain API results. This object, called a user space, is simply a buffer of contiguous, dedicated space to hold data. User space object manipulation—including creating, changing, and deleting a user space—is accomplished using a set of user space APIs. The user space APIs used in this example are:

- Create User Space (QUSCRTUS)

- Change User Space Attributes (QUSCUSAT)

- Retrieve Pointer to User Space (QUSPTRUS)

The Create User Space API

The Create User Space (QUSCRTUS) API creates a user space object used to hold the results of List APIs. The API accepts nine parameters, six that are required and three that are optional.

QUSCRTUS Parameters

The API receives six required parameters. The first optional parameter group accepts two additional parameters. A second optional parameter group accepts one additional parameter. Table 4.17 shows the QUSCRTUS API parameter groups.

Table 4.17: QUSCRTUS API Parameter List. Required Parameters			
Sequence	Parameter	I/O	Type
1	Qualified User Space Name	Input	Char(20)
2	Extended Attribute	Input	Char(10)
3	Initial Size	Input	Binary(4)
4	Initial Value	Input	Char(1)
5	Public Authority	Input	Char(10)
6	Text Description	Input	Char(50)
First Optional Parameter Group			
Sequence	Parameter	I/O	Type
7	Replace	Input	Char(10)
8	Error Code	I/O	Char(*)
Second Optional Parameter Group			
Sequence	Parameter	I/O	Type
9	Domain	Input	Char(10)

Qualified User Space Name

The first parameter is an input parameter containing the name and library name of the new user space being created. The first 10 characters are the user space name, followed

161

by the library name in the second 10 characters. The special value *CURLIB may be used in place of a library name.

Extended Attribute

The second parameter is an input parameter containing an extended attribute for the user space. This is similar to a file object having the possible extended attributes PF, LF, or DSPF. It is of little use for user space objects and is generally left blank.

Initial Size

The third parameter is an input parameter containing the initial size of the user space. The value can range from 1 to 16,776,704 bytes. Because the parameter is a four-byte binary, the field is defined as a 10-digit integer that occupies four bytes of space.

Initial Value

The fourth parameter is an input parameter containing a character that is to be used as the initial value of the entire user space. Blanks or hexadecimal zeros (x'00') are generally good options for initial values. Using an initial value of x'00' generally leads to slightly better system performance.

Public Authority

The fifth parameter is an input parameter containing a value that defines the default authority public users have when using the user space. The valid values are:

*ALL	Users can perform all operations on the user space.
Authorization List Name	The user space authority is determined by the authorization list specified.
*CHANGE	Users can read the object description and manipulate the contents of the user space.
*EXCLUDE	Users cannot access the user space in any way.
*LIBCRTAUT	The public authority level of the library is used as the authority level of the user space.
*USE	Users can read the user space contents but not change them.

Text Description

The sixth parameter is an input parameter containing a 50-character text description for the user space object.

Replace

The first parameter in the first optional parameter group specifies whether you want to replace an existing user space if the named space already exists. The valid values are:

*NO	Do not replace an existing user space if found.
*YES	The existing user space is deleted before the new space is created (provided the user is authorized to do so).

Error Code

The second parameter in the first optional parameter group is a standard parameter used by many APIs. It is a variable-length structure containing a number of error-related subfields. In an RPG program, the Error Code parameter is defined as a data structure having multiple defined subfields. Table 4.18 shows the subfields that comprise the standard Error Code parameter structure.

Table 4.18: Standard Error Code Parameter Subfields.

Sequence	Parameter	I/O	Type
1	Bytes Provided	Input	Binary(4)
2	Bytes Available	Output	Binary(4)
3	Exception ID	Output	Char(7)
4	Reserved	Output	Char(1)
5	Exception Data	Output	Char(*)

Bytes Provided

The Bytes Provided subfield is a four-byte binary input field identifying the total size of the error code structure. A 10-digit integer is used to define the four-byte field.

Bytes Available

The Bytes Available subfield is a four-byte binary output field containing the number of bytes of error information returned to the API. This field is commonly used by the calling program to determine if the API encountered an error. If the field value is zero, the API did not end in error. A 10-digit integer is used to define the four-byte field.

Exception ID

The Exception ID subfield is a seven-character output field containing the message identifier for the error encountered by the API. If the API did not encounter an error, the Exception ID is blank.

Reserved

The Reserved subfield is a one-character field reserved for future use.

Exception Data

The Exception Data subfield is a character field used to return the data associated with the returned error. Inclusion of this field is optional. If used, it can be a field of any size you desire. It is good practice to make the field large enough to hold return data that could be expected from most errors.

Domain

The first parameter in the second optional parameter group specifies whether you want to create the user space in the user or system domain. In most cases, you will create all user spaces in the user domain. The valid values are:

*USER	The user space is created in the user domain.
*SYSTEM	The user space is created in the system domain.
*DEFAULT	The system decides in which domain the user space is created. If this parameter is not specified, the value of *DEFAULT is used.

The Change User Space Attributes API

The Change User Space Attributes (QUSCUSAT) API changes the attributes of an existing user space object. It is used to change the initial size or initial value of the user space. Additionally, it is used to set the user space size to be automatically extended by the system when more space is needed.

QUSCUSAT Parameters

The API receives four required parameters, as shown in Table 4.19.

Table 4.19: QUSCUSAT API Parameter List. Required Parameters			
Sequence	Parameter	I/O	Type
1	Returned Library Name	Output	Char(10)
2	Qualified User Space Name	Input	Char(20)
3	Attributes to Change	Input	Char(*)
4	Error Code	I/O	Char(*)

Returned Library Name

The first parameter is an output parameter returned by the API. It contains the name of the library of the user space whose attributes were changed. This is useful when a special value of *LIBL or *CURLIB is specified in the qualified user space name parameter.

Qualified User Space Name

The second parameter is an input parameter containing the name and library name of the user space whose attributes are to be changed. The first 10 characters are the user space name, followed by the library name in the second 10 characters. The special values *CURLIB or *LIBL may be used in place of a library name.

Attributes to Change

The third parameter is an input parameter containing a variable-length structure that specifies the user space attributes to be changed. The structure consists of a four-byte binary field that specifies the number of attributes you are changing followed by a data group of three subfields for each attribute. The format of the data group depends on the attribute being changed. The data group for the Attributes to Change parameter consists of three subfields, as shown in Table 4.20.

Table 4.20: Attribute Data Group (Subfields).			
Sequence	Parameter	I/O	Type
1	Key for Attribute	Input	Binary(4)
2	Length of Attribute Data	Input	Binary(4)
3	Attribute Data Value	Input	Char(*)

Key for Attribute. The first subfield used for the Attribute to Change parameter is a key that specifies the attribute you want to change. Because the parameter is a four-byte binary, the field is defined as a 10-digit integer that occupies four bytes of space. There are three possible keys from which to select: the first to change the space size, the second to change the initial value, or the third to set the automatic extendibility.

Length of Attribute Data. The second subfield contains the size of the Attribute Data Value subfield. This length depends on which key value is selected. However, the length of the value should always maintain a four-byte boundary. For instance, if the data value is only one byte in length, you should add a three-byte filler to the end of the parameter to maintain the four-byte boundary.

Attribute Data Value. The third subfield contains the attribute data that corresponds with the key selected. The length of this subfield depends on the key being used. If a key value 1 is specified, the data value must be a four-byte binary value that specifies the new initial size of the user space. If a key value of 2 is specified, the value must be a one-character initial value. The final key value of 3 must be a one-character field that sets the automatic extendibility on or off. A value of '0' turns automatic extendibility off, while a '1' sets it on.

Error Code

The fourth and final parameter of the QUSCUSAT API is a standard error code structure. It is a variable-length structure containing a number of error-related sub-fields. In an RPG program, the Error Code parameter is defined as a data structure having multiple defined subfields and is used by many APIs.

The Retrieve Pointer to User Space API

The Retrieve Pointer to User Space (QUSPTRUS) API returns a basing pointer to the contents of a user space object. A basing pointer allows you to address the contents of a user space simply by basing a data structure on the pointer.

QUSPTRUS Parameters

The API receives two required parameters and one optional parameter, as in Table 4.21.

Table 4.21: QUSPTRUS API Parameter List. Required Parameters			
Sequence	Parameter	I/O	Type
1	Qualified User Space Name	Input	Char(20)
2	Pointer to User Space Contents	Output	Pointer
Optional Parameter			
Sequence	Parameter	I/O	Type
3	Error Code	I/O	Char(*)

Qualified User Space Name

The first parameter is an input parameter containing the name and library name of the user space whose address is to be returned as a basing pointer. The first 10 characters are the user space name, followed by the library name in the second 10 characters. The special values *CURLIB or *LIBL may be used in place of a library name.

Pointer to User Space Contents

The second parameter is an output parameter that receives a basing pointer that addresses the user space. The parameter field is defined in RPG as a pointer variable. The pointer variable is used in conjunction with a data structure having the based keyword specified. This causes the data structure subfields to be automatically loaded with the data residing in the address stored in the pointer variable.

Error Code

The third parameter is optional. It is a standard error code structure. It is a variable-length structure containing a number of error-related subfields. In an RPG program, the Error Code parameter is defined as a data structure having multiple defined subfields and is used by many APIs.

List API Output

When executed, List APIs produce output that is written to and stored in a user space object. The API output follows a standardized format, allowing you to use the same basic logic to process most List APIs. The data returned by List APIs is divided into sections.

Figure 4.12 shows the format of the standard List API output. The output generated by List APIs consists of the following four sections:

- Generic Header
- Input Parameter Section
- API Specific Header Section
- List Data Section

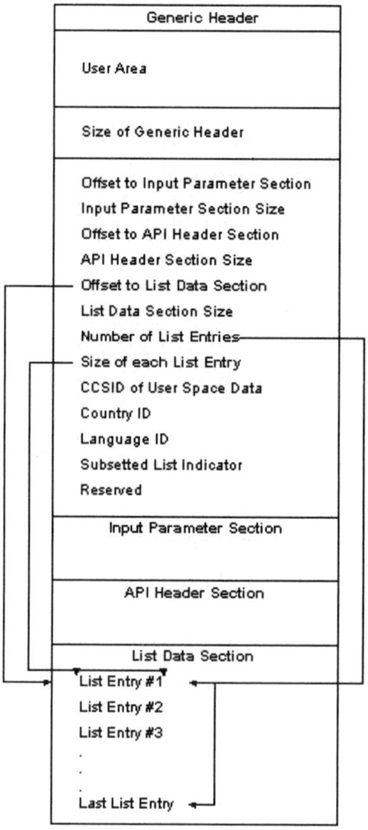

Generic Header

The Generic Header section of the user space contents provides information needed to access the data output by the List API. It provides offset values needed to access the information in all of the other sections. The Generic Header section is the map that guides you to the data within the user space. The fields of most value in the Generic Header section are the offset to the List Data section, the number of list entries in the List Data section, and the size of each list entry. Figure 4.13 shows the RPG definition of the Generic Header section.

Input Parameter Section

The Input Parameter section contains a mirror of the parameter values provided to the List API at the time of its execution.

Figure 4.12: The layout of the standard List API output.

API-Specific Header Section

Most List APIs provide a small amount of header-level information that is specific to the API.

List Data Section

The List Data section contains the resulting list entries output by the API. Each list entry appears consecutively as a string of data and is accessed using the offset and length of each entry information found in the Generic Header section.

```
*_____
*   Common List API Header
*_____
DAPIHeader0100      DS
D   HdrUserArea                    64A
D   HdrSize                        10I 0
D   HdrRelease                      4A
D   HdrFormat                       8A
D   HdrAPIName                     10A
D   HdrDateTime                    13A
D   HdrInfoSts                      1A
D   HdrUsrSpcSize                  10I 0
D   HdrOffInp                      10I 0
D   HdrSizeInput                   10I 0
D   HdrOffHdr                      10I 0
D   HdrSizeHdr                     10I 0
D   HdrOffList                     10I 0
D   HdrSizeList                    10I 0
D   HdrList#                       10I 0
D   HdrListSize                    10I 0
D   HdrCCSID                       10I 0
D   HdrCountry                      2A
D   HdrLanguage                     3A
D   HdrSubset                       1A
D   HdrReserved                    42A
```

Figure 4.13: An example definition of the List API Generic Header section.

Retrieving Data from a User Space

There are two commonly used methods to retrieve data from a user space. The first employs the Retrieve User Space API to return a portion of the user space contents when given a starting location and length. When using ILE RPG, there is an easier, better performing method. ILE RPG allows you to use basing pointers to address desired portions of the contiguous user space.

If you have not used pointers in an RPG program before, they are simply a way to address a specific storage location in memory. Pointers are used with data structures to parse the data residing in the pointer location into individual subfields. When coded on a data structure definition, the RPG BASED keyword specifies that the data structure is to be loaded with the data residing in the address provided by a pointer. Setting or changing the value of the pointer causes the contents of the data structure to automatically change.

169

The logic used to access List API data from a user space follows a basic flow of six steps, as follows:

1. Run the List API to load the user space.

2. Call the QUSPTRUS API to assign a pointer to the user space.

3. Because a data structure is based on the pointer, access the Generic Header data.

4. Add the offset to the List Data section to the pointer, assigning a list pointer to the location of the first list entry.

5. Because a second data structure is based on the list pointer, access the data for the first list entry.

6. To access subsequent list entries, add the length of each entry to the list pointer, automatically reloading the data structure with the next list entry.

The QUSLJOB API

The QUSLJOB API produces a list of system jobs meeting the specified criteria. The API returns all jobs or a subset based on the job name or job status. Entries meeting the desired criteria are written to a user space. The output information is available in two different formats: JOBL0100 for basic job information and JOBL0200 for basic job information with the selected keyed return values.

QUSLJOB Parameters

The API accepts four required parameters and has two optional parameter groups, as shown in Table 4.22.

Table 4.22: QUSLJOB API Parameter List. Required Parameters			
Sequence	Parameter	I/O	Type
1	Qualified User Space Name	Input	Char(20)
2	Format Name	Input	Char(8)
3	Qualified Job Name	Input	Char(26)
4	Status	Input	Char(10)

Table 4.22: QUSLJOB API Parameter List (continued).
Required Parameters

First Optional Parameter Group

Sequence	Parameter	I/O	Type
5	Error Code	I/O	Char(*)

Second Optional Parameter Group

Sequence	Parameter	I/O	Type
6	Job Type	Input	Char(1)
7	Number of Fields to Return	Input	Binary(4)
8	Key of Fields to Return	Input	Array of Binary(4)

Qualified User Space Name

The first parameter is an input parameter containing the name and library name of the user space that is to receive the API output. The first 10 characters are the user space name, followed by the library name in the second 10 characters. The special values *CURLIB or *LIBL may be used in place of a library name.

Format Name

The second parameter is an input parameter containing the name of the format to be used. The format name determines whether the API is to return basic job information or more basic information and values for supplied keys. The API offers two formats from which to choose: format JOBL0100 for basic information and format JOBL0200 for more detailed information.

Table 4.23 shows the layout for format JOBL0100, and Table 4.24 shows the layout for format JOBL0200.

Table 4.23: List Job API (Format JOBL0100).

Sequence	Parameter	I/O	Type
1	Job Name	Output	Char(10)
2	Job User	Output	Char(10)
3	Job Number	Output	Char(6)
4	Internal Job Identifier	Output	Char(16)
5	Status	Output	Char(10)
6	Job Type	Output	Char(1)
7	Job Subtype	Output	Char(1)
8	Reserved	Output	Char(2)

Table 4.24: List Job API (Format JOBL0200).

Sequence	Parameter	I/O	Type
	Entire JOBL0100 Format	Output	
9	Job Information Status	Output	Char(1)
10	Reserved	Output	Char(3)
11	Number of Fields Returned	Output	Binary(4)
12	Repeating Key Information Structure	Output	Char(*)

Repeating Key Information (Repeats for Each Key Field Selected).

Parameter	I/O	Type
Length of Information Returned	Output	Binary(4)
Key Field	Output	Binary(4)
Type of Data	Output	Char(1)
Reserved	Output	Char(3)
Length of Data	Output	Binary(4)
Data for Specified Key	Output	Char(*)
Reserved	Output	Char(*)

Qualified Job Name

The third parameter is a 26-character input parameter that specifies the name of the job to be retrieved by the API. Special values can be used to create a subset of jobs to be included. The following is a list of permissible special values:

Job Name

Occupies the first 10 bytes of the Qualified Job Name.

*	Returns information for the job running this API (job user and job number must be blank).
generic*	Returns information for jobs generically matching supplied name.
name	Returns information for jobs having a specific name.
*CURRENT	Returns information for jobs having the same name as the current job.
*ALL	Returns information for all job names.

User Name

Occupies the second 10 bytes of the Qualified Job Name.

generic*	Returns information for jobs generically matching the specified user.
name	Returns information for jobs having a specific user.
*CURRENT	Returns information for jobs having the same user name as current job.
*ALL	Returns information for all job user names.

Job Number

Occupies the last 6 bytes of the Qualified Job Name.

name	Returns information for jobs having a specific job number.
*ALL	Returns information for all job numbers.

Status

The fourth parameter is a 10-character input parameter that specifies the status of jobs to be returned. The following is a list of permissible special values:

*ACTIVE	Returns information for jobs having a status of *ACTIVE.
*JOBQ	Returns information for jobs having a status of *JOBQ.
*OUTQ	Returns information for jobs having a status of *OUTQ.
*ALL	Returns information for jobs having any status.

Error Code

The first optional parameter is a standard error code structure. It is a variable-length structure containing a number of error-related subfields. In an RPG program, the Error Code parameter is defined as a data structure having multiple defined subfields and is used by many APIs.

Job Type

The first parameter of the second optional parameter group is a one-character field that allows you to specify the type of job to be included in the list. The following is a list of permissible Job Type values:

*	List all job types
A	List autostart jobs
B	List batch jobs
I	List interactive jobs
M	List subsystem monitor jobs
R	List spooled reader jobs
S	List system jobs
W	List spooled writer jobs
X	List start-control-program-function (SCPF) system jobs

Number of Fields to Return

The second parameter of the second optional parameter group is a four-byte binary field that specifies the number of key fields you are specifying.

Key of Fields to Return

The third parameter of the second optional parameter group is an array of four-byte binary fields that specify the key fields that correspond with the data fields you want to retrieve. For example, to retrieve the job queue name and run priority, you would provide two binary fields having the values 1004 and 1802, respectively. The key 1004 means you want the job queue name and 1802 is the key for run priority. Table 4.25 lists all of the possible key values from which to choose.

Table 4.25: List Job API (Valid Key Values).

Key Description	Key	Returned Data Length
Active job status	0101	CHAR(4)
Break message handling	0201	CHAR(10)
Cancel key	0301	CHAR(1)
Coded character set ID	0302	BINARY(4)
Country ID	0303	CHAR(2)
Processing unit used	0304	BINARY(4)
Current user profile	0305	CHAR(10)
Completion status	0306	CHAR(1)
Current system pool identifier	0307	BINARY(4)
Character identifier control	0311	CHAR(10)
Date and time job became active	0401	CHAR(13)
Date and time job entered system	0402	CHAR(13)
Date and time job is scheduled to run	0403	CHAR(8)
Date and time job was put on this job queue	0404	CHAR(8)
Date format	0405	CHAR(4)
Date separator	0406	CHAR(1)
DBCS-capable	0407	CHAR(1)
DDM conversation handling	0408	CHAR(10)
Default wait	0409	BINARY(4)
Device recovery action	0410	CHAR(13)
Device name	0411	CHAR(10)
Default coded character set identifier	0412	BINARY(4)
Decimal format	0413	CHAR(1)
End severity	0501	BINARY(4)

Table 4.25: *List Job API (Valid Key Values) (continued)).*

Key Description	Key	Returned Data Length
End status	0502	CHAR(1)
Exit key	0503	CHAR(1)
Function name	0601	CHAR(10)
Function type	0602	CHAR(1)
Signed-on job	0701	CHAR(1)
Group profile name	0702	CHAR(10)
Group profile name - supplemental	0703	CHAR(150)
Inquiry message reply	0901	CHAR(10)
Job accounting code	1001	CHAR(15)
Job date	1002	CHAR(7)
Job description name	1003	CHAR(20)
Job queue name	1004	CHAR(20)
Job queue priority	1005	CHAR(2)
Job switches	1006	CHAR(8)
Job message queue full action	1007	HAR(10)
Job message queue maximum size	1008	BINARY(4)
Job user identity	1012	CHAR(10)
Job user identity setting	1013	CHAR(1)
Language ID	1201	CHAR(3)
Logging level	1202	CHAR(1)
Logging of CL programs	1203	CHAR(10)
Logging severity	1204	BINARY(4)
Logging text	1205	CHAR(10)
Mode name	1301	CHAR(8)
Maximum processing unit time	1302	BINARY(4)

Table 4.25: List Job API (Valid Key Values) (continued)).

Key Description	Key	Returned Data Length
Maximum temporary storage in kilo-bytes	1303	BINARY(4)
Maximum threads	1304	BINARY(4)
Maximum temporary storage in megabytes	1305	BINARY(4)
Number of auxiliary I/O requests	1401	BINARY(4)
Number of interactive transactions	1402	BINARY(4)
Number of database lock waits	1403	BINARY(4)
Number of internal machine lock waits	1404	BINARY(4)
Number of nondatabase lock waits	1405	BINARY(4)
Output queue name	1501	CHAR(20)
Output queue priority	1502	CHAR(2)
Print key format	1601	CHAR(10)
Print text	1602	CHAR(30)
Printer device name	1603	CHAR(10)
Purge	1604	CHAR(10)
Product return code	1605	BINARY(4)
Program return code	1606	BINARY(4)
Pending signal set	1607	CHAR(8)
Process ID number	1608	BINARY(4)
Response time total	1801	BINARY(4)
Run priority	1802	BINARY(4)
Routing data	1803	CHAR(80)
Sort sequence	1901	CHAR(20)
Status message handling	1902	CHAR(10)
Status of job on the job queue	1903	CHAR(10)

177

Table 4.25: List Job API (Valid Key Values) (continued)).

Key Description	Key	Returned Data Length
Submitter's job name	1904	CHAR(26)
Submitter's message queue name	1905	CHAR(20)
Subsystem description name	1906	CHAR(20)
System pool identifier	1907	BINARY(4)
Special environment	1908	CHAR(10)
Signal blocking mask	1909	CHAR(8)
Signal status	1910	BINARY(4)
Server type	1911	CHAR(30)
Time separator	2001	CHAR(1)
Time slice	2002	BINARY(4)
Time-slice end pool	2003	CHAR(10)
Temporary storage used in kilobytes	2004	BINARY(4)
Time spent on database lock waits	2005	CHAR(3)
Time spent on internal machine lock waits	2006	CHAR(3)
Time spent on nondatabase lock waits	2007	CHAR(3)
Thread count	2008	BINARY(4)
Temporary storage used in megabytes	2009	BINARY(4)
Unit of work ID	2101	CHAR(24)
User return code	2102	BINARY(4)

The ILE RPG Example

As you will recall, the example ILE RPG module API005R employs the QUSLJOB API to retrieve a list of jobs on the system meeting specified criteria. The example lists all jobs having a status of *OUTQ. It then prints a listing of jobs that ended with a severity greater than zero. Key values are provided on input to instruct the API to return the date and time the job became active and the ending severity.

Module API005R begins by creating the user space that is to receive the List API output. Figure 4.14 shows the call to the QUSCRTUS API and the definition of the API parameters.

```
 *_____
 *   Create User Space API Parameters
 *_____
DSpaceName       S            20A    Inz('USERSPC    QTEMP      ')
DSpaceAttrib     S            10A
DSpaceSize       S            10I 0  Inz(1024)
DSpaceInit       S             1A
DSpaceAuth       S            10A    Inz('*CHANGE')
DSpaceText       S            50A
DSpaceReplace    S            10A    Inz('*YES')
 *
 *_____
 *   Create User Space
 *_____
C                     Call      'QUSCRTUS'
C                     Parm                    SpaceName
C                     Parm                    SpaceAttrib
C                     Parm                    SpaceSize
C                     Parm                    SpaceInit
C                     Parm                    SpaceAuth
C                     Parm                    SpaceText
C                     Parm                    SpaceReplace
C                     Parm                    APIErrorDS
```

Figure 4.14: The module creates user space QTEMP/USERSPC.

The module continues with a call to the QUSCUSAT API. The API changes the user space to be automatically extendible. This means that the system will automatically increase the size of the user space if the available space is exceeded. Figure 4.15 shows the call to the QUSCUSAT API and the definition of the API parameters. Once the user space has been created and its attribute changed, the input parameters are initialized and the QUSLJOB API is called. Figure 4.16 shows the API call and associated parameter definitions.

```
 *_____
 *   Change User Space Attribute API Parameters
 *_____
DSpaceLibOut     S            10A
DSpaceChgAtt     DS
D  NbrAttrib                  10I 0  Inz(1)
D  KeyAttrib                  10I 0  Inz(3)
D  SizeAttrib                 10I 0  Inz(%Size(DataAttrib))
D  DataAttrib                  1A    Inz('1')
```

Figure 4.15: The module changes the user space to be automatically extendible.

```
     *_____
     *  Change User Space to be extendible
     *_____
     C                   Call      'QUSCUSAT'
     C                   Parm                    SpaceLibOut
     C                   Parm                    SpaceName
     C                   Parm                    SpaceChgAtt
     C                   Parm                    APIErrorDS
     *
```

Figure 4.15: The module changes the user space to be automatically extendible (continued).

```
     *_____
     *  List Jobs API Parameters (REQUIRED)
     *_____
     DJobLFormat       S              8A   Inz('JOBL0200')
     DJobLJobName      S             26A   Inz('*ALL        *ALL      *ALL  ')
     DJobLStatus       S             10A   Inz('*OUTQ      ')
     *_____
     *  List Jobs API Parameters (OPTIONAL GROUP 2)
     *_____
     DJobLType         S              1A   Inz('*')
     DJobL#Fields      S             10I 0 Inz(%Elem(JobLKeys))
     DJobLKeys         S             10I 0 Dim(2)

     *_____
     *  List job information entries to
     *  user space.
     *_____
     *
     C                   Eval      JobLKeys(1) = 0501
     C                   Eval      JobLKeys(2) = 0401
     *
     C                   Call      'QUSLJOB'
     C                   Parm                    SpaceName
     C                   Parm                    JobLFormat
     C                   Parm                    JobLJobName
     C                   Parm                    JobLStatus
     C                   Parm                    APIErrorDS
     C                   Parm                    JobLType
     C                   Parm                    JobL#Fields
     C                   Parm                    JobLKeys
```

Figure 4.16: The module calls the QUSLJOB API.

To access the data in the user space, the module needs a pointer to the user space. A call to the QUSPTRUS API establishes this pointer. Figure 4.17 shows the API call and associated parameter definitions. Because a data structure is defined based on the pointer, the data structure is automatically loaded when the pointer is assigned. The pointer addresses the first byte of the user space, which represents the Generic Header section of the List API output. Figure 4.18 shows the definition of the Generic Header data structure.

Once the pointer is assigned, the module has access to the information needed to retrieve list entries from the user space using fields from the Generic Header section. A second pointer, called LISTPTR, is assigned using the value of the user space pointer plus the offset to the first list entry. This addresses the pointer to the first byte of the first list entry.

```
     *
     DSpacePtr          S              *
     *_____
     *  Get a pointer to the user space
     *_____
     C                  Call      'QUSPTRUS'
     C                  Parm                     SpaceName
     C                  Parm                     SpacePtr
     C                  Parm                     APIErrorDS
     *
```

Figure 4.17: A pointer to the user space is established by calling an API.

```
     *_____
     *  Common List API Header
     *_____
     DAPIHeader0100     DS                        Based(SpacePtr)
     D  HdrUserArea                     64A
     D  HdrSize                         10I 0
     D  HdrRelease                       4A
     D  HdrFormat                        8A
     D  HdrAPIName                      10A
     D  HdrDateTime                     13A
     D  HdrInfoSts                       1A
     D  HdrUsrSpcSize                   10I 0
     D  HdrOffInp                       10I 0
     D  IldrSizeInput                   10I 0
     D  HdrOffHdr                       10I 0
     D  HdrSizeHdr                      10I 0
     D  HdrOffList                      10I 0
     D  HdrSizeList                     10I 0
     D  HdrList#                        10I 0
     D  HdrListSize                     10I 0
     D  HdrCCSID                        10I 0
     D  HdrCountry                       2A
     D  HdrLanguage                      3A
     D  HdrSubset                        1A
     D  HdrReserved                     42A
```

Figure 4.18: When the pointer is assigned, the contents of this data structure are loaded.

A data structure, FMTJOBL0200, is based on the pointer. This loads the data structure with the data of the first list entry. The layout of the data structure subfields matches the format selected when the List API was run. Figure 4.19 shows the pointer arithmetic and the data structure based on the pointer.

```
*_____
 *  API Format JOBL0200 Structure
 *_____
DFmtJOBL0200      DS                        Based(ListPtr)
D  JLJobName                      10A
D  JLJobUser                      10A
D  JLJob#                          6A
D  JLIntJobID                     16A
D  JLStatus                       10A
D  JLJobType                       1A
D  JLJobSubType                    1A
D  JLReserved1                     2A
D  JLJobInfoSts                    1A
D  JLReserved2                     3A
D  JL#Fields                      10I 0
 *_____
 *  Variable portion of return parameters.
 *  Depends upon keys you requested.
 *_____
D  JLKey1Len                      10I 0
D  JLKey1                         10I 0
D  JLKey1Type                      1A
D  JLKey1Reserve                   3A
D  JLKey1DataLen                  10I 0
D  JLEndSeverity                  10I 0
 *_____
 *  Second key value
 *_____
D  JLKey2Len                      10I 0
D  JLKey2                         10I 0
D  JLKey2Type                      1A
D  JLKey2Reserve                   3A
D  JLKey2DataLen                  10I 0
D  JLCentury                       1A
D  JLyymmdd                        6A
D  JLhhmmss                        6A
D  JLFiller3                       3A
 *
DSpacePtr          S                         *
DListPtr           S                         *
 *
 *_____
 *  Set position to first list entry
 *_____
C                     Eval      Listptr = SpacePtr + HdrOffList
```

Figure 4.19: The offset is added to the space pointer, addressing the first list entry.

Defining the Return Key Data

As you will recall from earlier in this example, data returned for the keys specified are provided in structures of variable length. The length of each key group varies because different keys return data of different lengths. For example, when the date and time the job became active, key 0401, is selected, the returned data is 13 characters. To return the job end severity, key 0501, the returned data is a four-byte binary field. The structure layout must be coded and formatted to appropriately accommodate the keys selected.

Maintaining a Four-Byte Boundary

Coding of the return data structure is complicated by the fact that each key data group must maintain a four-byte boundary. This means that, while each grouping varies in length, the total size of each group must be divisible by four. If the resulting length of the data group is not divisible by four, a filler field should be added to the end of the group having a length that makes the total divisible by four. The fixed portion of the data is 16-bytes long.

Suppose you are defining the return data group for the completion status key 0306. It has a length of one character. When added to the fixed portion of the group, the length of the group is 17 bytes. To observe a four-byte boundary, a three-byte filler field would be added to the end of the group.

This example defines two key values to return: a four-byte binary ending severity and a 13-character job activation date and time. When added to the 16-byte fixed portion of the data, the ending severity key data group is 20 bytes long. Because the length is divisible by four, no filler field definitions are necessary. The total length of the job activation date and time key data group is 29 bytes. To maintain the four-byte boundary, a three-byte filler field is added to the end of the group.

Completing the Module Logic

A control loop in the module executes detail logic for each list entry in the API. The field HDRLIST# from the Generic Header section tells you how many list entries were returned by the API and is the basis of the Do-Loop value. The detailed processing you desire for each job listing returned by the API is performed within the Do-Loop construct. The example module prints job information for each list entry using the RPG EXCPT op code. After each entry is processed, the pointer is advanced to the next entry by adding the length of each entry to the pointer value. Figure 4.20 shows the control construct used to process each individual list entry. When all entries have been processed, the module ends.

```
         *-----------------------------------------------------
         *  Loop for each entry.  Retrieve each
         *  entry from user space.
         *-----------------------------------------------------
         C                     Do           HdrList#      NumList
           *
         *-----------------------------------------------------
         *  This is where you would add your
         *  desired process for each list entry.
         *
         *  The example test the returned Job End
         *  severity.  Prints if greater than zero.
         *-----------------------------------------------------
         C                     If           JLEndSeverity  > 0
           *
         C                     Eval         JobName = %Trim(JLJobName) + '/' +
         C                                  %Trim(JLJobUser) + '/' +
         C                                  JLJob#
           *
         C                     Except       JobDtl
         C                     Endif
           *
         C                     If           NumList < HdrList#
         C                     Eval         Listptr = Listptr + HdrListSize
         C                     Endif
         C                     Enddo
```

Figure 4.20: Each list entry is processed using a Do-Loop construct.

EXAMPLE

Using the List Spooled Files API

The List Spooled Files (QUSLSPL) API is a powerful tool that allows you to retrieve information about spool files on your system. The ability to specify multiple selection criteria makes the API handy for many applications. The QUSLSPL API returns a list of spool files to a user space.

WHAT THE EXAMPLE DOES

The example ILE RPG module API006R employs the QUSLSPL API to retrieve a list of spool files on the system. Unlike the simplistic fixed-format interface of many List APIs, the QUSLSPL API allows you to specify the information you desire using key values.

The example prints a listing of all spool files found in any output queue for the current user running the example. Listing 4.6 shows the source member.

Listing 4.6: ILE RPG member API006R employs the QUSLSPL API.

```
FQPRINT    O   F  132         Printer OFLIND(*InOF)
   *
   *_____
   *  Create User Space API Parameters
   *_____
DSpaceName      S           20A    Inz('USERSPC    QTEMP     ')
DSpaceAttrib    S           10A
DSpaceSize      S           10I 0 Inz(1024)
DSpaceInit      S            1A
DSpaceAuth      S           10A    Inz('*CHANGE')
DSpaceText      S           50A
DSpaceReplace   S           10A    Inz('*YES')
   *
   *_____
   *  Change User Space Attribute API Parameters
   *_____
DSpaceLibOut    S           10A
DSpaceChgAtt    DS
D  NbrAttrib                10I 0 Inz(1)
D  KeyAttrib                10I 0 Inz(3)
D  SizeAttrib               10I 0 Inz(%Size(DataAttrib))
D  DataAttrib                1A   Inz('1')
   *_____
   *  List Spooled File API Parameters (REQUIRED)
   *_____
DSplFFormat     S            8A    Inz('SPLF0200')
DSplFUser       S           10A    Inz('*CURRENT  ')
DSplFOutQ       S           20A    Inz('*ALL')
DSplFForm       S           10A    Inz('*ALL')
DSplFUsrDta     S           10A    Inz('*ALL')
   *_____
   *  List Spooled File Parameters (OPTIONAL GROUP 2)
   *_____
DSplFJobName    S           26A
DSplF#Fields    S           10I 0 Inz(%Elem(SplFKeys))
DSplFKeys       S           10I 0 Dim(9)
   *_____
   *  Common List API Header
   *_____
DAPIHeader0100  DS                 Based(SpacePtr)
D  HdrUserArea             64A
D  HdrSize                 10I 0
D  HdrRelease               4A
D  HdrFormat                8A
```

Listing 4.6: ILE RPG member API006R employs the QUSLSPL API (continued).

```
D   HdrAPIName                10A
D   HdrDateTime               13A
D   HdrInfoSts                 1A
D   HdrUsrSpcSize             10I 0
D   HdrOffInp                 10I 0
D   HdrSizeInput              10I 0
D   HdrOffHdr                 10I 0
D   HdrSizeHdr                10I 0
D   HdrOffList                10I 0
D   HdrSizeList               10I 0
D   HdrList#                  10I 0
D   HdrListSize               10I 0
D   HdrCCSID                  10I 0
D   HdrCountry                 2A
D   HdrLanguage                3A
D   HdrSubset                  1A
D   HdrReserved               42A
 *
 *_____
 *   API Format SPLF0200 Structure
 *_____
DFmtSPLF0200      DS                        Based(ListPtr)
D   SF#Fields                 10I 0
 *_____
 *   Variable portion of return parameters.
 *   Depends upon keys you requested.
 *_____
D   SFKey1Len                 10I 0
D   SFKey1                     10I 0
D   SFKey1Type                 1A
D   SFKey1Reserve              3A
D   SFKey1DataLen             10I 0
D   SFFileName                10A
D   SFFiller1                  2A
 *_____
 *   Second key value
 *_____
 *
D   SFKey2Len                 10I 0
D   SFKey2                     10I 0
D   SFKey2Type                 1A
D   SFKey2Reserve              3A
D   SFKey2DataLen             10I 0
D   SFJobName                 10A
D   SFFiller2                  2A
 *_____
 *   Third key value
 *_____
```

**Listing 4.6: ILE RPG member *API006R*
employs the *QUSLSPL* API (continued).**

```
     *
D    SFKey3Len              10I 0
D    SFKey3                 10I 0
D    SFKey3Type              1A
D    SFKey3Reserve           3A
D    SFKey3DataLen          10I 0
D    SFUser                 10A
D    SFFiller3               2A
     *_____
     *  Fourth key value
     *_____
     *
D    SFKey4Len              10I 0
D    SFKey4                 10I 0
D    SFKey4Type              1A
D    SFKey4Reserve           3A
D    SFKey4DataLen          10I 0
D    SFJob#                  6A
D    SFFiller4               2A
     *_____
     *  Fifth key value
     *_____
     *
D    SFKey5Len              10I 0
D    SFKey5                 10I 0
D    SFKey5Type              1A
D    SFKey5Reserve           3A
D    SFKey5DataLen          10I 0
D    SFOutQ                 10A
D    SFFiller5               2A
     *_____
     *  Sixth key value
     *_____
     *
D    SFKey6Len              10I 0
D    SFKey6                 10I 0
D    SFKey6Type              1A
D    SFKey6Reserve           3A
D    SFKey6DataLen          10I 0
D    SFStatus               10A
D    SFFiller6               2A
     *_____
     *  Seventh key value
     *_____
     *
D    SFKey7Len              10I 0
D    SFKey7                 10I 0
D    SFKey7Type              1A
```

Listing 4.6: ILE RPG member API006R employs the QUSLSPL API (continued).

```
D   SFKey7Reserve              3A
D   SFKey7DataLen             10I 0
D   SF#Pages                  10I 0
 *_____
 *   Eighth key value
 *_____
 *
D   SFKey8Len                 10I 0
D   SFKey8                    10I 0
D   SFKey8Type                 1A
D   SFKey8Reserve              3A
D   SFKey8DataLen             10I 0
D   SFSize                    10I 0
 *_____
 *   Ninth key value
 *_____
 *
D   SFKey9Len                 10I 0
D   SFKey9                    10I 0
D   SFKey9Type                 1A
D   SFKey9Reserve              3A
D   SFKey9DataLen             10I 0
D   SFSizeMult                10I 0
 *_____
 *   Common API Error Structure
 *_____
DAPIErrorDS      DS
D   APIBytes                  10I 0 Inz(%Size(APIErrorDS))
D   APIBytesOut               10I 0
D   APIErrID                   7A
D   APIReserved                1A
D   APIErInDta               256A
 *
DSpacePtr        S              *
DListPtr         S              *
DNumList         S              9 0
DJobName         S             26A
DSpoolSize       S              9 0
 *
 *_____
 *   Create User Space
 *_____
C                 Call    'QUSCRTUS'
C                 Parm                SpaceName
C                 Parm                SpaceAttrib
C                 Parm                SpaceSize
C                 Parm                SpaceInit
C                 Parm                SpaceAuth
```

**Listing 4.6: ILE RPG member *API006R*
employs the *QUSLSPL* API (continued).**

```
C                 Parm                    SpaceText
C                 Parm                    SpaceReplace
C                 Parm                    APIErrorDS
 *
 *_____
 *  Change User Space to be extendible
 *_____
C                 Call       'QUSCUSAT'
C                 Parm                    SpaceLibOut
C                 Parm                    SpaceName
C                 Parm                    SpaceChgAtt
C                 Parm                    APIErrorDS
 *
 *_____
 *  List job information entries to
 *  user space.
 *_____
C*
C                 Eval       SplFKeys(1) = 0201
C                 Eval       SplFKeys(2) = 0202
C                 Eval       SplFKeys(3) = 0203
C                 Eval       SplFKeys(4) = 0204
C                 Eval       SplFKeys(5) = 0206
C                 Eval       SplFKeys(6) = 0210
C                 Eval       SplFKeys(7) = 0211
C                 Eval       SplFKeys(8) = 0223
C                 Eval       SplFKeys(9) = 0222
C*
C                 Call       'QUSLSPL'
C                 Parm                    SpaceName
C                 Parm                    SplFFormat
C                 Parm                    SplFUser
C                 Parm                    SplFOutQ
C                 Parm                    SplFForm
C                 Parm                    SplFUsrDta
C                 Parm                    APIErrorDS
C                 Parm                    SplFJobName
C                 Parm                    SplFKeys
C                 Parm                    SplF#Fields
 *
 *_____
 *  Get a pointer to the user space
 *_____
C                 Call       'QUSPTRUS'
C                 Parm                    SpaceName
C                 Parm                    SpacePtr
C                 Parm                    APIErrorDS
 *
```

Listing 4.6: ILE RPG member API006R employs the QUSLSPL API (continued).

```
    *_____
    *  Set position to first list entry
    *_____
    *
    C                     Eval      Listptr = SpacePtr + HdrOffList
    *
    C                     Except    Header1
    *
    *_____
    *  Loop for each entry.  Retrieve each
    *  entry from user space.
    *_____
    C                     Do        HdrList#      NumList
    *
    *_____
    *  This is where you would add your
    *  desired process for each list entry.
    *
    *  The example prints each entry.
    *_____
    *
    C                     Eval      JobName = %Trim(SFJobName) + '/' +
    C                                         %Trim(SFUser) + '/' +
    C                                         SFJob#
    *
    C                     Eval      SpoolSize = SFSize * SFSizeMult
    *
    C                     Except    SplDtl
    *
    C                     If        NumList < HdrList#
    C                     Eval      Listptr = Listptr + HdrListSize
    C                     Endif
    C                     Enddo
    *
    C                     Eval      *InLR = *On
    C                     Return
    *_____
    OQPRINT    E           Header1       2 01
    O                                              50 'Spool Files for the'
    O                                              64 'current user.'
    O                                              70 'Page:'
    O                           Page1         z    76
    O          E           Header1       1 1
    O                                               6 'Job'
    O                                              36 'Outq'
    O                                              49 'Status'
    O                                              64 '# Pages'
    O                                              78 'Size'
```

Listing 4.6: ILE RPG member APIOO6R
employs the QUSLSPL API (continued).

0	E	SplDtl	1	
0		JobName		30
0		SFOutQ		41
0		SFStatus		53
0		SF#Pages	1	64
0		SpoolSize	1	78

HOW THE EXAMPLE WORKS

List APIs allow you to retrieve multiple items from the system whose volume is undeterminable. To accomplish this, a mechanism called a user space is employed to contain the output contents of the List API.

The AS/400 User Space Object

APIs that produce lists of unpredictable size require a means of delivering the information to the requesting program. To accomplish this task, the AS/400 provides an object that represents space in memory to contain API results. This object, called a user space, is simply a buffer of contiguous, dedicated space to hold data.

User space object manipulation—including creating, changing, and deleting a user space—is accomplished using a set of user space APIs. The user space APIs used in this example are:

- Create User Space (QUSCRTUS)
- Change User Space Attributes (QUSCUSAT)
- Retrieve Pointer to User Space (QUSPTRUS)

The Create User Space API

The Create User Space (QUSCRTUS) API creates a user space object used to hold the results of List APIs. The API accepts nine parameters, six that are required and three that are optional.

The API receives six required parameters. The first optional parameter group accepts two additional parameters. A second optional parameter group accepts one additional parameter. Table 4.26 shows the QUSCRTUS API parameter groups.

Table 4.26: QUSCRTUS API Parameter List.
Required Parameters

Sequence	Parameter	I/O	Type
1	Qualified User Space Name	Input	Char(20)
2	Extended Attribute	Input	Char(10)
3	Initial Size	Input	Binary(4)
4	Initial Value	Input	Char(1)
5	Public Authority	Input	Char(10)
6	Text Description	Input	Char(50)
First Optional Parameter Group			
Sequence	Parameter	I/O	Type
7	Replace	Input	Char(10)
8	Error Code	I/O	Char(*)
Second Optional Parameter Group			
Sequence	Parameter	I/O	Type
9	Domain	Input	Char(10)

Qualified User Space Name

The first parameter is an input parameter containing the name and library name of the new user space being created. The first 10 characters are the user space name, followed by the library name in the second 10 characters. The special value *CURLIB may be used in place of a library name.

Extended Attribute

The second parameter is an input parameter containing an extended attribute for the user space. This is similar to a file object having the possible extended attributes PF, LF, or DSPF. It is of little use for user space objects and is generally left blank.

Initial Size

The third parameter is an input parameter containing the initial size of the user space. The value can range from 1 to 16,776,704 bytes. Because the parameter is a four-byte binary, the field is defined as a 10-digit integer that occupies four bytes of space.

Initial Value

The fourth parameter is an input parameter containing a character that is to be used as the initial value of the entire user space. Blanks or hexadecimal zeros (x'00') are generally good options for initial values. Setting the initial value to x'00' generally delivers slightly better system performance.

Public Authority

The fifth parameter is an input parameter containing a value that defines the default authority public users have when using the user space. The valid values are:

*ALL	Users can perform all operations on the user space.
Authorization List Name	The user space authority is determined by the authorization list specified.
*CHANGE	Users can read the object description and manipulate the contents of the user space.
*EXCLUDE	Users cannot access the user space in any way.
*LIBCRTAUT	The public authority level of the library is used as the authority level of the user space.
*USE	Users can read the user space contents but not change them.

Text Description

The sixth parameter is an input parameter containing a 50-character text description for the user space object.

Replace

The first parameter in the first optional parameter group specifies whether you want to replace an existing user space if the named space already exists. The valid values are:

*NO	Do not replace an existing user space if found.
*YES	The existing user space is deleted before the new space is created (provided the user is authorized to do so).

Error Code

The second parameter in the first optional parameter group is a standard parameter used by many APIs. It is a variable-length structure containing a number of error-related subfields. In an RPG program, the Error Code parameter is defined as a data structure having multiple defined subfields. Table 4.27 shows the subfields that comprise the Standard Error Code parameter structure.

Table 4.27: Standard Error Code Parameter Subfields.			
Sequence	Parameter	I/O	Type
1	Bytes Provided	Input	Binary(4)
2	Bytes Available	Output	Binary(4)
3	Exception ID	Output	Char(7)
4	Reserved	Output	Char(1)
5	Exception Data	Output	Char(*)

Bytes Provided

The Bytes Provided subfield is a four-byte binary input field identifying the total size of the error code structure. A 10-digit integer is used to define the four-byte field.

Bytes Available

The Bytes Available subfield is a four-byte binary output field containing the number of bytes of error information returned to the API. This field is commonly used by the calling program to determine if the API encountered an error. If the field value is zero, the API did not end in error. A 10-digit integer is used to define the four-byte field.

Exception ID

The Exception ID subfield is a seven-character output field containing the message identifier for the error encountered by the API. If the API did not encounter an error, the Exception ID is blank.

Reserved

The Reserved subfield is a one-character field reserved for future use.

Exception Data

The Exception Data subfield is a character field used to return the data associated with the returned error. Inclusion of this field is optional. If used, it can be a field of any size you desire. It is good practice to make the field large enough to hold return data that could be expected from most errors.

Domain

The first parameter in the second optional parameter group specifies whether you want to create the user space in the user or system domain. In most cases, you will create all user spaces in the user domain. The valid values are:

*USER	The user space is created in the user domain.
*SYSTEM	The user space is created in the system domain.
*DEFAULT	The system decides in which domain the user space is created. If this parameter is not specified, the value of *DEFAULT is used.

The Change User Space Attributes API

The Change User Space Attributes (QUSCUSAT) API changes the attributes of an existing user space object. It is used to change the initial size or initial value of the user space. Additionally, it is used to set the user space size to be automatically extended by the system when a more space is needed.

The API receives four required parameters, as shown in Table 4.28.

Table 4.28: QUSCUSAT API Parameter List.
Required Parameters

Sequence	Parameter	I/O	Type
1	Returned Library Name	Output	Char(10)
2	Qualified User Space Name	Input	Char(20)
3	Attributes to Change	Input	Char(*)
4	Error Code	I/O	Char(*)

Returned Library Name

The first parameter is an output parameter returned by the API. It contains the name of the library of the user space whose attributes were changed. This is useful when a special value of *LIBL or *CURLIB is specified in the qualified user space name parameter.

Qualified User Space Name

The second parameter is an input parameter containing the name and library name of the user space whose attributes are to be changed. The first 10 characters are the user space name, followed by the library name in the second 10 characters. The special values *CURLIB or *LIBL may be used in place of a library name.

Attributes to Change

The third parameter is an input parameter containing a variable-length structure that specifies the user space attributes to be changed. The structure consists of a four-byte binary field that specifies the number of attributes you are changing followed by a data group of three subfields for each attribute. The format of the data group depends on the attribute being changed. The data group for the Attributes to Change parameter consists of three subfields, as shown in Table 4.29.

	Table 4.29: Attribute Data Group Subfields.		
Sequence	Parameter	I/O	Type
1	Key for Attribute	Input	Binary(4)
2	Length of Attribute Data	Input	Binary(4)
3	Attribute Data Value	Input	Char(*)

Key for Attribute. The first subfield used for the Attribute to Change parameter is a key that specifies which attribute you want to change. Because the parameter is a four-byte binary, the field is defined as a 10-digit integer that occupies four bytes of space. There are three possible keys from which to select: the first to change the space size, the second to change the initial value, or the third to set the automatic extendibility.

Length of Attribute Data. The second subfield contains the size of the Attribute Data Value subfield. This length depends on which key value is selected. However, the length of the value should always maintain a four-byte boundary. For instance, if the data value is only one byte in length, you should add a three-byte filler to the end of the parameter to maintain the four-byte boundary.

Attribute Data Value. The third subfield contains the attribute data that corresponds with the key selected. The length of this subfield depends on the key being used. If a key value 1 is specified, the data value must be a four-byte binary value that specifies the new initial size of the user space. If a key value of 2 is specified, the value must be a one-character initial value. The final key value of 3 must be a one-character field that sets the automatic extendibility on or off. A value of '0' turns automatic extendibility off, while a '1' sets it on.

Error Code

The fourth and final parameter of the QUSCUSAT API is a standard error code structure. It is a variable-length structure containing a number of error-related subfields. In an RPG program, the Error Code parameter is defined as a data structure having multiple defined subfields and is used by many APIs.

The Retrieve Pointer to User Space API

The Retrieve Pointer to User Space (QUSPTRUS) API returns a basing pointer to the contents of a user space object. A basing pointer allows you to address the contents of a user space simply by basing a data structure on the pointer.

The API receives two required parameters and one optional parameter, as in Table 4.30.

Table 4.30: QUSPTRUS API Parameter List. Required Parameters			
Sequence	Parameter	I/O	Type
1	Qualified User Space Name	Input	Char(20)
2	Pointer to User Space Contents	Output	Pointer
Optional Parameter			
Sequence	Parameter	I/O	Type
3	Error Code	I/O	Char(*)

Qualified User Space Name

The first parameter is an input parameter containing the name and library name of the user space whose address is to be returned as a basing pointer. The first 10 characters are the user space name, followed by the library name in the second 10 characters. The special values *CURLIB or *LIBL may be used in place of a library name.

Pointer to User Space Contents

The second parameter is an output parameter that receives a basing pointer that addresses the user space. The parameter field is defined in RPG as a pointer variable. The pointer variable is used in conjunction with a data structure having the BASED keyword specified. This causes the data structure subfields to be automatically loaded with the data residing in the address stored in the pointer variable.

Error Code

The third parameter is optional. It is a standard error code structure. It is a variable-length structure containing a number of error-related subfields. In an RPG program, the Error Code parameter is defined as a data structure having multiple defined subfields and is used by many APIs.

List API Output

When executed, List APIs produce output that is written to and stored in a user space object. The API output follows a standardized format, allowing you to use the same basic logic to process most List APIs. The data returned by List APIs is divided into sections. Figure 4.21 shows the format of the standard List API output. The output generated by List APIs consists of the following four sections:

- Generic Header

- Input Parameter Section

- API Specific Header Section

- List Data Section

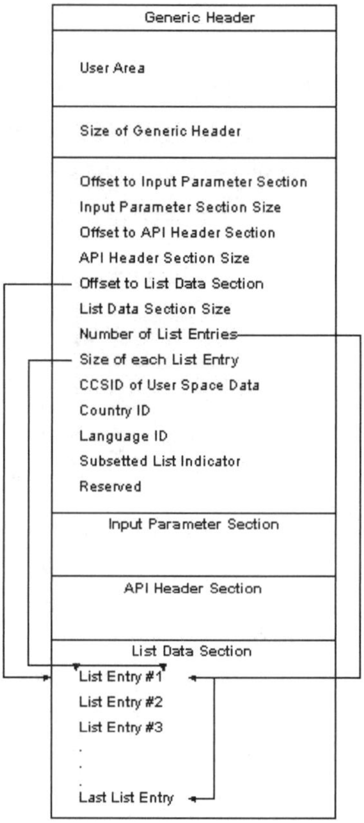

Generic Header

The Generic Header section of the user space contents provides information needed to access the data output by the list API. It provides offset values needed to access the information in all of the other sections. The Generic Header section is the map that guides you to the data within the user space. The fields of most value in the Generic Header section are the offset to the List Data section, the number of list entries in the List Data section, and the size of each list entry. Figure 4.22 shows the RPG definition of the Generic Header section.

Figure 4.21: The layout of the standard List API output.

Input Parameter Section

The Input Parameter section contains a mirror of the parameter values provided to the List API at the time of its execution.

```
*_____
*   Common List API Header
*_____
DAPIHeader0100    DS
D  HdrUserArea            64A
D  HdrSize                10I 0
D  HdrRelease              4A
D  HdrFormat               8A
D  HdrAPIName             10A
D  HdrDateTime            13A
D  HdrInfoSts              1A
D  HdrUsrSpcSize          10I 0
D  HdrOffInp              10I 0
D  HdrSizeInput           10I 0
D  HdrOffHdr              10I 0
D  HdrSizeHdr             10I 0
D  HdrOffList             10I 0
D  HdrSizeList            10I 0
D  HdrList#               10I 0
D  HdrListSize            10I 0
D  HdrCCSID               10I 0
D  HdrCountry              2A
D  HdrLanguage             3A
D  HdrSubset               1A
D  HdrReserved            42A
```

Figure 4.22: An example definition of the List API Generic Header section.

API Specific Header Section

Most List APIs provide a small amount of header-level information that is specific to the API.

List Data Section

The List Data section contains the resulting list entries output by the API. Each list entry appears consecutively as a string of data and is accessed using the offset and length of each entry information found in the Generic Header section.

Retrieving Data from a User Space

There are two commonly used methods to retrieve data from a user space. The first employs the Retrieve User Space API to return a portion of the user space contents when given a starting location and length. When using ILE RPG, there is an easier, better performing method. ILE RPG allows you to use basing pointers to address desired portions of the contiguous user space.

If you have not used pointers in an RPG program before, they are simply a way to address a specific storage location in memory. Pointers are used with data structures to parse the data residing in the pointer location into individual subfields. When coded on a data structure definition, the RPG BASED keyword specifies that the data structure is to be loaded with the data residing in the address provided by a pointer. Setting or changing the value of the pointer causes the contents of the data structure to automatically change.

The logic used to access List API data from a user space follows a basic flow of six steps, as follows:

1. Run the List API to load the user space.

2. Call the QUSPTRUS API to assign a pointer to the user space.

3. Because a data structure is based on the pointer, access the Generic Header data.

4. Add the offset to the List Data section to the pointer, assigning a list pointer to the location of the first list entry.

5. Because a second data structure is based on the list pointer, access the data for the first list entry.

6. To access subsequent list entries, add the length of each entry to the list pointer, automatically reloading the data structure with the next list entry.

The QUSLSPL API

The QUSLSPL API produces a list of spool files meeting the specified criteria. The API returns all spool files or a subset based on the output queue, form type, user data, or job name. Entries meeting the desired criteria are written to a user space. The output information is available in two different formats: SPLF0100 for basic file information and SPLF0200 for more detailed spool file information with the selected keyed return values.

QUSLSPL Parameters

The API accepts six required parameters and has three optional parameter groups, as shown in Table 4.31.

Table 4.31: QUSLSPL API Parameter List. Required Parameters			
Sequence	Parameter	I/O	Type
1	Qualified User Space Name	Input	Char(20)
2	Format Name	Input	Char(8)
3	User Name	Input	Char(10)
4	Qualified Output Queue Name	Input	Char(20)
5	Form Type	Input	Char(10)
6	User Data	Input	Char(10)
First Optional Parameter Group			
Sequence	Parameter	I/O	Type
7	Error Code	I/O	Char(*)
Second Optional Parameter Group			
Sequence	Parameter	I/O	Type
8	Qualified Job Name	Input	Char(26)
9	Key of Fields to Return	Input	Array of Binary(4)
10	Number of Fields to Return	Input	Binary(4)
Third Optional Parameter Group			
Sequence	Parameter	I/O	Type
11	Auxiliary Storage Pool (ASP)	Input	Binary(4)

Qualified User Space Name

The first parameter is an input parameter containing the name and library name of the user space that is to receive the API output. The first 10 characters are the user space name, followed by the library name in the second 10 characters. The special values *CURLIB or *LIBL may be used in place of a library name.

Format Name

The second parameter is an input parameter containing the name of the format to be used. The format name specifies whether the API is to return basic file information or specific data fields using key values. The API offers two formats from which to choose: format SPLF0100 for basic information and format SPLF0200 for specific information fields. Table 4.32 shows the layout for format SPLF0100 and Table 4.33 shows the layout for format SPLF0200.

Table 4.32: List Spooled Files API (Format SPLF0100).

Sequence	Parameter	I/O	Type
1	User Name	Output	Char(10)
2	Output Queue Name	Output	Char(10)
3	Output Queue Library Name	Output	Char(10)
4	Form Type	Output	Char(10)
5	User Data	Output	Char(10)
6	Internal Job Identifier	Output	Char(16)
7	Internal Spooled File Identifier	Output	Char(16)
8	Reserved	Output	Char(2)
9	Auxiliary Storage Pool	Output	Binary(4)

Table 4.33: List Spooled Files API (Format SPLF0200).

Sequence	Parameter	I/O	Type
1	Number of Fields Returned	Output	Binary(4)
2	Repeating Key Information Structure	Output	Char(*)

Repeating Key Information (Repeats for each key field selected).

Parameter	I/O	Type
Length of Information Returned	Output	Binary(4)
Key Field	Output	Binary(4)
Type of Data	Output	Char(1)
Reserved	Output	Char(3)
Length of Data	Output	Binary(4)
Data for Specified Key	Output	Char(*)
Reserved	Output	Char(*)

User Name

The third parameter is a 10-character input parameter that specifies the name of the user whose spool files are to be retrieved by the API. The following is a list of permissible special values:

name	Returns spool files created by a specific user.
*CURRENT	Returns spool files created by the current user.
*ALL	Returns spool files created by any user.

Qualified Output Queue Name

The fourth parameter is a 20-character input parameter that specifies the name of the output queue whose contained spool files are to be retrieved by the API. The first 10 bytes of the field contain the output queue name, followed by the output queue library in the second 10 bytes. The following is a list of permissible special values:

Output Queue Name	
name	Specifies an output queue name.
*ALL	Specifies all output queues.
Output Queue Library Name	
name	Specifies the output queue library name.
*CURLIB	Specifies the current library.
*LIBL	Specifies the output queue in the library list.

Form Type

The fifth parameter is a 10-character input parameter that specifies the name of the form types to be retrieved by the API. The following is a list of permissible special values:

name	Specifies the form type name to be included.
*ALL	Specifies that spool files of all form types are included.
*STD	Specifies that only spool files having the standard form type are included.

User Data

The sixth and final required parameter is a 10-character input parameter that specifies the user data values to be retrieved by the API. The following is a list of permissible special values:

name	Specifies the user data whose spool files are to be included.
*ALL	Specifies that spool files of all form types are included.
*STD	Specifies that only spool files having the standard form type are included.

Error Code

The first optional parameter is a standard error code structure. It is a variable-length structure containing a number of error-related subfields. In an RPG program, the Error Code parameter is defined as a data structure having multiple defined subfields and is used by many APIs.

Qualified Job Name

The first parameter of the second optional parameter group is a 26-character input parameter that specifies the name of the spool files to be retrieved by the API. Special values can be used to create a subset of files to be included. If left blank, the job name will not be used to determine the spool files to be included. The following is a list of permissible special values:

Job Name

Occupies the first 10 bytes of the Qualified Job Name.

*	Returns spool information for the job running this API (job user and job number must be blank).
name	Returns spool files for jobs having a specific name.

User Name

Occupies the second 10 bytes of the Qualified Job Name.

name	Returns spool files having a specific user.

Job Number

Occupies the last six bytes of the Qualified Job Name.

name	Returns information for files having a specific job number.

Key of Fields to Return

The second parameter of the second optional parameter group is an array of four-byte binary fields that specify the key fields that correspond with the data fields you want to retrieve. For example, to retrieve the spool file name and total pages, you would provide two binary fields having the values 0201 and 0211, respectively. The key 0201 means you want the spool file name and 0211 is the key for total pages. Table 4.34 lists all of the possible key values from which to choose.

Number of Fields to Return

The final parameter of the second optional parameter group is a four-byte binary field that specifies the number of key fields you are specifying.

Table 4.34: List Spooled Files API (Valid Key Values).		
Key Description	**Key**	**Returned Data Length**
Spool File Name	0201	CHAR(10)
Job Name	0202	CHAR(10)
User Name	0203	CHAR(10)
Job Number	0204	CHAR(6)
Spool File Number	0205	BINARY(4)
Output Queue Name	0206	CHAR(10)
Output Queue Library Name	0207	CHAR(10)
Device	0208	CHAR(10)
User Data	0209	CHAR(10)
Status	0210	CHAR(10)
Total Pages	0211	BINARY(4)
Current Page	0212	BINARY(4)
Copies Left to Produce	0213	BINARY(4)
Form Type	0214	CHAR(10)
Priority	0215	CHAR(2)
Date File was Opened	0216	CHAR(7)
Time File was Opened	0217	CHAR(6)
Internal Job Identifier	0218	CHAR(16)
Internal Spool File Identifier	0219	CHAR(16)
Device Type	0220	CHAR(10)
Date File Last Used	0221	CHAR(7)
Spooled File Size Multiplier	0222	BINARY(4)
Size of Spool File	0223	BINARY(4)
Auxiliary Storage Pool	0224	BINARY(4)

Auxiliary Storage Pool

The only parameter of the third optional parameter group is a four-byte binary field that specifies the auxiliary storage pool whose spool files are to be included. If omitted, the system does not use auxiliary storage pool as part of the selection criteria.

The ILE RPG Example

As you will recall, the example ILE RPG module API006R employs the QUSLSPL API to retrieve a list of spool files on the system meeting specified criteria. The example lists all spool files for the current user. Key values are provided on input to instruct the API to return the following nine values:

- Spool File Name
- Job Name
- Job User Name
- Job Number
- Output Queue Name
- Status
- Total Pages
- Spool File Size
- Spool File Size Multiplier

Module API006R begins by creating the user space that is to receive the List API output. Figure 4.23 shows the call to the QUSCRTUS API and the definition of the API parameters.

```
     *_____
     *   Create User Space API Parameters
     *_____
    DSpaceName        S            20A   Inz('USERSPC    QTEMP      ')
    DSpaceAttrib      S            10A
    DSpaceSize        S            10I 0 Inz(1024)
    DSpaceInit        S             1A
    DSpaceAuth        S            10A   Inz('*CHANGE')
    DSpaceText        S            50A
    DSpaceReplace     S            10A   Inz('*YES')
     *
     *_____
     *   Create User Space
     *_____
    C                     Call      'QUSCRTUS'
    C                     Parm                    SpaceName
    C                     Parm                    SpaceAttrib
    C                     Parm                    SpaceSize
    C                     Parm                    SpaceInit
    C                     Parm                    SpaceAuth
    C                     Parm                    SpaceText
    C                     Parm                    SpaceReplace
    C                     Parm                    APIErrorDS
```

Figure 4.23: The module creates user space QTEMP/USERSPC.

The module continues with a call to the QUSCUSAT API, which changes the user space to be automatically extendible. This means the system will automatically increase the size of the user space if the available space is exceeded. Figure 4.24 shows the call to the QUSCUSAT API and the definition of the API parameters.

```
      *_____
      *  Change User Space Attribute API Parameters
      *_____
     DSpaceLibOut       S              10A
     DSpaceChgAtt       DS
     D  NbrAttrib                      10I 0 Inz(1)
     D  KeyAttrib                      10I 0 Inz(3)
     D  SizeAttrib                     10I 0 Inz(%Size(DataAttrib))
     D  DataAttrib                      1A   Inz('1')

      *_____
      *  Change User Space to be extendible
      *_____
     C                   Call      'QUSCUSAT'
     C                   Parm                    SpaceLibOut
     C                   Parm                    SpaceName
     C                   Parm                    SpaceChgAtt
     C                   Parm                    APIErrorDS
      *
```

Figure 4.24: The module changes the user space to be automatically extendible.

Once the user space has been created and its attribute changed, the input parameters are initialized and the List Spooled Files API is called. Figure 4.25 shows the API call and associated parameter definitions.

```
      *_____
      *  List spool file information entries to
      *  user space.
      *_____

     C*
     C                   Eval      SplFKeys(1) = 0201
     C                   Eval      SplFKeys(2) = 0202
     C                   Eval      SplFKeys(3) = 0203
     C                   Eval      SplFKeys(4) = 0204
     C                   Eval      SplFKeys(5) = 0206
     C                   Eval      SplFKeys(6) = 0210
     C                   Eval      SplFKeys(7) = 0211
     C                   Eval      SplFKeys(8) = 0223
     C                   Eval      SplFKeys(9) = 0222
```

Figure 4.25: The module calls the QUSLSPL API.

```
C*
C                   Call      'QUSLSPL'
C                   Parm                  SpaceName
C                   Parm                  SplFFormat
C                   Parm                  SplFUser
C                   Parm                  SplFOutQ
C                   Parm                  SplFForm
C                   Parm                  SplFUsrDta
C                   Parm                  APIErrorDS
C                   Parm                  SplFJobName
C                   Parm                  SplFKeys
C                   Parm                  SplF#Fields
  *
```

Figure 4.25: The module calls the QUSLSPL API (continued).

To access the data in the user space, the module needs a pointer to the user space. A call to the QUSPTRUS API establishes this pointer. Figure 4.26 shows the API call and associated parameter definitions.

```
  *
DSpacePtr        S               *

  *_____
  *  Get a pointer to the user space
  *_____
C                   Call      'QUSPTRUS'
C                   Parm                  SpaceName
C                   Parm                  SpacePtr
C                   Parm                  APIErrorDS
  *
```

Figure 4.26: A pointer to the user space is established by calling an API.

Because a data structure is defined based on the pointer, the data structure is automatically loaded when the pointer is assigned. The pointer addresses the first byte of the user space, which represents the Generic Header section of the List API output. Figure 4.27 shows the definition of the Generic Header data structure.

```
*_____
*  Common List API Header
*_____
DAPIHeader0100     DS                      Based(SpacePtr)
D  HdrUserArea                   64A
D  HdrSize                       10I 0
D  HdrRelease                     4A
D  HdrFormat                      8A
D  HdrAPIName                    10A
D  HdrDateTime                   13A
D  HdrInfoSts                     1A
D  HdrUsrSpcSize                 10I 0
D  HdrOffInp                     10I 0
D  HdrSizeInput                  10I 0
D  HdrOffHdr                     10I 0
D  HdrSizeHdr                    10I 0
D  HdrOffList                    10I 0
D  HdrSizeList                   10I 0
D  HdrList#                      10I 0
D  HdrListSize                   10I 0
D  HdrCCSID                      10I 0
D  HdrCountry                     2A
D  HdrLanguage                    3A
D  HdrSubset                      1A
D  HdrReserved                   42A
```

Figure 4.27: When the pointer is assigned, the contents of this data structure are loaded.

Once the pointer is assigned, the module has access to the information needed to retrieve list entries from the user space using fields from the Generic Header section. A second pointer, called LISTPTR, is assigned using the value of the user space pointer plus the offset to the first list entry. This addresses the pointer to the first byte of the first list entry. A data structure, FMTSPLF0200, is based on the pointer. This loads the data structure with the data of the first list entry. The layout of the data structure subfields matches the format selected when the List API was run. Figure 4.28 shows the pointer arithmetic and the data structure based on the pointer.

```
*_____
*  API Format SPLF0200 Structure
*_____
DFmtSPLF0200       DS                      Based(ListPtr)
D  SF#Fields                     10I 0
*_____
*  Variable portion of return parameters.
*  Depends upon keys you requested.
```

Figure 4.28: The offset is added to the space pointer, addressing the first list entry.

```
 *-------------------------------------------------------
D  SFKey1Len                      10I 0
D  SFKey1                         10I 0
D  SFKey1Type                      1A
D  SFKey1Reserve                   3A
D  SFKey1DataLen                  10I 0
D  SFFileName                     10A
D  SFFiller1                       2A
 *-------------------------------------------------------
 *   Second key value
 *-------------------------------------------------------
 *
D  SFKey2Len                      10I 0
D  SFKey2                         10I 0
D  SFKey2Type                      1A
D  SFKey2Reserve                   3A
D  SFKey2DataLen                  10I 0
D  SFJobName                      10A
D  SFFiller2                       2A
 *-------------------------------------------------------
 *   Third key value
 *-------------------------------------------------------
 *
D  SFKey3Len                      10I 0
D  SFKey3                         10I 0
D  SFKey3Type                      1A
D  SFKey3Reserve                   3A
D  SFKey3DataLen                  10I 0
D  SFUser                         10A
D  SFFiller3                       2A
 *-------------------------------------------------------
 *   Fourth key value
 *-------------------------------------------------------
 *
D  SFKey4Len                      10I 0
D  SFKey4                         10I 0
D  SFKey4Type                      1A
D  SFKey4Reserve                   3A
D  SFKey4DataLen                  10I 0
D  SFJob#                          6A
D  SFFiller4                       2A
 *-------------------------------------------------------
 *   Fifth key value
 *-------------------------------------------------------
 *
D  SFKey5Len                      10I 0
D  SFKey5                         10I 0
D  SFKey5Type                      1A
D  SFKey5Reserve                   3A
D  SFKey5DataLen                  10I 0
D  SFOutQ                         10A
D  SFFiller5                       2A
```

Figure 4.28: The offset is added to the space pointer, addressing the first list entry (cont.).

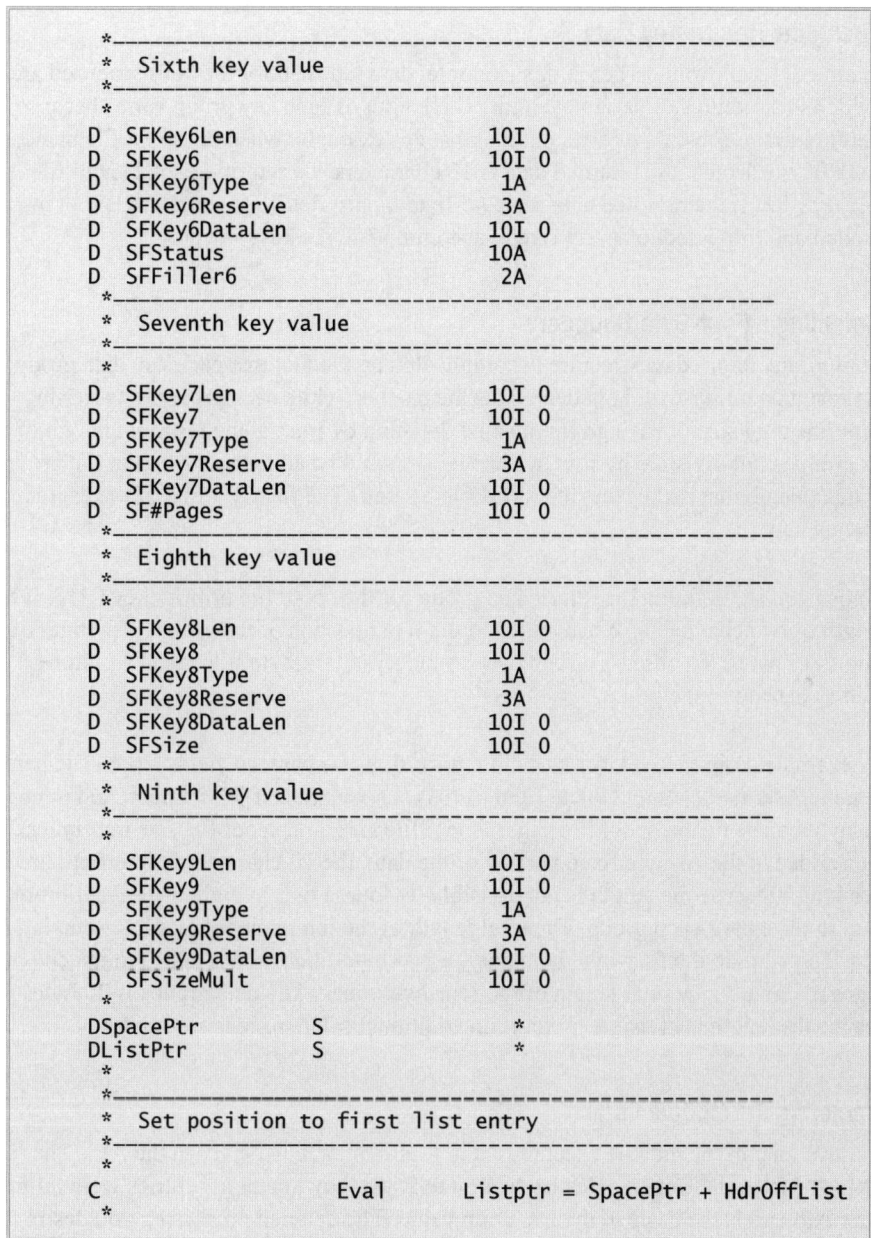

```
*_____
*   Sixth key value
*_____
*
D   SFKey6Len                        10I 0
D   SFKey6                           10I 0
D   SFKey6Type                        1A
D   SFKey6Reserve                     3A
D   SFKey6DataLen                    10I 0
D   SFStatus                         10A
D   SFFiller6                         2A
*_____
*   Seventh key value
*_____
*
D   SFKey7Len                        10I 0
D   SFKey7                           10I 0
D   SFKey7Type                        1A
D   SFKey7Reserve                     3A
D   SFKey7DataLen                    10I 0
D   SF#Pages                         10I 0
*_____
*   Eighth key value
*_____
*
D   SFKey8Len                        10I 0
D   SFKey8                           10I 0
D   SFKey8Type                        1A
D   SFKey8Reserve                     3A
D   SFKey8DataLen                    10I 0
D   SFSize                           10I 0
*_____
*   Ninth key value
*_____
*
D   SFKey9Len                        10I 0
D   SFKey9                           10I 0
D   SFKey9Type                        1A
D   SFKey9Reserve                     3A
D   SFKey9DataLen                    10I 0
D   SFSizeMult                       10I 0
*
DSpacePtr          S                  *
DListPtr           S                  *
*
*_____
*   Set position to first list entry
*_____
*
C                   Eval      Listptr = SpacePtr + HdrOffList
*
```

Figure 4.28: The offset is added to the space pointer, addressing the first list entry (cont.).

Defining the Return Key Data

As you will recall from earlier in this example, data returned for the keys specified are provided in structures of variable length. The length of each key group varies because different keys return data of different lengths. For example, when the spool file name, key 0201, is selected, the returned data is 10 characters. To return the total spool file pages, key 0211, the returned data is a four-byte binary field. The structure layout must be coded and formatted to appropriately accommodate the keys selected.

Maintaining a Four-Byte Boundary

Coding of the return data structure is complicated by the fact that each key data group must maintain a four-byte boundary. This means that, while each grouping varies in length, the total size of each group must be divisible by four. If the resulting length of the data group is not divisible by four, a filler field should be added to the end of the group having a length that makes the total divisible by four. The fixed portion of the data is 16-bytes long.

Suppose you are defining the return data group for the spool file priority key 0215. It has a length of two characters. When added to the fixed portion of the group, the length of the group is 18 bytes. To observe a four-byte boundary, a two-byte filler field would be added to the end of the group.

This example defines nine key values to return: five 10-character fields (spool file name, job name, user name, output queue, and status); a six-character job number; and three four-byte binary fields (spool file pages, spool file size, and spool file size multiplier). When added to the 16-byte fixed portion of the data, the 10-character field groups are 26 bytes long. Because the length is not divisible by four, a two-byte filler field definition is added to the end of each group. The total length of the job number key data group is 22 bytes. To maintain the four-byte boundary, a two-byte filler field is added to the end of the group. Finally, the total length of the four-byte binary key data groups is 20 bytes. Because the length is divisible by four, no additional filler space is required.

Completing the Module Logic

A control loop in the module executes detail logic for each list entry in the API. The field HDRLIST# from the Generic Header section tells you how many list entries were returned by the API and is the basis of the Do-Loop value. The detailed processing you desire for each spool file listing returned by the API is performed within the Do-Loop construct. The example module prints spool file information for each list entry using the RPG EXCPT op code. After each entry is processed, the pointer is advanced to the next entry by adding the length of each entry to the pointer value. Figure 4.29 shows the control construct used to process each individual list entry. When all entries have been processed, the module ends.

```
       *_____
       *  Loop for each entry.  Retrieve each
       *  entry from user space.
       *_____
       C                    Do        HdrList#      NumList
       *
       *_____
       *  This is where you would add your
       *  desired process for each list entry.
       *
       *  The example prints each entry.
       *_____
       *
       C                    Eval      JobName = %Trim(SFJobName) + '/' +
       C                                        %Trim(SFUser) + '/' +
       C                                        SFJob#
       *
       C                    Eval      SpoolSize = SFSize * SFSizeMult
       *
       C                    Except    SplDtl
       *
       C                    If        NumList < HdrList#
       C                    Eval      Listptr = Listptr + HdrListSize
       C                    Endif
       C                    Enddo
       *
```

Figure 4.29: Each list entry is processed using a Do-Loop construct.

EXAMPLE

Using the Random Number Generation API

The Random Number Generation (CEERAN0) API belongs to a category of APIs known as bindable APIs. Unlike the other APIs presented in this chapter, bindable APIs are callable only from ILE languages. The set of bindable APIs (often referred to as CEE APIs because of their naming convention) are not programs. Rather, they are procedures that are bound to your program.

The CEERAN0 API generates a random number between 0 and 1.

WHAT THE EXAMPLE DOES

This example is intended to serve as a shell that can be adapted for your use as necessary. The example ILE RPG module API007R employs the CEERAN0 API to generate a random number integer between 0 and 9, which is then displayed to the user. Listing 4.7 shows the source member.

Listing 4.7: ILE RPG member API007R employs the CEERAN0 API.

```
     *
     *_____
     *   Procedure Prototype
     *_____
DCEERAN0          PR
D   Seed                          10I 0
D   RandomNumber                   8F
D   Feedback                      12A    Options(*Omit)
     *
     *_____
     *   API Parameters
     *_____
DSeed             S              10I 0 Inz(0)
DRandomNumber     S               8F
DRandom           S               1  0
     *
C                 Callp    CEERAN0(Seed: RandomNumber: *Omit)
     *
C                 Eval     Random = RandomNumber * 10
     *
C                 dsply                     Random
C*
C                 Return
```

HOW THE EXAMPLE WORKS

The CEERAN0 API is a member of the ILE Math API group. It generates a random number between 0 and 1. The API accepts a seed value used to initialize the random number calculation.

To call a bindable API from an ILE RPG module, the procedure should first be prototyped. A prototype is simply a definition of the procedure's interface and parameters. It defines the length and type of each parameter and how the procedure is to be called. For more information about prototypes, see chapter 1.

CEERAN0 Parameters

The API receives two required parameters and one optional parameter, as shown in Table 4.35.

Table 4.35: CEERAN0 API Parameter List. Required Parameters			
Sequence	Parameter	I/O	Type
1	Seed	I/O	Int(4)
2	Random Number	Output	Float8
Optional Parameter			
Sequence	Parameter	I/O	Type
3	Feedback	Output	Char(12)

Seed Parameter

The first parameter is a four-byte integer field that contains the initial seed value for the random number calculation. After the API completes execution, the system returns a new value in the Seed parameter. This is done so that if the API is called again, a different seed value is used. This ensures that if the API is called repetitively, the same seed value is not used for each call.

As you will recall from the discussion at the beginning of this chapter, an integer field can be defined in RPG as 3, 5, 10, or 20 digits in length. An integer defined as three digits long results in the creation of a one-byte field. Five-digit integers are two bytes long, 10-digit integers are four bytes long, and 20-digit integers are eight bytes in length. Therefore, APIs that call for four-byte integer parameters are best defined as 10-digit integers.

The valid range of numbers that can be used as seed values is zero to 2,147,483,646. If the seed value is zero, the system uses the current Greenwich Mean Time as the starting seed value.

Random Number Parameter

The second parameter is an eight-digit floating point field that returns the random number generated by the API. RPG supports floating point fields for applications using a data type F in the field definition specification. The number of decimal positions in the definition specification is always left blank when defining floating point fields.

Feedback Parameter

The third parameter, which is optional, is a 12-character field that receives a condition token from the API. When omitted, API errors will result in a hard error being signaled to the condition manager.

The ILE RPG Example

The example source member API007R generates a random number using the CEERAN0 API. The module defines a prototype for the API based on information researched from the *System API Reference Manual*. The definition of the prototype is shown in Figure 4.30.

```
 *_____
 *   Procedure Prototype
 *_____
DCEERAN0          PR
D   Seed                        10I 0
D   RandomNumber                 8F
D   Feedback                    12A    Options(*Omit)
```

Figure 4.30: The prototype for the CEERAN0 procedure.

The example then calls the API using the RPG Call Procedure (CALLP) op code. The special value of *OMIT is specified as the Feedback parameter, meaning the parameter is not being used. The module multiplies the returned random number by 10 to derive a single-digit integer value. This logic is shown in Figure 4.31. The module concludes by displaying the resulting random number and ending.

```
 C                   Callp       CEERAN0(Seed: RandomNumber: *Omit)
 *
 C                   Eval        Random = RandomNumber * 10
 *
 C                   dsply                   Random
 C*
 C                   Return
```

Figure 4.31: The random number is generated and displayed to the user.

EXAMPLE

Using the ILE Date APIs

The example determines the day of week for a given date using the ILE Convert Date to Lillian Format (CEEDAYS) and Convert Lillian Date to Character Format (CEEDATE) APIs. These APIs belong to a category of APIs known as bindable APIs. Unlike the other APIs presented in this chapter, bindable APIs are callable only from ILE languages. The set of bindable APIs (often referred to as CEE APIs because of their naming convention) are not programs. Rather, they are procedures that are bound to your program.

WHAT THE EXAMPLE DOES

The example ILE RPG module API008R employs the ILE Date and Time APIs to determine the character representation of the day of week for a date passed to the module as an input parameter. The day of week is displayed to the user by the DSPLY RPG op code. Listing 4.8 shows the source member.

Listing 4.8: ILE RPG member API008R calls the CEEDAYS and CEEDATE APIs.

```
 *
 *_____
 *   Procedure Prototype
 *_____
DCEEDAYS         PR                    Opdesc
D  InputDate                 32767A    Options(*Varsize)
D  DateFormat                32767A    Options(*Varsize)
D  LillianOut                  10I 0
D  Feedback                    12A     Options(*Omit)
 *
DCEEDATE         PR                    Opdesc
D  LillianIn                   10I 0
D  DateString                32767A    Options(*Varsize)
D  DateOut                   32767A    Options(*Varsize)
D  Feedback                    12A     Options(*Omit)
 *
 *_____
 *   API Parameters
 *_____
DDateInput        S            8A
DDateFmt          S            8A     Inz('MMDDYYYY')
DLillianOut       S           10I 0
DOutFmt           S           10A     Inz('WWWWWWWWW')
DWeekDay          S           10A
```

Listing 4.8: ILE RPG member API008R
calls the CEEDAYS and CEEDATE APIs (continued).

```
 *
D@Error          C                       'Error found on API'
DErrorMsg        S              50A
 *
DFeedback        DS
D  FBSeverity               5I 0
D  FBMsgNumber              5I 0
D  FBFlags                  1A
D  FBFacId                  3A
D  FBIsi                   10I 0
 *
C     *Entry     Plist
C                Parm                    DateInput
 *
C                Callp     CEEDAYS(DateInput:
C                            DateFmt:
C                            LillianOut:
C                            Feedback)
 *
C                If        FBSeverity > 0
C                Eval      ErrorMsg = @Error
 *
C                Dsply                   ErrorMsg
C                Else
C                Callp     CEEDATE(LillianOut:
C                            OutFmt:
C                            WeekDay:
C                            *Omit)
 *
C                Dsply                   WeekDay
C                Endif
 *
C                Return
```

HOW THE EXAMPLE WORKS

The CEEDAYS API is a member of the ILE Date and Time API group. It accepts an input date in one of many possible formats and returns the Lillian representation of the date. The Lillian format represents the number of days since October 14, 1582. The Lillian format is handy for performing date arithmetic such as adding or subtracting days from a date. Many of the date APIs require the use of the Lillian format to perform a desired function. After a Lillian representation of the input date is derived, it is passed as input to the CEEDATE API to determine the day of week.

To call a bindable API from an ILE RPG module, the procedure should first be prototyped. A prototype is simply a definition of the procedure's interface and parameters. It defines the length and type of each parameter and how the procedure is to be called. For more information about prototypes, see chapter 1.

CEEDAYS Parameters

The API receives three required parameters and one optional parameter, as shown in Table 4.36.

Table 4.36: CEEDAYS API Parameter List. Required Parameters			
Sequence	Parameter	I/O	Type
1	Input Character Date	Input	VSTRING
2	Picture String for Input Date	Input	VSTRING
3	Output Lillian Date	Output	INT4
Optional Parameter			
Sequence	Parameter	I/O	Type
4	Feedback	Output	Char(12)

Input Character Date Parameter

The first parameter is a variable-length character input field that supplies the date to be converted to Lillian format. The date can be supplied in one of numerous formats. Valid dates are within the range October 15, 1582, to December 31, 9999.

Picture String for Input Date Parameter

The second parameter is a variable-length character input field that supplies a picture string that indicates the format of the Input Character Date parameter. If the Picture String field is left blank, the system will interpret the input date using the current job value of COUNTRY ID. For the United States the default format is mm/dd/yyyy. Table 4.37 shows a list of valid picture strings. Valid strings can include many combinations of the picture string shown.

Table 4.37: Convert Date to Lillian Format API (Valid Picture Strings).

Picture	Example
MM	2 Digit Month — 01-12
ZM	Either a 1 or 2 Digit Month — 1-12
RRRR	Roman Numeral Month — I-XII
RRRz	
MMM	JAN
Mmm	Jan
MMMMMMMMMMMMMMM	FEBRUARY
Mmmmmmmmmmmmmmm	March
MMMMMMMMMMMMMMMZ	JUNE (no trailing blanks)
Mmmmmmmmmmmmmmmz	July (no trailingm—ixed case)
DD	Day of month — 01-31
ZD	1-31
DDD	Day of year — 001-366
HH	Hour — 00-23
ZH	1-23
MI	Minute — 00-59
SS	Second — 00-59
9	1/10 second — 0-9
99	1/100 second — 00-99
999	1/1000 second — 000-999
AP	AM or PM
Ap	Am or Pm
A.P.	A.M. or P.M.
a.p.	a.m. or p.m.
W	Day of week — S, M, T, W, T, F, S
WWW	SAT
Www	Sat
WWWWWWWWWW	MONDAY
Wwwwwwwwww	Tuesday
WWWWWWWWWWZ	WEDNESDAY (no trailing blanks)
Wwwwwwwwwwz	Wednesday (no trailing blanks)
YYMMDD	991231
YYYYMMDD	20020101
YYYY-MM-DD	2005-10-29

Table 4.37: Convert Date to Lillian Format API (Valid Picture Strings) (continued)).

Picture	Example
MMDDYY	010101
MM/DD/YY	01/15/03
ZM/zD/YY	1/7/99
MM/DD/YYYY	10/29/2006
MM/DD/Y	10/29/4
DD.MM.YY	01.10.02
MM-RRRR-YY	01—X—99
DD MMM YY	20 MAY 99
DD Mmmmmmmmmmmmmmmm YY	15 January 02
ZD Mmmmmmmmmmmmmmmm YY	2 February 05
Mmmmmmmmmmmmmmmz ZD, YYYY	March 1, 2000
ZDMMMMMMMMMMMMMMMZYY	6JULY03
YY.DDD	03.115
YYDDD	03115
YYYY/DDD	2003/115
YYMMDDHHMISS	991231235959
YYYYMMDDHHMISS	19991231235959
YYYY-MM-DD HH:MI:SS.999	1999-12-31 23:59:59.999
WWW, ZM/ZD/YY HH:MI AP	TUE, 11/23/99 16:21 PM
Wwwwwwwwwz, DD Mmm YYYY, ZH:MI AP	Tuesday, 23 Nov 1999, 16:22 PM

Output Lillian Date Parameter

The third parameter is a four-byte integer field that returns the Lillian date representation of the input date passed to the API. If the input date was not valid, a zero is returned as the Lillian date and an error is returned in the Feedback parameter.

As you will recall, an integer field can be defined in RPG as 3, 5, 10, or 20 digits in length. An integer defined as three digits long results in the creation of a one-byte field. Five-digit integers are two bytes long, 10-digit integers are four bytes long, and 20-digit integers are eight-bytes in length. Therefore, APIs that call for four-byte integer parameters are best defined as 10-digit integers.

Feedback Parameter

The fourth parameter, which is optional, is a 12-character field that receives a condition token from the API. When omitted, API errors will result in a hard error being signaled to the condition manager.

The CEEDATE API

The CEEDATE API, also a member of the ILE Date and Time API group, is the inverse of the CEEDAYS API. It accepts an input date in Lillian format and returns the desired character representation of the date. The Lillian format represents the number of days since October 14, 1582. The Lillian format, which is handy for performing date arithmetic such as adding or subtracting days from a date, is derived using the CEEDAYS API. After a Lillian date is derived, it is passed as input to the CEEDATE API to determine the day of week.

An alternative to using the CEEDATE API to determine a date's day of week is to use the CEEDYWK API. However, it only returns a numeric value to represent the day of week. To return the name of the day, this example employs the more flexible CEEDATE API.

To call a bindable API from an ILE RPG module, the procedure should first be prototyped. A prototype is simply a definition of the procedure's interface and parameters. It defines the length and type of each parameter and how the procedure is to be called. For more information about prototypes, see chapter 1.

CEEDATE Parameters

The API receives three required parameters and one optional parameter, as shown in Table 4.38.

Table 4.38: CEEDATE API Parameter List. Required Parameters			
Sequence	Parameter	I/O	Type
1	Input Lillian Date	Input	INT4
2	Picture String for Output Date	Input	VSTRING
3	Output Character Date	Output	VSTRING
Optional Parameter			
Sequence	Parameter	I/O	Type
4	Feedback	Output	Char(12)

Input Lillian Date Parameter

The first parameter is a four-byte integer field that inputs a Lillian date to the API. As you will recall, an integer field can be defined in RPG as 3, 5, 10, or 20 digits in length. An integer defined as three digits long results in the creation of a one-byte field.

Five-digit integers are two bytes long, 10-digit integers are four bytes long, and 20-digit integers are eight bytes in length. Therefore, APIs that call for four-byte integer parameters are best defined as 10-digit integers.

Picture String for Output Date Parameter

The second parameter is a variable-length character input field that supplies a picture string that indicates the desired format of the Output Character Date parameter. If the Picture String field is left blank, the system will return the output date using the current job value of country id. For the United States, the default format is mm/dd/yyyy. Valid picture strings, previously listed in Table 4.37, can include many combinations of the picture strings shown.

Output Character Date Parameter

The third parameter is a variable-length character field that returns the character date representation of the Lillian date passed to the API. The returned date is in the format specified by the picture string.

Feedback Parameter

The fourth parameter, which is optional, is a 12-character field that receives a condition token from the API. When omitted, API errors will result in a hard error being signaled to the condition manager.

The ILE RPG Example

The example source member API008R accepts an input parameter date in the format mmddyyyy and displays the day of week for the input date. The module defines prototypes for the bindable APIs based on information researched from the *System API Reference Manual*. The prototype definitions are shown in Figure 4.32.

```
     *_____
     *   Procedure Prototype
     *_____
DCEEDAYS          PR                    Opdesc
D  InputDate                   32767A   Options(*Varsize)
D  DateFormat                  32767A   Options(*Varsize)
D  LilllanOut                    10I 0
D  Feedback                      12A    Options(*Omit)
     *
DCEEDATE          PR                    Opdesc
D  LillianIn                     10I 0
D  DateString                  32767A   Options(*Varsize)
D  DateOut                     32767A   Options(*Varsize)
D  Feedback                      12A    Options(*Omit)
```

Figure 4.32: The prototype definitions for the CEEDAYS and CEEDATE procedures.

Because the variable-length character fields can accept large strings of unknown size, the prototype uses a size of 32,767 bytes. This is the largest possible string to hold within a character field. The *System API Reference Manual* specifies that the API parameters be passed by descriptor. Because of this specification, the Operational Descriptor (OPDESC) keyword is specified on the prototype definitions.

Operational Descriptors

An operational descriptor is simply a precise description of the data type associated with a procedure's parameters. Some APIs require that you pass operational descriptors with the parameters being passed. Without the descriptors, the API being called does not know precisely what type of string is being passed to it. The *System API Reference Manual* will tell if a parameter requires operation descriptors by listing "by descriptor" next to the parameter description.

The Example Module Logic

The example calls the CEEDAYS API using the RPG Call Procedure (CALLP) op code. The value of the feedback parameter is tested to verify that the API successfully completed. Figure 4.33 shows the API call and parameter definitions.

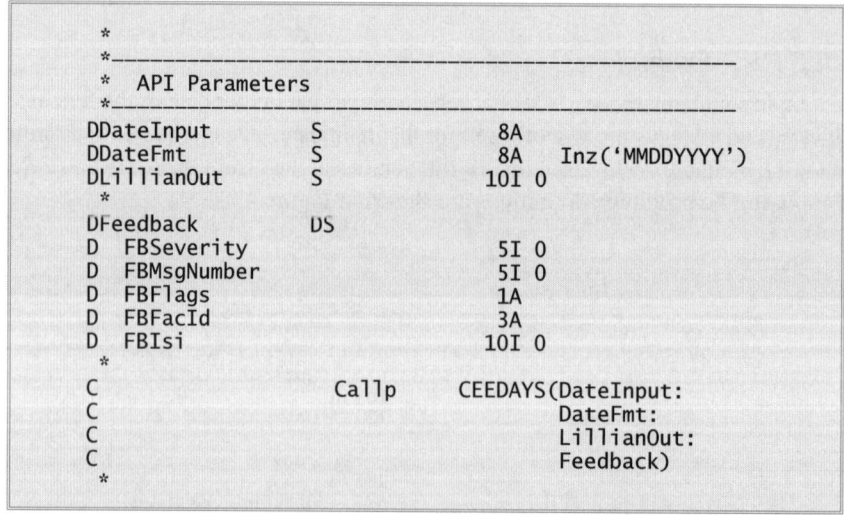

```
 *
 *_____
 *  API Parameters
 *_____
DDateInput        S            8A
DDateFmt          S            8A    Inz('MMDDYYYY')
DLillianOut       S           10I 0
 *
DFeedback        DS
D  FBSeverity                  5I 0
D  FBMsgNumber                 5I 0
D  FBFlags                     1A
D  FBFacId                     3A
D  FBIsi                      10I 0
 *
C                     Callp     CEEDAYS(DateInput:
C                                       DateFmt:
C                                       LillianOut:
C                                       Feedback)
 *
```

Figure 4.33: The CEEDAYS API converts the input date to the Lillian format.

 If the Feedback parameter returns an error from the CEEDAYS API, an error message is displayed to the user. If no error occurred, the Lillian date is used as input to call the CEEDATE API. The picture format of 'WWWWWWWWWW' is used, instructing the API to return the uppercase day of week. Upon completion, the module displays the result to the user and ends execution, as shown in Figure 4.34.

```
     *
     C              If        FBSeverity > 0
     C              Eval      ErrorMsg = @Error
     *
     C              Dsply                       ErrorMsg
     C              Else
     C              Callp     CEEDATE(LillianOut:
     C                            OutFmt:
     C                            WeekDay:
     C                            *Omit)
     *
     C              Dsply                       WeekDay
     C              Endif
     *
     C              Return
```

Figure 4.34: The day of week is returned and displayed.

Part 2

Database Examples

T he AS/400 has long been recognized as a very good database machine, and to its credit, IBM doesn't appear to be resting on its laurels. DB2 for OS/400, based on its strength, flexibility, and reliability, has evolved to become a truly world-class business database. The contents of this section include:

Chapter 5: Database Constraints

Chapter 6: Database Triggers

Chapter 7: Using SQL

5

DATABASE CONSTRAINTS

Today's computing environments are far more complex than those seen only a few years ago. In the past, most programmers performed data validation and business rule enforcement at the application level. That is, the acceptable values allowed in the database were commonly hard coded within the entry programs themselves. Some would call those the good old days, when input was accepted only from a green-screen input terminal application written in RPG or COBOL. Today's data input may come from a number of new sources, such as client/server or Web-based applications written in Visual Basic or Java.

Maintaining the integrity of your database is simply not as easy to accomplish as it once was. Relying on each client application to enforce database rules becomes far less desirable in a distributed computing world. Luckily, DB2/400 provides tools called *constraints* that enable you to define the validation rules for your data directly within the database itself. This approach guarantees compliance to the defined rules, regardless of the source of the input. Two types of constraints—*Check constraints* and *Referential Integrity constraints*—are presented in this chapter.

CHECK CONSTRAINTS

DB2/400 Check constraints allow you to restrict the values of a specific field within a record. Every time a record is added or updated, the value restrictions defined by the Check constraints are enforced. Check constraints allow you to define the validation rules for your data within the database itself, mandating compliance by any and all input sources. Any attempt to add or update a field with a value that violates the rules of the constraint is rejected by the AS/400 Database Manager with a system error message. Within a Check constraint, you can validate a field against one or more specific values, against a range of values, or against another field in the same record.

REFERENTIAL INTEGRITY CONSTRAINTS

DB2/400 Referential Integrity (RI) constraints allow you to restrict the values of a specific field within a record based on its relationship with a record in a second file. The most common use for RI Constraints is to guarantee the relationship between master- and detail-, or *parent-* and *dependent-*, level files. For example, an order detail record should never exist for a customer whose customer number is not in the Customer Master File. You can use RI constraints to define how records being added, updated, or deleted in these two files are handled.

GENERAL CONSIDERATIONS

Once added, a constraint becomes part of the database file object. Constraints are thus saved along with the file object during normal backup procedures. When a file having defined constraints is rebuilt—such as to add a new field to the file—all constraints must be re-created. For this reason, it is good practice to code your constraint commands into a CL program, allowing you to easily call the program and reestablish the defined constraints. As of this writing, a file is limited to 300 total constraints. Because constraints are tested every time a record is added, updated, or deleted, they can impact performance and should not be added indiscriminately.

Constraints can be added to a file in several ways, three of the most common of which are using the CL Add Physical File Constraint (ADDPFCST) command, the Create Table or Alter Table SQL statements, or the Table Properties tab of AS/400 Operations Navigator. Because constraints are defined at the file level, adding one to an existing file requires that all existing data comply with the constraint being added. You might need to perform data cleanup prior to introducing a constraint to the file. If you try adding a constraint to a file already containing data that violates the constraint, the constraint is added in a check pending status.

Check Pending Status

A constraint having a status of check pending doesn't become enabled until after the data in violation of the constraint is corrected and the constraint re-added. To identify and correct the records in violation, two CL commands exist to assist you—Work with Physical File Constraints (WRKPFCST) and Display Check Pending Constraint (DSPCPCST).

The WRKPFCST command, as shown in Figure 5.1, displays a list of all constraints existing for a given file. The list shows the check pending status of each constraint. Selecting option 6, Display Records in Check Pending, presents you with a prompt for the DSPCPCST command. When executed, the command will display or optionally print a list of the records in the file that violate the rules of the constraint. An example of the DSPCPCST display is shown in Figure 5.2. After correcting the problematic records, the constraint remains in check pending status until it is re-added.

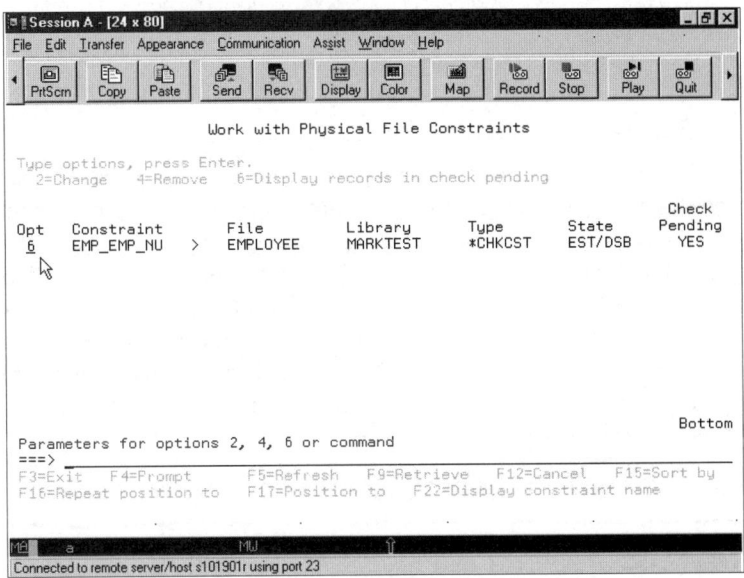

Figure 5.1: The WRKPFCST command lets you work with a file's constraints.

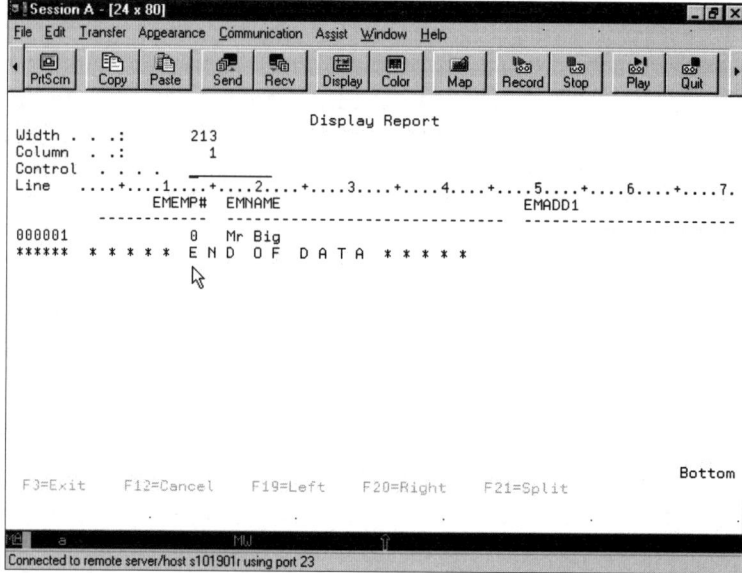

Figure 5.2: The DSPCPCST command lets you view records causing a check pending status.

Constraint States

Constraints added to a file can have a state of either *enabled* or *disabled*. This state can be conceptualized as a toggle switch for the constraint. When set to disabled, the rules of the constraint are not enforced. If a constraint is added in a check pending status, the state is automatically set to disabled. An active constraint can be temporarily disabled using the State parameter of the Change Physical File Constraint (CHGPFCST) command. This can, in certain cases, come in handy for performing mass batch updates where performance gains can be significant if rules are validated by the application rather than by the database. A word of caution: When a state is changed from disabled back to enabled, the contents of the file are revalidated.

EXAMPLE

Using a Check Constraint to Validate a Single Value

This example employs a Check constraint to perform simple, single value data validation on an Employee Master File called EMPLOYEE. The file contains fields you would expect to see in a simple employee file, such as employee number, name, address, job code, salary, etc. Figure 5.3 shows the complete layout for the file. The constraint is added to the file via CL command in the program shown in Listing 5.1.

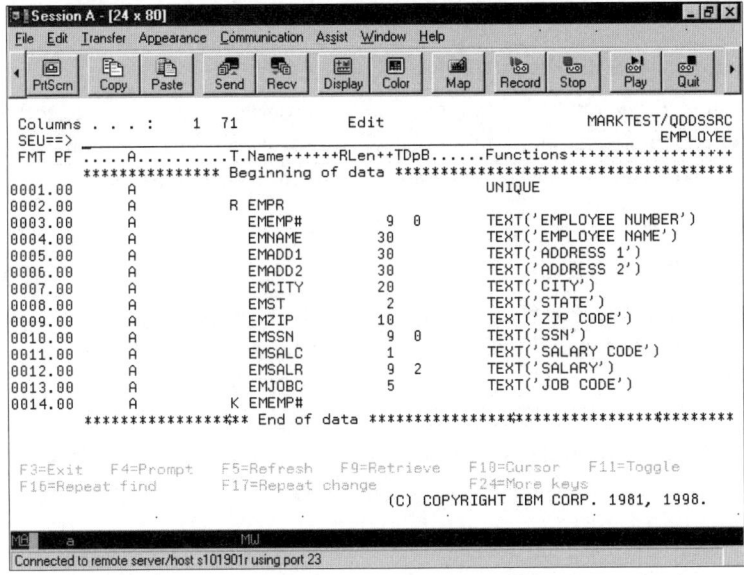

Figure 5.3: This Employee Master File is used to demonstrate constraint usage.

Listing 5.1: CL program DB001C uses ADDPFCST to add a constraint.

```
        PGM

/*-----------------------------------------------------------------*/
/*    Add a check constraint to the Employee Master File.          */
/*       Require a value in the employee number field.             */
/*-----------------------------------------------------------------*/

        ADDPFCST    FILE(EMPLOYEE) TYPE(*CHKCST) +
                      CST(EMP_EMP_NUMBER) CHKCST('EMEMP# > 0')


        ENDPGM
```

WHAT THE EXAMPLE DOES

The example program DB001C uses the ADDPFCST command to define a Check constraint for an Employee Master File called Employee. The constraint restricts the permissible values for the employee number field (EMEMP#).

HOW THE EXAMPLE WORKS

When executed, the ADDPFCST command listed in program DB001C permanently restricts the value of the employee number field for all records in the file to contain a value greater than zero. The ADDPFCST command uses the following parameters:

The Type (TYPE) Parameter

The ADDPFCST command provides a parameter, TYPE, that allows you to specify the type of constraint being added to the file. To define a Check constraint, the TYPE parameter is set to *CHKCST. The permissible values for the TYPE parameter are:

*CHKCST	Defines a Check constraint
*REFCST	Defines a Referential constraint
*UNQCST	Defines a Unique Key Value constraint
*PRIKEY	Defines a Primary Key (unique) constraint

The Constraint Name (CST) Parameter

The CST parameter allows you to specify the name of the constraint being added to the file. The name you provide is used only to provide a unique identifier for the constraint. It is good practice to give each constraint a name that provides a meaningful clue as to its purpose.

The Check Constraint (CHKCST) Parameter

The CHKCST parameter allows you to specify the expression that defines the rules of the constraint. The expression, enclosed by single quotes, uses standard SQL syntax and can be simple or complex in its composition. The example uses the following entry to restrict the value of the employee number field (EMEMP#) to a number greater than zero:

```
'EMEMP# > 0'
```

EXAMPLE
Using a Check Constraint to Validate Complex Values

This example employs a Check constraint to perform complex data validation on an Employee Master File called EMPLOYEE. The file contains fields you would expect to see in a simple employee file, such as employee number, name, address, job code, salary, etc. Figure 5.3 shows the complete layout for the file. The constraint is added to the file via a CL command in the program shown in Listing 5.2.

Listing 5.2: CL program DB002C uses ADDPFCST to add a constraint.

```
PGM

/*--------------------------------------------------------------*/
/*   Add a check constraint to the Employee Master File.        */
/*      Allow only the following values for the Salary Code     */
/*      and set appropriate maximum salaries for each:          */
/*         H = Hourly  Maximum salary = $100                    */
/*         M = Monthly Maximum salary = $10,000                 */
/*         Y = Yearly  Maximum salary = $120,000                */
/*--------------------------------------------------------------*/

         ADDPFCST    FILE(EMPLOYEE) TYPE(*CHKCST) +
                     CST(EMP_SALARY_MAXIMUMS) CHKCST('EMSALC = +
                     ''H'' And EMSALR <= 100 or EMSALC = ''M'' +
                     And EMSALR <= 10000 or EMSALC = ''Y'' And +
                     EMSALR <= 120000')

         ENDPGM
```

WHAT THE EXAMPLE DOES
The example program DB002C uses the ADDPFCST command to define a Check constraint for an Employee Master File called EMPLOYEE. The constraint restricts the permissible values for both the salary code field (EMSALC) and the salary amount field (EMSALR).

HOW THE EXAMPLE WORKS
When executed, the ADDPFCST command listed in program DB002C permanently restricts the value of the salary code and salary amount fields for all records in the file. The salary code field is limited to values of H (hourly), M (monthly), or Y (yearly). Each value has an associated maximum for the salary amount field. The ADDPFCST command uses the following parameters:

The Type (TYPE) Parameter

The ADDPFCST command provides a parameter, TYPE, that allows you to specify the type of constraint being added to the file. To define a Check constraint, the TYPE parameter is set to *CHKCST. The permissible values for the TYPE parameter are:

*CHKCST	Defines a Check constraint
*REFCST	Defines a Referential constraint
*UNQCST	Defines a Unique Key Value constraint
*PRIKEY	Defines a Primary Key (unique) constraint

The Constraint Name (CST) Parameter

The CST parameter allows you to specify the name of the constraint being added to the file. The name you provide is used only to provide a unique identifier for the constraint. It is good practice to give each constraint a name that provides a meaningful clue as to its purpose.

The Check Constraint (CHKCST) Parameter

The CHKCST parameter allows you to specify the expression that defines the rules of the constraint. The expression, enclosed by single quotes, uses standard SQL syntax and can be simple or complex in its composition. The example uses the following entry to restrict the values of the salary code (EMSALC) and the salary amount (EMSALR):

```
'EMSALC = "H" And EMSALR <= 100 or
 EMSALC = "M" And EMSALR <= 10000 or
 EMSALC = "Y" And EMSALR <= 120000'
```

EXAMPLE

Using a Check Constraint with Field-to-Field Validation

This example employs a Check constraint to perform data validation on an Employee Master File called EMPLOYEE. The file contains fields you would expect to see in a simple employee file, such as employee number, name, address, job code, salary, etc. Figure 5.3 shows the complete layout for the file. The constraint is added to the file via a CL command in the program shown in Listing 5.3.

Listing 5.3: CL program DB003C uses ADDPFCST to add a constraint.

```
            PGM

/*─────────────────────────────────────────────────────────────*/
/*   Add a check constraint to the Employee Master File.      */
/*     Require the Employee Number field to match the Social  */
/*     Security Number field.                                 */
/*─────────────────────────────────────────────────────────────*/

            ADDPFCST   FILE(EMPLOYEE) TYPE(*CHKCST) +
                       CST(EMP_EMP#_SSN) CHKCST('EMEMP#    +
                       = EMSSN')


            ENDPGM
```

WHAT THE EXAMPLE DOES

The example program DB003C uses the ADDPFCST command to define a Check constraint for an Employee Master File called EMPLOYEE. The constraint restricts the permissible values for the employee number field (EMEMP#).

HOW THE EXAMPLE WORKS

When executed, the ADDPFCST command listed in program DB003C permanently restricts the value of the employee number field for all records in the file. The employee number field must have the same value as that in the social security number field (EMSSN). This demonstrates the ability of Check constraints to restrict the value of one field to maintain a defined relationship with the value of other fields in the same record. The ADDPFCST command uses the following parameters:

The Type (TYPE) Parameter

The ADDPFCST command provides a parameter, TYPE, that allows you to specify the type of constraint being added to the file. To define a Check constraint, the TYPE parameter is set to *CHKCST. The permissible values for the TYPE parameter are:

*CHKCST	Defines a Check constraint
*REFCST	Defines a Referential constraint
*UNQCST	Defines a Unique Key Value constraint
*PRIKEY	Defines a Primary Key (unique) constraint

The Constraint Name (CST) Parameter

The CST parameter allows you to specify the name of the constraint being added to the file. The name you provide is used only to provide a unique identifier for the constraint. It is good practice to give each constraint a name that provides a meaningful clue as to its purpose.

The Check Constraint (CHKCST) Parameter

The CHKCST parameter allows you to specify the expression that defines the rules of the constraint. The expression, enclosed by single quotes, uses standard SQL syntax and can be simple or complex in its composition. The example uses the following entry to restrict the value of the employee number (EMEMP#) to be equal to the social security number (EMSSN):

```
'EMEMP#  =  EMSSN'
```

EXAMPLE

Using a Check Constraint with an Embedded Function

This example employs a Check constraint to perform data validation on an Employee Master File called EMPLOYEE. The file contains fields you would expect to see in a simple employee file, such as employee number, name, address, job code, salary, etc. Figure 5.3 shows the complete layout for the file. The constraint is added to the file via a CL command in the program shown in Listing 5.4.

Listing 5.4: CL program DB004C uses ADDPFCST to add a constraint.

```
            PGM

/*-----------------------------------------------------------*/
/*   Add a check constraint to the Employee Master File.     */
/*     Use CURRENT DATE function to restrict birth date to   */
/*     a value less than today's date and greater than       */
/*     1-1-1900.                                             */
/*-----------------------------------------------------------*/

            ADDPFCST    FILE(EMPLOYEE) TYPE(*CHKCST) +
                        CST(EMP_BIRTH_DATE) CHKCST('EMBDATE  +
                        < CURDATE() AND EMBDATE > ''1900-01-01''')

            ENDPGM
```

WHAT THE EXAMPLE DOES

The example program DB004C uses the ADDPFCST command to define a Check constraint for an Employee Master File called EMPLOYEE. The constraint restricts the permissible values for the employee birth date field (EMBDATE).

HOW THE EXAMPLE WORKS

When executed, the ADDPFCST command listed in program DB004C permanently restricts the value of the employee birth date field for all records in the file. As has been demonstrated in the previous examples, field values can be validated against hard-coded values or against the values of other fields in the record using constraints. Another capability of constraints allows you to use built-in functions for validation. For this example, the employee birth date is tested for a reasonable value using the current date (CURDATE) function. The birth date is restricted to a value that is greater than 1/1/1900 and less than the current date. The ADDPFCST command uses the following parameters:

The Type (TYPE) Parameter

The ADDPFCST command provides a parameter, TYPE, that allows you to specify the type of constraint being added to the file. To define a Check constraint, the TYPE parameter is set to *CHKCST. The permissible values for the TYPE parameter are:

*CHKCST	Defines a Check constraint
*REFCST	Defines a Referential constraint
*UNQCST	Defines a Unique Key Value constraint
*PRIKEY	Defines a Primary Key (unique) constraint

The Constraint Name (CST) Parameter

The CST parameter allows you to specify the name of the constraint being added to the file. The name you provide is used only to provide a unique identifier for the constraint. It is good practice to give each constraint a name that provides a meaningful clue as to its purpose.

The Check Constraint (CHKCST) Parameter

The CHKCST parameter allows you to specify the expression that defines the rules of the constraint. The expression, enclosed by single quotes, uses standard SQL syntax and can be simple or complex in its composition. SQL provides numerous special functions to perform date and time operations. The example uses the following entry to restrict the value of the employee birth date (EMBDATE):

```
'EMBDATE < CURDATE() AND EMBDATE > ''1900-01-01'''
```

EXAMPLE

Using a Referential Integrity Constraint

This example employs a Referential Integrity (RI) constraint to maintain the desired parent-dependent relationship between an Employee Master File and a Job Code description file. The EMPLOYEE file contains fields you would expect to see in a simple employee file, such as employee number, name, address, job code, salary, etc. Figure 5.3 shows the complete layout for the file. The Job Code description file (JOBCODES) contains one record for each valid job code—along with its appropriate description. The constraint is added to both files via CL commands in the program shown in Listing 5.5.

Listing 5.5: CL program DB005C uses ADDPFCST to add an RI constraint.

```
            PGM

/*----------------------------------------------------------*/
/*    Add referential integrity constraints to the Employee  */
/*       Master File and Job Code Description File.  Do not   */
/*       allow Employee records to have a job code not found in */
/*       the Job Code Description File.                       */
/*----------------------------------------------------------*/

            ADDPFCST   FILE(JOBCODES) TYPE(*PRIKEY) KEY(JMJOBC) +
                         CST(JOB_CODE_KEY)

            ADDPFCST   FILE(EMPLOYEE) TYPE(*REFCST) KEY(EMJOBC) +
                         CST(EMP_JOB_CODE_RI) PRNFILE(JOBCODES) +
                         DLTRULE(*RESTRICT) UPDRULE(*RESTRICT)

            ENDPGM
```

WHAT THE EXAMPLE DOES

The example program DB005C uses the ADDPFCST command to define two constraints: a Primary Key constraint for a Job Code description file (JOBCODES) and an RI constraint for an Employee Master File (EMPLOYEE). This combination of constraints establishes the Job Code file as parent and the Employee Master File as dependent. This is because the Job Code file contains only unique records for each job code, while the Employee file may have multiple entries for each job code. To maintain this relationship, constraints mandate that only job codes found in the Job Code file may be entered in the Employee file. Further, it defines the system action to be performed whenever a record in the Job Code file is changed or deleted when there are matching records for the Job Code in the Employee file.

HOW THE EXAMPLE WORKS

When executed, the first ADDPFCST command listed in program DB005C establishes a Primary Key constraint on the JOBCODES file. To be defined as a parent file having a dependent file, the Job Code file must be assured of having unique key values. If you do not add either a Primary Key constraint or a Unique Key constraint to the parent file, the system will attempt to implicitly add one at the time the RI constraint is added to the dependent file. To maintain meaningful constraint naming, it is good practice to manually add a Primary Key constraint to the file rather than let the system assign it automatically.

The second constraint, an RI constraint, is added to the dependent the EMPLOYEE file. For RI constraints, the ADDPFCST command allows you to specify the action that is to be taken when a user attempts to change or delete a record in the parent whose value appears in the dependent file. For example, if there are three employee records having job code '123', what happens when someone tries to delete record '123' from the job code file? The ADDPFCST command uses the following parameters:

The Type (TYPE) Parameter

The ADDPFCST command provides a parameter, TYPE, that allows you to specify the type of constraint being added to the file. To define a Primary Key constraint, the TYPE parameter is set to *PRIKEY. To define a Referential constraint, the TYPE parameter is set to *REFCST. The permissible values for the TYPE parameter are:

*CHKCST	Defines a Check constraint
*REFCST	Defines a Referential constraint
*UNQCST	Defines a Unique Key constraint
*PRIKEY	Defines a Primary Key (unique) constraint

The Constraint Name (CST) Parameter

The CST parameter allows you to specify the name of the constraint being added to the file. The name you provide is used only to provide a unique identifier for the constraint. It is good practice to give each constraint a name that provides a meaningful clue as to its purpose.

The Constraint Key (KEY) Parameter

The KEY parameter allows you to specify the field or fields that provide linkage between parent and dependent files. For the example, the Job Code field in the Employee file (EMJOBC) is defined as the RI key field. Its attributes must match those of the unique or primary key in the job code file.

The Parent File (PRNFILE) Parameter

The PRNFILE parameter allows you to specify the qualified name of the file that is to be the parent file. The parent file must be created as a single member file (MAXMBRS(1)). For this example, the Job Code file is defined as the parent.

The Delete Rule (DLTRULE) Parameter

The ADDPFCST command provides a parameter, DLTRULE, that allows you to specify how the system is to react when a job attempts to delete a parent file record. If the record being deleted does not have dependent records of the same key value, the delete is always allowed. The permissible values for the DLTRULE parameter are:

*CASCADE	System performs a cascading delete
*RESTRICT	System restricts the delete if in dependent file
*NOACTION	System restricts delete but performs before trigger
*SETNULL	System allows delete and sets dependent to null
*SETDFT	System allows delete and sets dependent to a default value

The Cascading Delete Rule

When *CASCADE is specified as the delete rule, the system performs a cascading delete. This means that the record is deleted from the parent file, and all matching records in the dependent file are also deleted. So, for the example where there are three employee records having job code '123' and you attempt to delete record '123' from the Job Code file, the Job Code record is deleted, as are the three '123' employee records.

The Restricted Delete Rule

When *RESTRICT is specified as the delete rule, the system will not allow deletion of the parent record. The system issues error CPF503A, Referential Constraint Violation, if you attempt to delete a parent with match dependencies. Unlike the No Action Delete Rule, any delete triggers associated with the file are not called.

The No Action Delete Rule

When *NOACTION is specified as the delete rule, the system will not allow deletion of the parent record. The system issues error CPF503A, Referential Constraint Violation, if you attempt to delete a parent with match dependencies. Unlike the Restricted Delete Rule, any delete triggers associated with the file are called.

The Set Null Delete Rule

When *SETNULL is specified as the delete rule, the system will allow deletion of the parent record. This means that the record is deleted from the parent file, and all matching records in the dependent file have their key values set to NULL. This is only true if a NULL key valued record exists in the parent file. So, for the example where there are three employee records having job code '123' and you attempt to delete record '123' from the Job Code file, the Job Code record is deleted. The job code field in all three '123' employee records is changed to NULL (provided the field supports NULL values).

The Set Default Delete Rule

When *SETDFT is specified as the delete rule, the system will allow deletion of the parent record. This means that the record is deleted from the parent file, and all matching records in the dependent file have their key values set to their defined default value. This is only true if a record exists in the parent file having a key value equal to the default value. So, for the example where there are three employee records having job code '123' and you attempt to delete record '123' from the Job Code file, the Job Code record is deleted. The job code field in all three '123' employee records is changed to their default value, which happens to be blanks. This is allowed only if there is a record in the parent file with a job code of blanks.

The Update Rule (UPDRULE) Parameter

The ADDPFCST command provides a parameter, UPDRULE, that allows you to specify how the system is to react when a job attempts to update a parent file record. If the record being changed does not have dependent records of the same key value, the update is always allowed. The permissible values for the UPDRULE parameter are:

```
*RESTRICT System restricts the update if in dependent file
*NOACTION System restricts update but performs before trigger
```

The Restricted Update Rule

When *RESTRICT is specified as the update rule, the system will not allow you to change the key value of the parent record if there are records in the dependent file matching that value being changed. The system issues error CPF503A, Referential Constraint Violation, if you attempt to update a parent with match dependencies. Unlike the No Action Update Rule, any update triggers associated with the file are not called.

The No Action Update Rule

When *NOACTION is specified as the update rule, the system will not allow you to change the key value of the parent record if there are records in the dependent file matching that value being changed. The system issues error CPF503A, Referential Constraint Violation, if you attempt to update a parent with match dependencies. Unlike the Restricted Update Rule, any update triggers associated with the file are called.

6

DATABASE TRIGGERS

The previous chapter presented powerful tools, constraints, to assist you with the arduous task of keeping your database clean. Another powerhouse of a tool, called a *database trigger*, allows you to perform the same functions as constraints, and even takes you a step further. So what are triggers and what can you do with them?

A trigger is simply a program you write in RPG, COBOL, CL, or even C. The unique feature of a trigger is not in the code, but in the way it is called. A trigger program is called automatically by the system every time an operation is performed on a specific file. Remember in the previous chapter how Check constraints can be defined to validate your data fields every time a record is changed or added? As an alternative or even companion to constraints, you can instruct the system to call your trigger program whenever a record is added, changed, or deleted. Because a program is being called, the logic may be simple or very complex. Execution of the trigger program is automatic, so it is guaranteed to happen—regardless of the interface used to interact with the file.

When you add a constraint to an existing file, the rules of the constraint are enforced against existing file records. This is not the case when you are adding a database trigger.

Records already in the file when the trigger is added do not cause the trigger to be called and are unaffected by the introduction of the trigger program.

WHAT CAN YOU DO WITH A TRIGGER?

Database triggers have many useful applications, some of the most common of which include:

- Security and auditing
- Data validation
- Auto-assignment of data values
- Extended transaction processing

Security and Auditing

Because a trigger program execution, called *firing*, is an automated system event that cannot be bypassed, triggers are attractive tools for implementing database security and auditing features. Applications that require security enforcement more flexible than normal object-level authorization are good candidates for trigger-level implementation.

Triggers are uniquely suited to performing detailed auditing at the record- or field-level. Whenever a record in a triggered file is changed, the trigger program has access to both the before and after images of the changed record. This allows detailed interrogation or reporting of changes that are made.

Data Validation

Because triggers are guaranteed to execute, or *fire*, whenever a specific file action is performed, they are excellent mechanisms for enforcing your rules of data validation. Because you write the trigger program, you decide how validation is enforced. You may choose to reject records that do not pass your validation, log attempted violations, or simply replace values with accepted defaults.

Auto-Assignment of Data Values

Triggers are effective mechanisms for strictly enforcing default value assignments or to provide application-generated data such as unique record numbers or unique keys such as account numbers.

Extended Transaction Processing

If your application has value-added processes that are performed every time a record is added, changed, or deleted in a file, it may be a good candidate for encapsulation in a trigger program. For example, if you wish to send a welcome letter to all new customers, a trigger on the customer file may be a good place to generate the letter anytime a new record is added.

TRIGGER PROGRAM PARAMETERS

All trigger programs are called in the same way. Regardless of the interface or mechanism used to insert, alter, or delete records in a file, all trigger programs are called by the system database manager. When called, trigger programs are passed a common set of parameters by the system. Every trigger program receives two parameters when fired: a trigger buffer parameter and the length of the trigger buffer parameter.

The Trigger Buffer

The first parameter passed to all trigger programs is called the *trigger buffer*. The trigger buffer contains a great deal of information about the action being performed. Embedded within the trigger buffer is the before image and after image of the record that caused the trigger to fire. Because the record length may be different for each file you assign a trigger to, the length of the trigger buffer also varies. Table 6.1 shows a complete list of fields embedded within the trigger buffer.

Table 6.1: Contents of the Trigger Buffer.		
Description	Length	Data Type
File Name	10	Character
File Library Name	10	Character
File Member Name	10	Character
Trigger Event (1–Insert, 2–Delete, 3–Update)	1	Character
Trigger Time (1=After, 2=Before)	1	Character
Commit Control Level	1	Character
Reserved	3	Character

Table 6.1: Contents of the Trigger Buffer (continued).

Description	Length	Data Type
CCSID	4	Binary
Relative Record Number	4	Binary
Reserved	4	Character
Before Image Record Offset (Location of before image within trigger buffer)	4	Binary
Before Image Record Length	4	Binary
Before Image Null Byte Map Offset	4	Binary
Before Image Null Byte Map Length	4	Binary
After Image Record Offset (Location of after image within trigger buffer)	4	Binary
After Image Record Length	4	Binary
After Image Null Byte Map Offset	4	Binary
After Image Null Byte Map Length	4	Binary
Reserved	16	Character
Before Image Record	Varies	Varies
Before Image Null Byte Map	Varies	Character
After Image Record	Varies	Varies
After Image Null Byte Map	Varies	Character

ADDING A TRIGGER TO A FILE

Triggers can be added to a file in several ways, two of the most common of which are using the CL Add Physical File Trigger (ADDPFTRG) command or the Table Properties tab of the AS/400 Operations Navigator. When adding a trigger to a file, you specify both the type of action that fires the trigger and whether the trigger fires before or after the action.

GENERAL CONSIDERATIONS

Once added, the trigger assignment becomes part of the database file object. The program itself does not, however. Trigger programs are therefore not saved along with the file object during normal backup procedures. When a file having defined triggers is rebuilt—such as to add a new field to the file—all triggers must be re-added. For this reason, it is good practice to code your add trigger commands into a CL program, allowing you to easily call the program and reestablish the defined triggers.

As of this writing, a file is limited to six total triggers. When fired, triggers always execute as part of the job that caused it to fire. By default, the trigger executes using the authority, library list, and QTEMP library contents of the user who performed the action that caused the trigger to fire. Further, trigger programs run synchronously. Control passes from the user to the trigger and does not return to the user until the trigger completes execution. This is an important performance factor that needs to be considered when you are designing trigger programs.

EXAMPLE

Using a Trigger to Auto-Generate a Key Value

This example employs a trigger program to automatically generate a unique employee number every time a new record is added to an Employee Master File called EMPLOYEE. The file contains fields you would expect to see in a simple employee file, such as employee number, name, address, job code, salary, etc. Figure 6.1 shows the complete layout for the file.

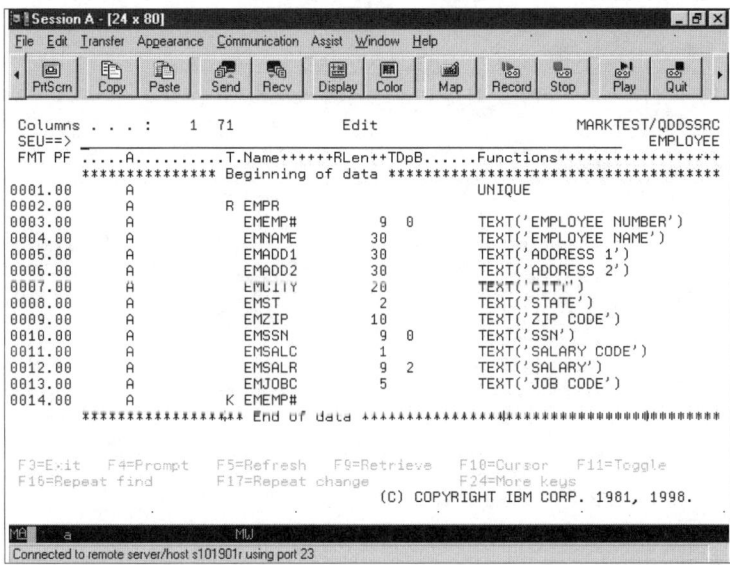

Figure 6.1: This Employee Master File is used to demonstrate trigger usage.

The trigger program is added to the file via a CL command in the program DB006C, as shown in Listing 6.1.

Listing 6.1: CL program DB006C uses ADDPFTRG to add a trigger.

```
PGM
/*_____*/
/*  Add trigger DB006R to file Employee to auto-generate  */
/*  the employee number key.                              */
/*_____*/


            ADDPFTRG   FILE(EMPLOYEE) TRGTIME(*BEFORE) +
                       TRGEVENT(*INSERT) PGM(DB006R) ALWREPCHG(*YES)

            ENDPGM
```

The trigger program DB006R is shown in Listing 6.2.

Listing 6.2: ILE RPG program DB006R is a trigger for file EMPLOYEE.

```
     *_____
     *    Data Area EmployeeDA contains the last employee number
     *    used.
     *_____
    DEmployeeDA      DS                  Dtaara(EmployeeDA)
    D  Last#                       9S 0
     *
    DpBefore         S             *
    DpAfter          S             *
     *
    DBefore          E DS                 ExtName(EMPLOYEE) Prefix(B_)
    D                                     Based(pBefore)
    DAfter           E DS                 ExtName(EMPLOYEE) Prefix(A_)
    D                                     Based(pAfter)
    D*
     *_____
     *    Trigger Buffer and Trigger Buffer Length Declarations
     *_____
    DBufferLen       S            10I 0
    DTrigBuff        DS
    D  TrigFile                   10A
    D  TrigLib                    10A
    D  TrigMbr                    10A
    D  TrigEvent                   1A
    D  TrigTime                    1A
    D  TrigCommit                  1A
    D  TrigRes1                    3A
```

Listing 6.2: ILE RPG program DB006R is a trigger for file EMPLOYEE (continued).

```
D  TrigCCSID                      10I 0
D  TrigRRN                        10I 0
D  TrigRes2                        4A
D  TrigB4OS                       10I 0
D  TrigB4Len                      10I 0
D  TrigB4NBM                      10I 0
D  TrigB4NBL                      10I 0
D  TrigAftOS                      10I 0
D  TrigAftLen                     10I 0
D  TrigAfNBM                      10I 0
D  TrigAfNBL                      10I 0
    *_____
    *    Trigger Constants
    *_____
D@Insert          C                   '1'
D@Delete          C                   '2'
D@Update          C                   '3'
D@Before          C                   '2'
D@After           C                   '1'
    *_____
    *    Input parameters are passed automatically when the trigger
    *    fires.  Passed are the trigger buffer and trigger buffer length.
    *_____
C     *Entry       PList
C                  Parm                      TrigBuff
C                  Parm                      BufferLen
    *
    *_____
    *    Map the data structures for the before and after images to
    *    the offset location in the trigger buffer using pointers.
    *_____
C                  Eval      pBefore = %Addr(TrigBuff) + TrigB4OS
C                  Eval      pAfter  = %Addr(TrigBuff) + TrigAftOS
    *
    *_____
    *    Only assign employee number on inserts.
    *_____
C                  If        TrigEvent = @Insert
    *_____
    *    Get the last employee number from the data area.  Increment
    *    it and update data area and trigger buffer with new number.
    *_____
C     *Lock        In        EmployeeDA
C                  Eval      Last# = Last# + 1
C                  Out       EmployeeDA
C                  Eval      A_EMEMP# = Last#
C                  Endif
    *
C                  Return
```

WHAT THE EXAMPLE DOES

The example program DB006C uses the ADDPFTRG command to add the trigger program DB006R to file EMPLOYEE. The trigger is fired every time a new record is added to the EMPLOYEE file. The program generates a unique employee number and inserts the value into the record.

HOW THE EXAMPLE WORKS

When executed, the ADDPTFRG command listed in program DB006C adds trigger program DB006R to the employee file. The ADDPFTRG command uses the following parameters.

The Physical File (FILE) Parameter

The FILE parameter is required and specifies the qualified name of the file to which the trigger is to be added.

The Trigger Time (TRGTIME) Parameter

The TRGTIME parameter is required and specifies the timing of the firing of the trigger program. The permissible values for the TRGTIME parameter are:

```
*BEFORE   The trigger executes before the record is processed
*AFTER    The trigger executes after the record is processed
```

The example uses the value *BEFORE, meaning the trigger runs before the new employee records are written to the file.

The Trigger Event (TRGEVENT) Parameter

The TRGEVENT parameter is required and defines the file event that causes the trigger program to fire. The permissible values for the TRGEVENT parameter are:

```
*INSERT   The trigger executes when a new record is added
*UPDATE   The trigger executes when a record is updated
*DELETE   The trigger executes when a record is deleted
```

The example uses the value *INSERT, meaning the trigger runs after an application writes new employee records but before the new employee records are written to the file by the system database manager.

252

The Program Name (PGM) Parameter

The PGM parameter is required and specifies the qualified name of the trigger program to be added.

The Replace Trigger (RPLTRG) Parameter

The RPLTRG parameter specifies whether the new trigger is to replace any existing trigger defined for the file, time, and event combination. The permissible values for the RPLTRG parameter are:

*YES	The new trigger will replace an existing trigger
*NO	The new trigger will not replace an existing trigger

The example uses the value *NO.

The Allow Repeated Change (ALWREPCHG) Parameter

The ALWREPCHG parameter specifies whether the new trigger has the capability to change the original record that caused the trigger to fire. The permissible values for the ALWREPCHG parameter are:

*YES	The trigger program can alter the original record
*NO	The trigger program cannot alter the original record

The example uses the value *YES, allowing it to generate a new value for the employee number field before the record is written to the file.

The Trigger Update Condition (TRGUPDCND) Parameter

The TRGUPDCND is used only for triggers having a trigger event of *UPDATE. The parameter specifies if the trigger is to be fired only when a field is actually changed by an update operation. The permissible values for the trgupdcnd parameter are:

*CHANGE	The trigger fires only if fields have changed
*ALWAYS	The trigger fires on all update operations

Because the example has a trigger event of *INSERT it does not use this parameter.

The ILE RPG Trigger Program

When executed, the trigger program DB006R retrieves the last employee number from an external data area, increments the number, and inserts the new employee number into the record before it is written to the file. This program can be used as an example of how to use a trigger program to alter the original record that was passed to it.

The program (actually an ILE RPG module) begins with a definition of the external data area used to contain the last sequential employee number used. The data area, EMPLOYEEDA, contains a nine-digit number defined by the subfield LAST#. See Figure 6.2.

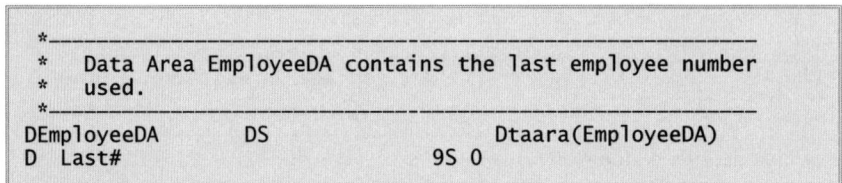

```
*_____
*   Data Area EmployeeDA contains the last employee number
*   used.
*_____
DEmployeeDA      DS                    Dtaara(EmployeeDA)
D  Last#                         9S 0
```

Figure 6.2: These definition specs define the external data area EMPLOYEEDA.

Defining the Trigger Buffer

The code that is common to all trigger programs defines the layout of the trigger buffer parameter. A simple coding technique employing *pointers* defines the trigger buffer in a flexible and reliable way. If you have not used pointers in an RPG program before, they are simply a way to address a specific storage location. As discussed earlier in this chapter, the trigger buffer parameter passed to your program varies in length because the length of the trigger record varies from file to file. Pointers allow you to soft code the location of the record images with the trigger buffer using the offset values also found in the parameter. Figure 6.3 shows the definition of the pointers and data structures that define the input parameters.

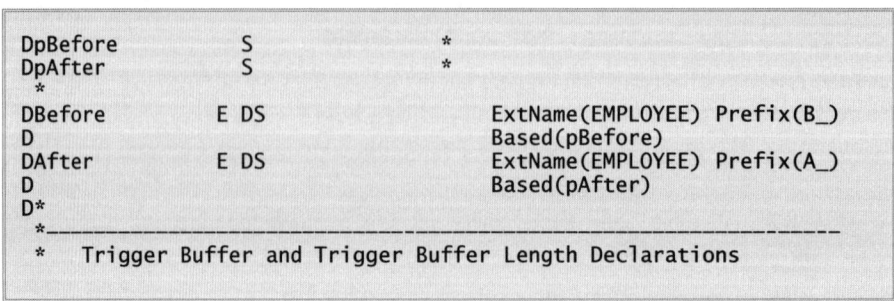

```
DpBefore         S                     *
DpAfter          S                     *
*
DBefore          E DS                  ExtName(EMPLOYEE) Prefix(B_)
D                                      Based(pBefore)
DAfter           E DS                  ExtName(EMPLOYEE) Prefix(A_)
D                                      Based(pAfter)
D*
*_____
*   Trigger Buffer and Trigger Buffer Length Declarations
```

Figure 6.3: These specs define the pointers and data structures used for the trigger buffer.

```
 *_____ _____
DBufferLen         S              10I 0
DTrigBuff          DS
D  TrigFile                        10A
D  TrigLib                         10A
D  TrigMbr                         10A
D  TrigEvent                        1A
D  TrigTime                         1A
D  TrigCommit                       1A
D  TrigRes1                         3A
D  TrigCCSID                       10I 0
D  TrigRRN                         10I 0
D  TrigRes2                         4A
D  TrigB4OS                        10I 0
D  TrigB4Len                       10I 0
D  TrigB4NBM                       10I 0
D  TrigB4NBL                       10I 0
D  TrigAftOS                       10I 0
D  TrigAftLen                      10I 0
D  TrigAfNBM                       10I 0
D  TrigAfNBL                       10I 0
 *_____
 *   Input parameters are passed automatically when the trigger
 *   fires.  Passed are the trigger buffer and trigger buffer length.
 *_____
C        *Entry        PList
C                      Parm                    TrigBuff
C                      Parm                    BufferLen
```

Figure 6.3: These specs define the pointers and data structures used for the trigger buffer (continued).

The input parameter TRIGBUFF is defined as a data structure, with subfields parsing out each individual field within the fixed length portion of the buffer. The offset values, provided in the subfields TRIGB4OS and TRIGAFTOS, tell your program the starting positions within the buffer for the before and after record images.

To avoid the hard coding of the subfields of the EMPLOYEE record within both the before and after images, the file is used to create two external data structures called BEFORE and AFTER. The data structure definitions use the DTAARA keyword to base the layout of the structure on the Employee file. The PREFIX keyword is used on each to add a unique prefix of either 'B_' or 'A_' to the field names. The BASED keyword specifies that the data structure is to be loaded with the data residing in the address provided by the pointers PBEFORE and PAFTER.

The before and after record images are loaded into the data structures by setting the pointers to the address locations of the records within the trigger buffer. This is performed in Figure 6.4 using the RPG Address-Of function. The appropriate offset is added to the address of the buffer and is loaded into the pointer variable. Because the data structures BEFORE and AFTER are based on the pointer variables, they reflect the proper values.

```
*_____
*   Map the data structures for the before and after images to
*   the offset location in the trigger buffer using pointers.
*_____
C                           Eval        pBefore = %Addr(TrigBuff) +
TrigB4OS
C                           Eval        pAfter  = %Addr(TrigBuff) +
TrigAftOS
```

Figure 6.4: The before and after record images are retrieved from the buffer using pointers.

Employing pointers to define the record images in the trigger buffer is a flexible, soft-coded approach to use for all your trigger programs. Figure 6.5 provides a further conceptual look at the technique.

The Remaining Trigger Logic

Once the trigger buffer has been defined, allowing easy access to the before and after record images, the main program logic assigns a unique employee number. Figure 6.6 shows the remaining code.

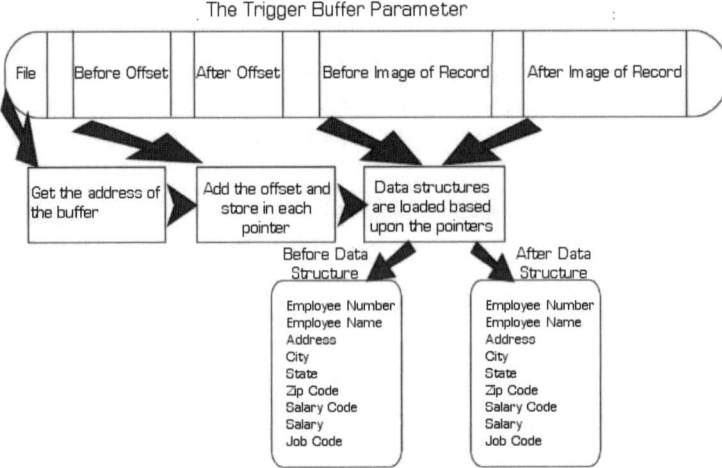

Figure 6.5: A conceptual view of the use of pointers and data structures within a trigger.

```
 *_____
 *  Only assign employee number on inserts.
 *_____
C                     If          TrigEvent = @Insert
 *_____
 *  Get the last employee number from the data area.  Increment
 *  it and update data area and trigger buffer with new number.
 *_____
C       *Lock         In          EmployeeDA
C                     Eval        Last# = Last# + 1
C                     Out         EmployeeDA
C                     Eval        A_EMEMP# = Last#
C                     Endif
 *
C                     Return
```

Figure 6.6: The trigger program assigns a unique employee number.

The main trigger logic begins by verifying the trigger event in a new record that is being added. If it is an insert, the code locks the data area and retrieves the contents to ensure a unique value. The last used number is incremented by one and the new value written back out to the data area. Finally, the new employee number is moved to the employee number field (A_EMEMP#) within the after image of the employee record. This image is what is written to the file by the system database manager.

Additional Considerations

When you create your trigger programs in ILE, you need to decide how it will fit into your overall ILE strategy. What is the appropriate activation group the trigger should run under? It depends on the type of applications that will be calling it. It is generally appropriate to create your trigger programs to run under a specific named activation group.

EXAMPLE

Using a Trigger for Security Monitoring

This example employs a trigger program to monitor changes made to the salary field in an Employee Master File. The file contains fields you would expect to see in a simple employee file, such as employee number, name, address, job code, salary, etc. Figure 6.7 shows the complete layout for the file.

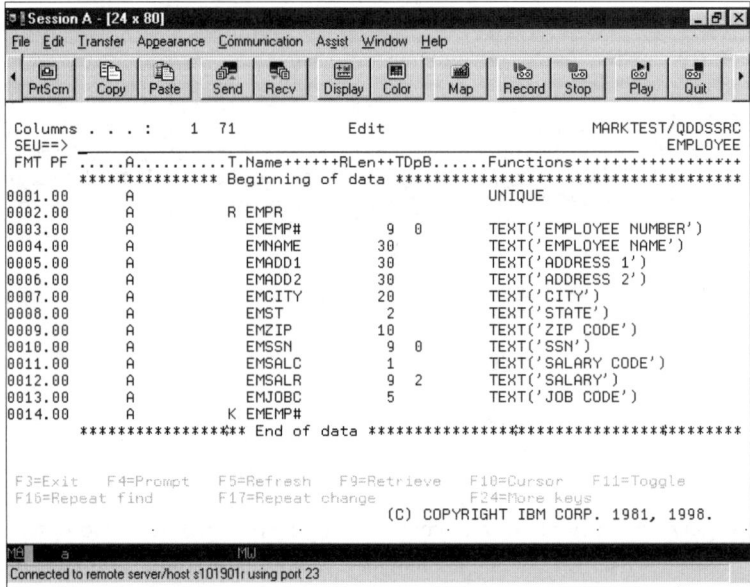

Figure 6.7: This Employee Master File is used to demonstrate trigger use.

The trigger program is added to the file via a CL command in the program DB007C, as shown in Listing 6.3.

Listing 6.3: CL program DB007C uses ADDPFTRG to add a trigger.

```
         PGM
/*-----------------------------------------------------------*/
/*  Add trigger DB007R to file Employee to send alert         */
/*  message when employee salary is increased by more than 20%. */
/*-----------------------------------------------------------*/

         ADDPFTRG    FILE(EMPLOYEE) TRGTIME(*AFTER) +
                     TRGEVENT(*UPDATE) PGM(DB007R) +
                     ALWREPCHG(*NO) TRGUPDCND(*CHANGE)

         ENDPGM
```

The trigger program DB007R is shown in Listing 6.4.

Listing 6.4: ILE RPG program *DB007R* is a trigger for the *EMPLOYEE* file.

```
 *
DpBefore          S              *
DpAfter           S              *
 *
DBefore           E DS                      ExtName(EMPLOYEE) Prefix(B_)
D                                           Based(pBefore)
DAfter            E DS                      ExtName(EMPLOYEE) Prefix(A_)
D                                           Based(pAfter)
D*
D#PctChg          S              7  4
D*
/*────────────────────────────────────────────────────────────────*/
 *    Trigger Buffer and Trigger Buffer Length Declarations
/*────────────────────────────────────────────────────────────────*/
DBufferLen        S             10I 0
DTrigBuff         DS
D  TrigFile                     10A
D  TrigLib                      10A
D  TrigMbr                      10A
D  TrigEvent                     1A
D  TrigTime                      1A
D  TrigCommit                    1A
D  TrigRes1                      3A
D  TrigCCSID                    10I 0
D  TrigRRN                      10I 0
D  TrigRes2                      4A
D  TrigB4OS                     10I 0
D  TrigB4Len                    10I 0
D  TrigB4NBM                    10I 0
D  TrigB4NBL                    10I 0
D  TrigAftOS                    10I 0
D  TrigAftLen                   10I 0
D  TrigAfNBM                    10I 0
D  TrigAfNBL                    10I 0
/*────────────────────────────────────────────────────────────────*/
 *    Trigger Constants
/*────────────────────────────────────────────────────────────────*/
D@Insert          C                         '1'
D@Delete          C                         '2'
D@Update          C                         '3'
D@Before          C                         '2'
D@After           C                         '1'
/*────────────────────────────────────────────────────────────────*/
 *    API Declarations
/*────────────────────────────────────────────────────────────────*/
DSMMsgId          S              7
DSMMsgFile        S             20
DSMMsgTxt         S            100
```

Listing 6.4: ILE RPG program DB007R is a trigger for the EMPLOYEE file (continued).

```
DSMMsgLen        S               10I 0 Inz(%Size(SMMsgTxt))
DSMMsgType       S               10    Inz('*INFO')
DSMMsgQ          S               20    Inz('CFO         *LIBL      ')
DSMMsgQ#         S               10I 0 Inz(1)
DSMReplyQ        S               20
DSMMsgKey        S                4
 *
DAPIErrorDS      DS
D  APIBytes                      10I 0 Inz(%Size(APIErrorDS))
D  APIBytesOut                   10I 0
D  APIErrID                       7A
D  APIReserved                    1A
D  APIErInDta                   256A
 /*—————————————————————————————————————————————————————————*/
 *  Input parameters are passed automatically when the trigger
 *  fires.  Passed are the trigger buffer and trigger buffer length.
 /*—————————————————————————————————————————————————————————*/
C     *Entry        PList
C                   Parm                    TrigBuff
C                   Parm                    BufferLen
 *
 /*—————————————————————————————————————————————————————————*/
 *  Map the data structures for the before and after images to
 *  the offset location in the trigger buffer using pointers.
 /*—————————————————————————————————————————————————————————*/
C                   Eval      pBefore = %Addr(TrigBuff) + TrigB4OS
C                   Eval      pAfter  = %Addr(TrigBuff) + TrigAftOS
 *
C                   If        TrigEvent = @Update
 /*—————————————————————————————————————————————————————————*/
 *  If salary was increased:  If it was zero before or if it
 *  was increased by more than 20% - send an alert message.
 /*—————————————————————————————————————————————————————————*/
C                   If        A_EMSALR > B_EMSALR
C                   If        B_EMSALR = 0
C                   Exsr      SendAlert
C                   Else
C                   Eval(R)   #PctChg = (A_EMSALR / B_EMSALR) - 1
C                   If        #PctChg > .20
C                   Exsr      SendAlert
C                   Endif
C                   Endif
C                   Endif
 *
C                   Endif
 *
C                   Return
```

**Listing 6.4: ILE RPG program DB007R
is a trigger for the EMPLOYEE file (continued).**

```
/*———————————————————————————————————————————*/
 *   Salary has been increased by more than 20%  -  Use QMHSNDM API
 *   to send an alert message to the company C.F.O.
/*———————————————————————————————————————————*/
C     SendAlert    Begsr
C                  Eval      SMMsgTxt = 'Alert-Salary for '+
C                                       %Trimr(B_EMNAME)    +
C                                       ' Increased More than 20%.'
C*
C                  Call      'QMHSNDM'
C                  Parm                 SMMsgId
C                  Parm                 SMMsgFile
C                  Parm                 SMMsgTxt
C                  Parm                 SMMsgLen
C                  Parm                 SMMsgType
C                  Parm                 SMMsgQ
C                  Parm                 SMMsgQ#
C                  Parm                 SMReplyQ
C                  Parm                 SMMsgKey
C                  Parm                 APIErrorDS
C*
C                  Endsr
```

WHAT THE EXAMPLE DOES

The example program DB007C uses the ADDPFTRG command to add the trigger program DB007R to the EMPLOYEE file. The trigger is fired every time a record in the EMPLOYEE file is changed. The program checks the salary field. If the value was increased by more than 20 percent, an alert message is sent to the company's chief financial officer (CFO).

HOW THE EXAMPLE WORKS

When executed, the ADDPFTRG command listed in program DB007C adds trigger program DB007R to the EMPLOYEE file. The ADDPFTRG command uses the following parameters:

The Physical File (FILE) Parameter. The FILE parameter is required and specifies the qualified name of the file to which the trigger is to be added.

The Trigger Time (TRGTIME) Parameter. The TRGTIME parameter is required and specifies the timing of the firing of the trigger program. The permissible values for the TRGTIME parameter are:

*BEFORE	The trigger executes before the record is processed
*AFTER	The trigger executes after the record is processed

The example uses the value *AFTER, meaning the trigger runs after the EMPLOYEE record changes are written to the file.

The Trigger Event (TRGEVENT) Parameter. The TRGEVENT parameter is required and defines the file event that causes the trigger program to fire. The permissible values for the TRGEVENT parameter are:

*INSERT	The trigger executes when a new record is added
*UPDATE	The trigger executes when a record is updated
*DELETE	The trigger executes when a record is deleted

The example uses the value *UPDATE, meaning the trigger runs after an application changes one or more values in an employee record.

The Program Name (PGM) Parameter. The PGM parameter is required and specifies the qualified name of the trigger program to be added.

The Replace Trigger (RPLTRG) Parameter. The RPLTRG parameter specifies whether the new trigger is to replace any existing trigger defined for the file, time, and event combination. The permissible values for the RPLTRG parameter are:

*YES	The new trigger will replace an existing trigger
*NO	The new trigger will not replace an existing trigger

The example uses the value *NO.

The Allow Repeated Change (ALWREPCHG) Parameter. The ALWREPCHG parameter specifies whether the new trigger has the capability to change the original record that caused the trigger to fire. The permissible values for the ALWREPCHG parameter are:

*YES	The trigger program can alter the original record
*NO	The trigger program cannot alter the original record

The example uses the value *NO, restricting it from changing any of the values in the Employee record.

The Trigger Update Condition (TRGUPDCND) Parameter. The TRGUPDCND is used only for triggers having a trigger event of *UPDATE. The parameter specifies if the trigger is to be fired only when a field is actually changed by an update operation. The permissible values for the TRGUPDCND parameter are:

```
*CHANGE   The trigger fires only if fields have changed
*ALWAYS   The trigger fires on all update operations
```

The example uses the value *CHANGE, specifying that one or more field values must actually be changed to fire the trigger.

The ILE RPG Trigger Program

When executed, the trigger program DB007R compares the before image of the salary field to the after image. If the salary was increased by more than 20 percent, the program sends a message to the CFO's message queue. This program can be used as an example of how to use a trigger program to test the data that has been changed and of how to employ the Send Non-Program Message API.

Defining the Trigger Buffer

The code that is common to all trigger programs defines the layout of the trigger buffer parameter. A simple coding technique employing pointers defines the trigger buffer in a flexible and reliable way. If you have not used pointers in an RPG program before, they are simply a way to address a specific storage location. As discussed earlier in this chapter, the trigger buffer parameter passed to your program varies in length because the length of the trigger record varies from file to file. Pointers allow you to soft code the location of the record images with the trigger buffer using the offset values also found in the parameter. Figure 6.8 shows the definition of the pointers and data structures that define the input parameters.

```
DpBefore          S              *
DpAfter           S              *
 *
DBefore         E DS                   ExtName(EMPLOYEE) Prefix(B_)
D                                      Based(pBefore)
DAfter          E DS                   ExtName(EMPLOYEE) Prefix(A_)
D                                      Based(pAfter)
D*
```

Figure 6.8: These specs define the pointers and data structures used for the trigger buffer.

```
    *_____
    *    Trigger Buffer and Trigger Buffer Length Declarations
    *_____
DBufferLen         S            10I 0
DTrigBuff          DS
D  TrigFile                     10A
D  TrigLib                      10A
D  TrigMbr                      10A
D  TrigEvent                     1A
D  TrigTime                      1A
D  TrigCommit                    1A
D  TrigRes1                      3A
D  TrigCCSID                    10I 0
D  TrigRRN                      10I 0
D  TrigRes2                      4A
D  TrigB4OS                     10I 0
D  TrigB4Len                    10I 0
D  TrigB4NBM                    10I 0
D  TrigB4NBL                    10I 0
D  TrigAftOS                    10I 0
D  TrigAftLen                   10I 0
D  TrigAfNBM                    10I 0

D  TrigAfNBL                    10I 0
    *_____
    *   Input parameters are passed automatically when the trigger
    *   fires.  Passed are the trigger buffer and trigger buffer length.
    *_____
C      *Entry       PList
C                   Parm                       TrigBuff
C                   Parm                       BufferLen
```

Figure 6.8: These specs define the pointers and data structures used for the trigger buffer (cont.).

The input parameter TRIGBUFF is defined as a data structure, with subfields parsing out each individual field within the fixed-length portion of the buffer. The offset values, provided in the subfields TRIGB4OS and TRIGAFTOS, tell your program the starting positions within the buffer for the before and after record images.

To avoid the hard coding of the subfields of the employee record within both the before and after images, the file is used to create two external data structures called BEFORE and AFTER. The data structure definitions use the DTAARA keyword to base the layout of the structure on the EMPLOYEE file. The PREFIX keyword is used on each to add a unique prefix of either 'B_' or 'A_' to the field names. The BASED keyword specifies that the data structure is to be loaded with the data residing in the address provided by the pointers PBEFORE and PAFTER.

The before and after record images are loaded into the data structures by setting the pointers to the address locations of the records within the trigger buffer. This is performed in Figure 6.9 using the RPG Address-Of function. The appropriate offset is added to the address of the buffer and is loaded into the pointer variable. Because the data structures BEFORE and AFTER are based on the pointer variables, they reflect the proper values.

```
*_____
*   Map the data structures for the before and after images to
*   the offset location in the trigger buffer using pointers.
*_____
C                     Eval      pBefore = %Addr(TrigBuff) + TrigB4OS
C                     Eval      pAfter  = %Addr(TrigBuff) + TrigAftOS
```

Figure 6.9: The before and after record images are retrieved from the buffer using pointers.

Employing pointers to define the record images in the trigger buffer is a flexible, soft-coded approach to use for all your trigger programs. Figure 6.10 provides a further conceptual look at the technique.

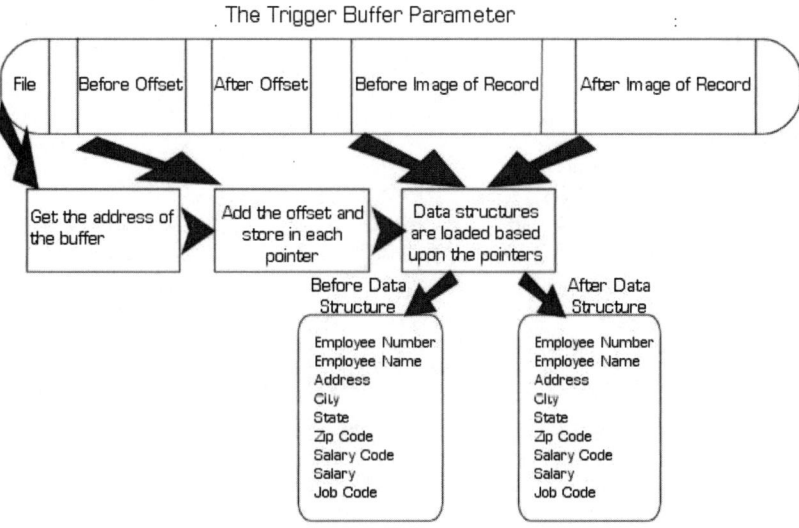

Figure 6.10: A conceptual view of the use of pointers and data structures within a trigger.

The Remaining Trigger Logic

Once the trigger buffer has been defined, allowing easy access to the before and after re-cord images, the main program logic compares the before and after values of the salary field. Figure 6.11 shows the code for the comparison.

```
C                  If         TrigEvent = @Update
 *_____
 *  If salary was increased:  If it was zero before or if it
 *  was increased by more than 20% - send an alert message.
 *_____
C                  If         A_EMSALR > B_EMSALR
C                  If         B_EMSALR = 0
C                  Exsr       SendAlert
C                  Else
C                  Eval(R)    #PctChg = (A_EMSALR / B_EMSALR) - 1
C                  If         #PctChg > .20
C                  Exsr       SendAlert
C                  Endif
C                  Endif
C                  Endif
 *
C                  Endif
C                  Return
```

Figure 6.11: The trigger program tests the salary field for an increase of more than 20 percent.

The main trigger logic begins by verifying the trigger event in a record update. If it is an up-date, the code tests the before and after change values of the salary field. If the number was increased, further tests are made. If the number was originally zero, an alert message is sent by executing the subroutine SENDALERT. If the salary was not previously zero, the percent-age of change is calculated. If the percentage is greater than 20, an alert message is sent by executing subroutine SENDALERT. The subroutine SENDALERT is shown in Figure 6.12.

```
C     SendAlert    Begsr
C                  Eval       SMMsgTxt = 'Alert-Salary for '+
C                                        %Trimr(B_EMNAME)    +
C                                        ' Increased More than 20%.'
C*
C                  Call       'QMHSNDM'
C                  Parm                   SMMsgId
C                  Parm                   SMMsgFile
C                  Parm                   SMMsgTxt
C                  Parm                   SMMsgLen
C                  Parm                   SMMsgType
C                  Parm                   SMMsgQ
C                  Parm                   SMMsgQ#
C                  Parm                   SMReplyQ
C                  Parm                   SMMsgKey
C                  Parm                   APIErrorDS
C*
C                  Endsr
```

Figure 6.12: The SENDALERT subroutine sends an alert message to message queue CFO.

To send a message to a nonprogram message queue, the RPG program could call a CL program that would use a Send Message (SNDMSG) command to send the desired alert. However, it is just as easy and more flexible to employ a system API to do the same thing. For more detailed explanations of API use, please refer to chapter 4.

The system API, QMHSNDM, sends a message to a nonprogram message queue. The API parameters are defined in the program definition specifications and provide details used to instruct message delivery when the API is called. Figure 6.13 shows the definition of the API parameters.

```
*_____
*    API Declarations
*_____
DSMMsgId         S              7
DSMMsgFile       S             20
DSMMsgTxt        S            100
DSMMsgLen        S             10I 0 Inz(%Size(SMMsgTxt))
DSMMsgType       S             10    Inz('*INFO')
DSMMsgQ          S             20    Inz('CFO        *LIBL     ')
DSMMsgQ#         S             10I 0 Inz(1)
DSMReplyQ        S             20
DSMMsgKey        S              4
*
DAPIErrorDS      DS
D  APIBytes                    10I 0 Inz(%Size(APIErrorDS))
D  APIBytesOut                 10I 0
D  APIErrID                     7A
D  APIReserved                  1A
D  APIErInDta                 256A
```

Figure 6.13: The parameters used by the API to send a message to message queue CFO.

Additional Considerations

When you create your trigger programs in ILE, you need to decide how it will fit into your overall ILE strategy. What is the appropriate activation group the trigger should run under? It really depends on the type of applications that will be calling it. It is generally appropriate to create your trigger programs to run under a specific named activation group.

Some applications may require the exchange of information between the trigger program and the calling program. Objects such as data areas, data queues, and user spaces created in the QTEMP library are useful to accommodate this requirement.

EXAMPLE

Using a Trigger for Data Validation

This example employs a trigger program to validate data field values entered on new or changed CUSTOMER file records. The file contains fields you would expect to see in a simple customer file, such as customer number, company name, contact name, address, etc. Figure 6.14 shows the complete layout for the file.

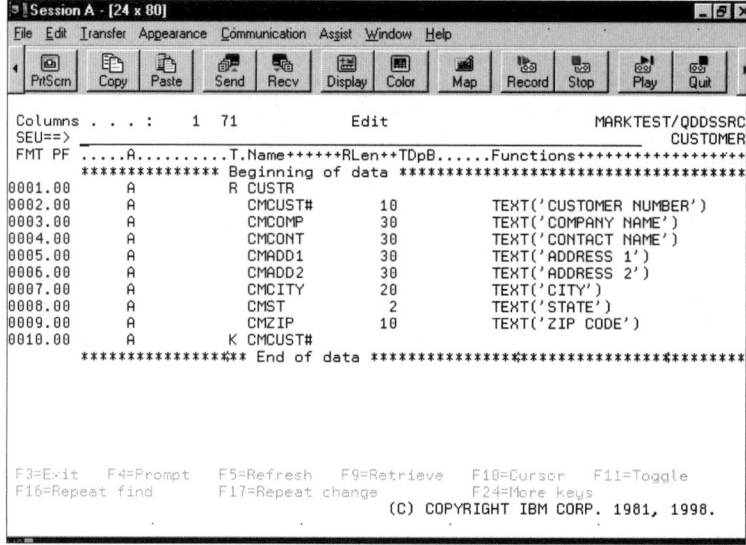

Figure 6.14: This CUSTOMER file is used to demonstrate trigger use.

The trigger program is added to the file via a CL command in the program DB008C shown in Listing 6.5.

Listing 6.5: CL program DB008C uses ADDPFTRG to add a trigger.

```
PGM
/*-----------------------------------------------------------------*/
/*  Add trigger DB008R to file Customer to perform data            */
/*  validation.                                                    */
/*-----------------------------------------------------------------*/

        ADDPFTRG   FILE(CUSTOMER) TRGTIME(*BEFORE) +
                     TRGEVENT(*INSERT) PGM(DB008R) ALWREPCHG(*NO)
```

Listing 6.5: CL program DB008C uses ADDPFTRG to add a trigger (continued).

```
ADDPFTRG   FILE(CUSTOMER) TRGTIME(*BEFORE) +
             TRGEVENT(*UPDATE) PGM(DB008R) ALWREPCHG(*NO)

ENDPGM
```

The trigger program DB008R is shown in Listing 6.6.

Listing 6.6: ILE RPG program DB008R is a trigger for the CUSTOMER file.

```
FStates     CT   F    2          Disk
DStateCodes      S              2A    Dim(100) Perrcd(1) Fromfile(States)
 *_____
 *   I'm using pointers instead of SUBSTR because %Addr
 *   retains packed data.  Substr doesn't handle embedded
 *   packed data fields.
 *_____
 *
DpBefore         S              *
DpAfter          S              *
 *
DBefore     E DS                     ExtName(CUSTOMER) Prefix(B_)
D                                    Based(pBefore)
DAfter      E DS                     ExtName(CUSTOMER) Prefix(A_)
D                                    Based(pAfter)
D*
DX               S              3  0
 *
/*_____*/
 *   Trigger Buffer and Trigger Buffer Length Declarations
/*_____*/
DBufferLen       S             10I 0
DTrigBuff        DS
D  TrigFile                    10A
D  TrigLib                     10A
D  TrigMbr                     10A
D  TrigEvent                    1A
D  TrigTime                     1A
D  TrigCommit                   1A
D  TrigRes1                     3A
D  TrigCCSID                   10I 0
D  TrigRRN                     10I 0
D  TrigRes2                     4A
D  TrigB4OS                    10I 0
D  TrigB4Len                   10I 0
D  TrigB4NBM                   10I 0
D  TrigB4NBL                   10I 0
D  TrigAftOS                   10I 0
```

➔

Listing 6.6: ILE RPG program *DB008R* is a trigger for the CUSTOMER file (continued).

```
D   TrigAftLen                      10I 0
D   TrigAfNBM                       10I 0
D   TrigAfNBL                       10I 0
 *_____
 *    Trigger Constants
 *_____
D@Insert          C                        '1'
D@Delete          C                        '2'
D@Update          C                        '3'
D@Before          C                        '2'

D@After           C                        '1'
 *_____
 *    API Declarations
 *_____
DSMMsgId          S               7        Inz('CPF9898')
DSMMsgFile        S              20        Inz('QCPFMSG    *LIBL')
DSMMsgTxt         S             100
DSMMsgLen         S              10I 0 Inz(%Size(SMMsgTxt))
DSMMsgType        S              10        Inz('*ESCAPE')
DSMMsgQ           S              10        Inz('*')
DSMStack#         S              10I 0 Inz(1)
DSMMsgKey         S               4
 *
DAPIErrorDS       DS
D   APIBytes                      10I 0 Inz(%Size(APIErrorDS))
D   APIBytesOut                   10I 0
D   APIErrID                       7A
D   APIReserved                    1A
D   APIErInDta                   256A
 *_____
 *    Error Message Constants
 *_____
D@Error1          C                        'Customer Number cannot be blank'
D@Error2          C                        'Company Name cannot be blank'
D@Error3          C                        'Contact Name cannot be blank'
D@Error4          C                        'Address cannot be blank'
D@Error5          C                        'City cannot be blank'
D@Error6          C                        'Zip Code cannot be blank'
D@Error7          C                        'State cannot be blank'
D@Error8          C                        'Invalid State Entered'
 *_____
 *    Input parameters are passed automatically when the trigger
 *    fires.  Passed are the trigger buffer and trigger buffer length.
 *_____
C       *Entry        PList
C                     Parm                  TrigBuff
C                     Parm                  BufferLen
```

270

Listing 6.6: ILE RPG program DB008R
is a trigger for the Customer file (continued).

```
*_____
* Map the data structures for the before and after images to
* the offset location in the trigger buffer using pointers.
*_____
C                 Eval      pBefore = %Addr(TrigBuff) + TrigB4OS
C                 Eval      pAfter  = %Addr(TrigBuff) + TrigAftOS
*
C                 If        TrigEvent = @Update Or
C                           TrigEvent = @Insert
*_____
* Validate entire record.  Send an error message for each
* violation found.
*_____
C                 If        A_CMCUST# = *Blanks
C                 Movel(p)  @Error1            SMMsgTxt
C                 Exsr      SendError
C                 Endif
*
C                 If        A_CMCOMP = *Blanks
C                 Movel(p)  @Error2            SMMsgTxt
C                 Exsr      SendError
C                 Endif
*
C                 If        A_CMCONT = *Blanks
C                 Movel(p)  @Error3            SMMsgTxt
C                 Exsr      SendError
C                 Endif
*
C                 If        A_CMADD1 = *Blanks
C                 Movel(p)  @Error4            SMMsgTxt
C                 Exsr      SendError
C                 Endif
*
C                 If        A_CMCITY = *Blanks
C                 Movel(p)  @Error5            SMMsgTxt
C                 Exsr      SendError
C                 Endif
*
C                 If        A_CMZIP = *Blanks
C                 Movel(p)  @Error6            SMMsgTxt
C                 Exsr      SendError
C                 Endif
*
C                 If        A_CMST   = *Blanks
C                 Movel(p)  @Error7            SMMsgTxt
C                 Exsr      SendError
C                 Else
C                 Eval      X = 1
```

Listing 6.6: ILE RPG program DB008R is a trigger for the CUSTOMER file (continued).

```
C       A_CMST      Lookup    StateCodes(X)                        90
C                   If        Not(*In90)
C                   Movel(p)  @Error8        SMMsgTxt
C                   Exsr      SendError
C                   Endif
C                   Endif
   *
C                   Endif
   *
C                   Return
   *_____
   *  If any exceptions were found  -  Use QMHSNDPM API to send
   *  a hard error back.
   *_____
C       SendError   Begsr
C*
C                   Call      'QMHSNDPM'
C                   Parm                    SMMsgId
C                   Parm                    SMMsgFile
C                   Parm                    SMMsgTxt
C                   Parm                    SMMsgLen
C                   Parm                    SMMsgType
C                   Parm                    SMMsgQ
C                   Parm                    SMStack#
C                   Parm                    SMMsgKey
C                   Parm                    APIErrorDS
C*
C                   Endsr
```

WHAT THE EXAMPLE DOES

The example program DB008C uses the ADDPFTRG command to add the trigger program DB008R to the CUSTOMER file. The trigger is fired every time a record in the CUSTOMER file is added or changed. Because the trigger monitors both insert and update events, the trigger is added twice. The program checks and validates the input data, returning an error message if the data does not pass.

HOW THE EXAMPLE WORKS

When executed, the ADDPFTRG command listed in program DB008C adds trigger program DB008R to the CUSTOMER file. The ADDPFTRG command uses the following parameters.

The Physical File (FILE) Parameter. The FILE parameter is required and specifies the qualified name of the file to which the trigger is to be added.

The Trigger Time (TRGTIME) Parameter. The TRGTIME parameter is required and specifies the timing of the firing of the trigger program. The permissible values for the TRGTIME parameter are:

```
*BEFORE    The trigger executes before the record is processed
*AFTER     The trigger executes after the record is processed
```

The example uses the value *BEFORE, meaning the trigger runs before the employee record changes or additions are written to the file. This allows you to reject records that do not meet the validation criteria.

The Trigger Event (TRGEVENT) Parameter. The TRGEVENT parameter is required and defines the file event that causes the trigger program to fire. The permissible values for the TRGEVENT parameter are:

```
*INSERT    The trigger executes when a new record is added
*UPDATE    The trigger executes when a record is updated
*DELETE    The trigger executes when a record is deleted
```

The example adds two triggers, one having the value *UPDATE, meaning the trigger runs before an application's record changes are written. The second trigger has a value of *INSERT, meaning the trigger runs before new records are written to the CUSTOMER file.

The Program Name (PGM) Parameter. The PGM parameter is required and specifies the qualified name of the trigger program to be added.

The Replace Trigger (RPLTRG) Parameter. The RPLTRG parameter specifies whether the new trigger is to replace any existing trigger defined for the file, time, and event combination. The permissible values for the RPLTRG parameter are:

```
*YES    The new trigger will replace an existing trigger
*NO     The new trigger will not replace an existing trigger
```

The example uses the value *NO.

The Allow Repeated Change (ALWREPCHG) Parameter. The ALWREPCHG parameter specifies whether the new trigger has the capability to change the original record that caused the trigger to fire. The permissible values for the ALWREPCHG parameter are:

*YES	The trigger program can alter the original record
*NO	The trigger program cannot alter the original record

The example uses the value *NO, restricting it from changing any of the values in the Customer record.

The Trigger Update Condition (TRGUPDCND) Parameter. The TRGUPDCND is used only for triggers having a trigger event of *UPDATE. The parameter specifies if the trigger is to be fired only when a field is actually changed by an update operation. The permissible values for the TRGUPDCND parameter are:

*CHANGE	The trigger fires only if fields have changed
*ALWAYS	The trigger fires on all update operations

The example uses the value *CHANGE, specifying that one or more field values must actually be changed to fire the trigger.

The ILE RPG Trigger Program

When executed, the trigger program DB008R validates the data being added or changed in the CUSTOMER file. If any field does not meet the validation requirements, the program sends an escape error message to the program message queue. This results in a hard error for the application that initiated the add or change. This program can be used as an example of how to use a trigger program to perform data validation and of how to employ the Send Program Message API.

Defining the Trigger Buffer

The code that is common to all trigger programs defines the layout of the trigger buffer parameter. A simple coding technique employing pointers defines the trigger buffer in a flexible and reliable way. If you have not used pointers in an RPG program before, they are simply a way to address a specific storage location. As discussed earlier in this chapter, the trigger buffer parameter passed to your program varies in length because the length of the trigger record varies from file to file. Pointers allow you to soft code the location of the record images with the trigger buffer using the offset values also found in the parameter. Figure 6.15 shows the definition of the pointers and data structures that define the input parameters.

274

```
DpBefore          S                    *
DpAfter           S                    *
 *
DBefore           E DS                 ExtName(CUSTOMER) Prefix(B_)
D                                      Based(pBefore)
DAfter            E DS                 ExtName(CUSTOMER) Prefix(A_)
D                                      Based(pAfter)
D*
 *_____
 *   Trigger Buffer and Trigger Buffer Length Declarations
 *_____
DBufferLen        S                    10I 0
DTrigBuff         DS
D  TrigFile                            10A

D  TrigLib                             10A

D  TrigMbr                             10A

D  TrigEvent                            1A

D  TrigTime                             1A

D  TrigCommit                           1A
D  TrigRes1
D  TrigCCSID                           10I 0
D  TrigRRN                             10I 0
D  TrigRes2                             4A
D  TrigB4OS                            10I 0
D  TrigB4Len                           10I 0
D  TrigB4NBM                           10I 0
D  TrigB4NBL                           10I 0
D  TrigAftOS                           10I 0
D  TrigAftLen                          10I 0
D  TrigAfNBM                           10I 0
D  TrigAfNBL                           10I 0
 *_____
 *   Input parameters are passed automatically when the trigger
 *   fires.  Passed are the trigger buffer and trigger buffer
length.
 *_____
C       *Entry         PList
C                      Parm                    TrigBuff
C                      Parm                    BufferLen
```

Figure 6.15: These specs define the pointers and data structures used for the trigger buffer.

The input parameter TRIGBUFF is defined as a data structure, with subfields parsing out each individual field within the fixed-length portion of the buffer. The offset values, provided in the subfields TRIGB4OS and TRIGAFTOS, tell your program the starting positions within the buffer for the before and after record images.

To avoid the hard coding of the subfields of the customer record within both the before and after images, the file is used to create two external data structures called BEFORE and AFTER. The data structure definitions use the DTAARA keyword to base the layout of the structure on the Customer file. The PREFIX keyword is used on each to add a unique prefix of either 'B_' or 'A_' to the field names. The BASED keyword specifies that the data structure is to be loaded with the data residing in the address provided by the pointers PBEFORE and PAFTER.

The before and after record images are loaded into the data structures by setting the pointers to the address locations of the records within the trigger buffer. This is performed in Figure 6.16 using the RPG Address-Of function. The appropriate offset is added to the address of the buffer and is loaded into the pointer variable. Because the data structures BEFORE and AFTER are based on the pointer variables, they reflect the proper values.

```
 *_____
 *  Map the data structures for the before and after images to
 *  the offset location in the trigger buffer using pointers.
 *_____
 C                    Eval      pBefore = %Addr(TrigBuff) + TrigB4OS
 C                    Eval      pAfter  = %Addr(TrigBuff) + TrigAftOS
```

Figure 6.16: The before and after record images are retrieved from the buffer using pointers.

Employing pointers to define the record images in the trigger buffer is a flexible, soft-coded approach to use for all your trigger programs. Figure 6.17 provides a further conceptual look at the technique.

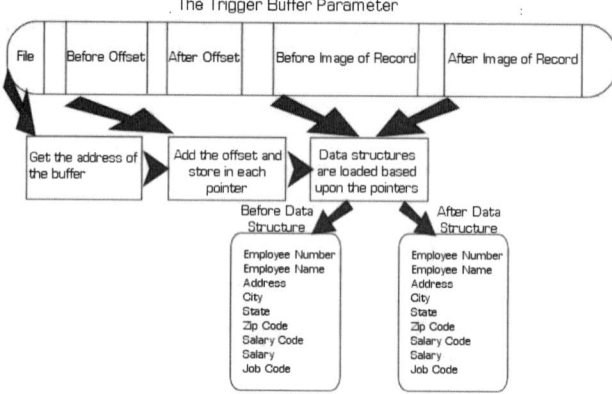

Figure 6.17: A conceptual view of the use of pointers and data structures within a trigger.

The Remaining Trigger Logic

Once the trigger buffer has been defined, allowing easy access to the before and after record images, the main program logic validates each data field. Figure 6.18 shows the validation code.

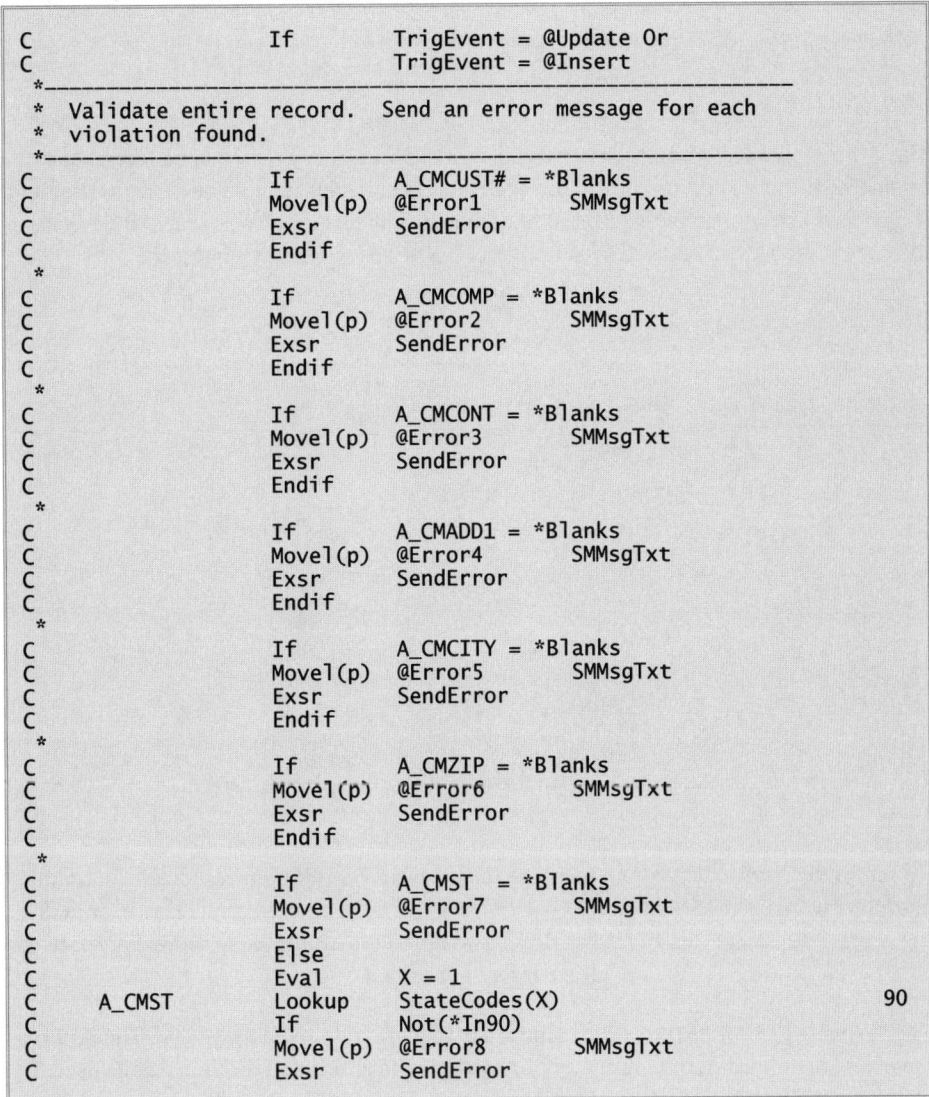

```
C                       If        TrigEvent = @Update Or
C                                 TrigEvent = @Insert
 *_____
 *  Validate entire record.  Send an error message for each
 *  violation found.
 *_____
C                       If        A_CMCUST# = *Blanks
C                       Movel(p)  @Error1        SMMsgTxt
C                       Exsr      SendError
C                       Endif
 *
C                       If        A_CMCOMP = *Blanks
C                       Movel(p)  @Error2        SMMsgTxt
C                       Exsr      SendError
C                       Endif
 *
C                       If        A_CMCONT = *Blanks
C                       Movel(p)  @Error3        SMMsgTxt
C                       Exsr      SendError
C                       Endif
 *
C                       If        A_CMADD1 = *Blanks
C                       Movel(p)  @Error4        SMMsgTxt
C                       Exsr      SendError
C                       Endif
 *
C                       If        A_CMCITY = *Blanks
C                       Movel(p)  @Error5        SMMsgTxt
C                       Exsr      SendError
C                       Endif
 *
C                       If        A_CMZIP = *Blanks
C                       Movel(p)  @Error6        SMMsgTxt
C                       Exsr      SendError
C                       Endif
 *
C                       If        A_CMST  = *Blanks
C                       Movel(p)  @Error7        SMMsgTxt
C                       Exsr      SendError
C                       Else
C                       Eval      X = 1
C       A_CMST          Lookup    StateCodes(X)                90
C                       If        Not(*In90)
C                       Movel(p)  @Error8        SMMsgTxt
C                       Exsr      SendError
```

Figure 6.18: The trigger program tests each individual data field.

```
C                    Endif
C                    Endif
 *
C                    Endif
 *
C                    Return
```

Figure 6.18: The trigger program tests each individual data field (continued).

The main trigger logic begins by verifying that the trigger event is either a record update or an add. If it is an add or update, the code tests the after-change value of each data field. If any field does not meet the desired requirements, an error message is sent by executing the subroutine SENDERROR. The subroutine SENDERROR is shown in Figure 6.19.

```
 *_____
 *  If any exceptions were found  -  Use QMHSNDPM API to send
 *  a hard error back.
 *_____
C      SendError    Begsr
C*
C                   Call      'QMHSNDPM'
C                   Parm                   SMMsgId
C                   Parm                   SMMsgFile
C                   Parm                   SMMsgTxt
C                   Parm                   SMMsgLen
C                   Parm                   SMMsgType
C                   Parm                   SMMsgQ
C                   Parm                   SMStack#
C                   Parm                   SMMsgKey
C                   Parm                   APIErrorDS
C*
C                   Endsr
```

Figure 6.19: The SENDERROR subroutine sends a program error message.

To send a message to a program message queue, the RPG program could call a CL program that would use a SNDPGMMSG command to send the desired error. However, it is just as easy and more flexible to employ a system API to do the same thing. For more detailed explanations of API use, please refer to chapter 4.

The system API QMHSNDPM sends a message to a program message queue. The API parameters are defined in the program definition specifications and provide details used to instruct message delivery when the API is called. Figure 6.20 shows the definition of the API parameters.

```
*-----------------------------------------------------------
*   API Declarations
*-----------------------------------------------------------
DSMMsgId          S              7       Inz('CPF9898')
DSMMsgFile        S             20       Inz('QCPFMSG    *LIBL')
DSMMsgTxt         S            100
DSMMsgLen         S             10I 0 Inz(%Size(SMMsgTxt))
DSMMsgType        S             10       Inz('*ESCAPE')
DSMMsgQ           S             10       Inz('*')
DSMStack#         S             10I 0 Inz(1)
DSMMsgKey         S              4
*
DAPIErrorDS       DS
D  APIBytes                     10I 0 Inz(%Size(APIErrorDS))
D  APIBytesOut                  10I 0
D  APIErrID                      7A
D  APIReserved                   1A
D  APIErInDta                  256A
```

Figure 6.20: The parameters used by the API to send an error message.

Additional Considerations

When you create your trigger programs in ILE, you need to decide how it will fit into your overall ILE strategy. What is the appropriate activation group the trigger should run under? It really depends on what type of applications that will be calling it. It is generally appropriate to create your trigger programs to run under a specific named activation group.

7

USING SQL

If you have been creating, managing, and manipulating database files on an AS/400 for more than a couple of years, you have probably done so using DDS specifications, CL commands, and RPG op codes. This is called the native database interface. Another interface, SQL, which is widely used on non-AS/400 platforms, also is available to AS/400 developers.

SQL is a standardized database access language used by the majority of relational data base products available today. It is an extremely powerful tool that should not be overlooked on the AS/400. Regardless of whether you purchase the optional SQL development environment, SQL support is included with the base OS/400 operating system. If you have an AS/400, you also have SQL.

SQL, the language of relational databases, is constructed in a manner similar to another language: English. SQL statements are like sentences, but instead of having nouns and verbs, they are made up of verbs and clauses. SQL verbs perform a number of database functions, including creating libraries and files, and adding, updating, and deleting records within the files.

WHAT CAN YOU DO WITH SQL?

If you have experience with native AS/400 database access, you are familiar with methods such as the Create Physical File (CRTPF) CL command and RPG op codes such as CHAIN, READ, WRITE, and UPDATE. The native interface is designed to provide access to AS/400 data one record at a time. SQL is different. It is a tool designed to work with sets of records. This design makes it especially well suited for performing mass file updates, creating test data and test environments, combining and summarizing data, and servicing client/server and distributed applications.

SQL TERMINOLOGY

Because SQL is a widely used industry standard tool, its terminology is not AS/400 specific. The terms used within the SQL interface differ slightly from those of the native AS/400 interface. Table 7.1 lists some of the most commonly used SQL terms, along with their native counterparts.

Table 7.1: SQL and Native Terminology.

Native Term	SQL Term
Library	Collection (Except that a collection includes journals and SQL Catalog Files within the library)
Library (Including the objects it contains)	Schema (A schema is the collection plus the objects in the collection)
Physical File	Table
Logical File (used to combine or filter records from one or more physical files)	View
Logical File (used to set the key of a physical file)	Index
Record	Row
Field	Column

SQL STATEMENTS

SQL statements fall into four broad categories: data definition, data manipulation, dynamic, and miscellaneous. These statements perform operations that create and manage database objects and manipulate the data residing in these objects. SQL statements used to create database objects such as libraries and files are not significantly different from those created with native commands such as Create Library (CRTLIB) and CRTPF. The files you create natively using DDS and CRTPF can be altered and manipulated using SQL. Conversely, the files (tables) you create with SQL can be manipulated by an HLL program using normal native techniques.

SQL is a complex and powerful database language. Indeed, there are hundreds of books dedicated to a thorough and complete explanation of the topic. The goal of this book is not to be an all-inclusive SQL reference. Instead, it demonstrates the techniques that can be the most helpful to you, the AS/400 professional. This chapter presents examples that employ three types of SQL statements—data definition, data manipulation, and dynamic. The most commonly used SQL statements are listed in Tables 7.2 and 7.3.

Table 7.2: Commonly used Data Definition SQL Statements.

SQL Statement	Description	Similar CL Command	
Alter Table	Adds, changes, and deletes fields from an existing file; also adds and removes constraints and adds, changes or deletes keys	CHGPF CRTPF ADDPFCST RMVPFCST	
Create Alias	Directs to a specific qualified file or member	OVRDBF (except that it becomes permanent)	
Create Collection	Creates a new library with catalog files and journal	CRTLIB	
Create Index	Creates a keyed access path	CRTLF	OPNQRYF
Create Procedure	Creates a stored procedure	None	
Create Table	Creates a new physical file (allows you to define fields and add constraints)	CRTPF	ADDPFCST
Create View	Creates a view that can combine data from more than one file or include only a portion of a file	CRTLF	OPNQRYF
Drop Alias	Deletes an alias	DLTOVR	
Drop Collection	Deletes a collection	DLTLIB	
Drop Index	Deletes an index	DLTF	
Drop Procedure	Deletes a stored procedure	None	

Table 7.2: Commonly used Data Definition SQL Statements. (continued)

SQL Statement	Description	Similar CL Command
Drop Table	Deletes a file	DLTF
Drop View	Deletes a view	DLTF
Grant Procedure	Grants authority to a procedure	None
Grant Table	Grants authority to a file	GRTOBJAUT
Label On	Changes object text for files. Also changes column headings for fields	CHGOBJD CHGPF
Rename	Renames a file	RNMOBJ
Revoke Procedure	Revokes authority to a stored procedure	None
Revoke Table	Revokes authority to a file	RVKOBJAUT

Table 7.3: Commonly Used Data Manipulation SQL Statements.

SQL Statement	Description	Similar RPG Op Code
Close	Closes a cursor (a marker for position within a file)	CLOSE
Commit	Writes pending transactions	COMMIT
Declare Cursor	Defines a cursor for use	None
Delete	Deletes one or more records from a file	DELETE
Fetch	Reads a record	READ
Insert	Writes one or more records to a file	WRITE
Open	Opens a cursor	OPEN
Rollback	Rolls back pending transactions	ROLLBACK
Select	Retrieves one or more records from a file	READ CHAIN
Update	Changes one or more records in a file	UPDATE

Most SQL statements have *clauses* that further define the characteristics of the operations. Clauses are similar in concept to the parameters that accompany common CL commands.

Ways to Run SQL Statements

On the AS/400, there are several different ways to execute SQL statements. The optional licensed product DB2/400 Query Manager and SQL Development Kit includes a full interactive runtime interface that allows you to key SQL statements into a command line. The product also includes an interpreter that performs multiple statements that have been keyed into a source file. To integrate the use of SQL with your RPG development, you can embed SQL statements within an RPG program.

The AS/400 Operations Navigator also provides an interface to perform interactive SQL operations. Further, it allows you to analyze the performance of SQL statements by creating an SQL Monitor.

EXAMPLE

Using SQL to Create a Library and Files

This example employs SQL statements to create a library, two physical files, and a unique key logical file on the AS/400. The first file created contains fields you would expect to see in a simple student file, such as student number, name, address, birth date, and teacher, as shown in Figure 7.1. The second physical file contains information about schoolteachers, as shown in Figure 7.2.

```
                                    File Layout

            File:        STUDENTS
            Library:     SCHOOLLIB

                                     Beginning   Ending     Column
            Field Name   Type   Length  Position  Position   Heading
            STUDENT#     Zoned  5,0        1         5        STUDENT#
            FIRSTNAME    Char   12         6        17        FIRSTNAME
            LASTNAME     Char   20        18        37        LASTNAME
            ADDRESS      Char   30        38        67        ADDRESS
            CITY         Char   15        68        82        CITY
            STATE        Char    2        83        84        STATE
            ZIP          Char   10        85        94        ZIP
            BIRTHDATE    Date   10        95       104        BIRTHDATE
            TEACHER      Zoned  3,0      105       107        TEACHER


            Key
            Arrival

            Logical Files   Key        Unique?
            LSTUDENTS1      STUDENT#     Yes
```

Figure 7.1: This STUDENT file is used to demonstrate SQL use.

```
                              File Layout

        File:        TEACHERS
        Library:     SCHOOLLIB

                                      Beginning  Ending    Column
        Field Name   Type    Length   Position   Position  Heading
        TEACHER#     Zoned   3 , 0      1          3        TEACHER#
        TEACHERNAME  Char    30         4         33        TEACHERNAME
        HIREDATE     Date    10        34         43        HIREDATE
        PHONE        Char    8         44         51        PHONE




        Key
        TEACHER#        UNIQUE

        Logical Files   Key          Unique?
        NONE
```

Figure 7.2: This TEACHER file is used to demonstrate SQL use.

The SQL statements used to create the SCHOOLLIB library, the STUDENTS physical file, the LSTUDENTS1 unique keyed logical file, and the TEACHERS physical file are shown in Listing 7.1.

Listing 7.1: Source member DB009T uses SQL to create database objects.

```
CREATE COLLECTION SCHOOLLIB

CREATE TABLE SCHOOLLIB/STUDENTS
(STUDENT# NUMERIC (5, 0) NOT NULL WITH DEFAULT,
 FIRSTNAME CHAR (12) NOT NULL WITH DEFAULT,
 LASTNAME CHAR (20) NOT NULL WITH DEFAULT,
 ADDRESS CHAR (30) NOT NULL WITH DEFAULT,
 CITY CHAR (15) NOT NULL WITH DEFAULT,
 STATE CHAR (2) NOT NULL WITH DEFAULT,
 ZIP CHAR (10) NOT NULL WITH DEFAULT,
 BIRTHDATE DATE NOT NULL WITH DEFAULT,
 TEACHER NUMERIC (3, 0) NOT NULL WITH DEFAULT)

CREATE UNIQUE INDEX SCHOOLLIB/LSTUDENTS1 ON SCHOOLLIB/STUDENTS

(STUDENT#)
CREATE TABLE SCHOOLLIB/TEACHERS
(TEACHER# NUMERIC (3, 0) NOT NULL WITH DEFAULT,
 TEACHERNAME CHAR (30) NOT NULL WITH DEFAULT,
 HIREDATE DATE NOT NULL,
 PHONE CHAR (8) NOT NULL WITH DEFAULT,
 PRIMARY KEY (TEACHER#))
```

WHAT THE EXAMPLE DOES

The example source member DB009T uses the CREATE COLLECTION SQL statement to create a new library, SCHOOLLIB. The CREATE TABLE statement defines fields used to create the STUDENTS file in the SCHOOLLIB library. When the physical file is created, it is not keyed. A logical file, LSTUDENTS1, is created using the CREATE UNIQUE INDEX statement to establish the student number field as a unique key. The CREATE TABLE statement is used a second time to create the TEACHERS file in the SCHOOLLIB library. A primary key constraint is added, establishing the teacher number field as the primary, unique key.

HOW THE EXAMPLE WORKS

When executed, the CREATE COLLECTION statement listed in source member DB009T creates an SQL Collection called SCHOOLLIB. An SQL collection is simply a library that includes a set of database catalog files and a system journal.

Database Catalog

When you use SQL to create an AS/400 library, a number of system files are also automatically created. These files provide access to information about the database objects that are subsequently created in the library. Whenever a new file is created in the library, the system automatically stores information describing the file in the catalog files. The contents of these files are a handy tool for obtaining information about your database. Table 7.4 shows the catalog files automatically created as part of an SQL collection.

Table 7.4: Catalog Files Created with a Collection.

Logical File Name	File Purpose
SYSTABLES	Lists all physical files
SYSCOLUMNS	Lists all fields with definition
SYSINDEXES	Lists all indexes (keyed logical files)
SYSKEYS	Lists all key fields for all logical files
SYSVIEWS	Lists all views (logical files that combine or restrict data)
SYSVIEWDEP	Lists all logical file dependencies
SYSCST	Lists all database constraints
SYSCSTCOL	Lists the fields having defined constraints
SYSCSTDEP	Lists constraint dependencies
SYSCHKCST	Lists all check constraints
SYSKEYCST	Lists all key constraints
SYSREFCST	Lists all referential constraints
SYSPACKAGE	Lists defined SQL packages

The CREATE COLLECTION statement uses the following clauses:

The IN ASP Clause

The optional IN ASP clause allows you to specify the Auxiliary Storage Pool in which the collection is to be created. If omitted, the collection is created in the main ASP, ASP 1. Although not specified in this example, the following is a representation of how the clause can be specified:

```
CREATE COLLECTION SCHOOLLIB IN ASP 1
```

The WITH DATA DICTIONARY Clause

The optional WITH DATA DICTIONARY clause allows you to create a data dictionary in the new library. Data dictionaries are files that contain database object definitions to be used with the system Interactive Data Definition Utility (IDDU). IDDU data dictionaries supply database information to system tools such as Query/400, Officevision/400, and Data File Utility (DFU). Although not specified in this example, the following is a representation of how the clause can be specified:

```
CREATE COLLECTION SCHOOLLIB WITH DATA DICTIONARY
```

The CREATE TABLE Statement

When executed, the CREATE TABLE statement listed in source member DB009T creates two physical files called STUDENTS and TEACHERS. Files created using the SQL CREATE TABLE statement are not significantly different than those created using specifications keyed into a source member using DDS.

The Column Definition

The CREATE TABLE statement accepts one or more column definitions to specify the name and attributes of each field. A table column definition allows you to provide a field name, data type, length, default value, null capability, constraint and primary key, or unique key. The first field defined in the example STUDENT file is the student number. It is a five-digit zoned numeric field that does not accept null values and has a default value of zero. The field is defined as follows:

```
STUDENT# NUMERIC (5, 0) NOT NULL WITH DEFAULT
```

The example also defines several character fields, including the student first name, as follows:

```
FIRSTNAME CHAR (12) NOT NULL WITH DEFAULT
```

The student birth date is defined in the example as a date type field. It is defined as follows:

```
BIRTHDATE DATE NOT NULL WITH DEFAULT
```

In addition to the column definitions, the CREATE TABLE statement commonly uses the following constraint clauses (for more information about constraints, see chapter 5):

The PRIMARY KEY Clause

The optional PRIMARY KEY clause allows you to identify the field or fields that are to comprise a unique and primary key for the file. This clause can only be specified once on a CREATE TABLE statement. This clause is employed in the CREATE TABLE statement for the TEACHERS file. It establishes the field TEACHER# as the primary key:

```
PRIMARY KEY (TEACHER#)
```

The UNIQUE Clause

The optional UNIQUE clause allows you to identify the field or fields that are to comprise a unique key constraint for the file. This clause can be specified multiple times on a CREATE TABLE statement. Although not specified in this example, the following is a representation of how the clause can be specified:

```
UNIQUE (STUDENT#)
```

The CREATE INDEX Statement

When executed, the CREATE INDEX statement listed in source member DB009T creates a logical file called LSTUDENTS1. The file provides a unique key over the STUDENTS physical file.

The UNIQUE Clause

The optional UNIQUE clause allows you to specify that the keys defined further in the index are to allow only unique values. When UNIQUE is specified, the file is restricted from having duplicate key values, even in cases where the keys contain null values. By adding the clause UNIQUE WHERE NOT NULL, you can allow enforcement of unique keys only when the value is not null.

The ON Clause

The ON clause allows you to identify the name of the physical file over which the logical is to be created. The clause includes one or more field names that are to comprise the key of the logical file. Each field name listed can optionally include a sort sequence identifier of ascending (ASC) or descending (DESC). If omitted, the sort sequence defaults to ascending value.

The CREATE INDEX statement used to create a unique keyed logical file over the students physical file is as follows:

```
CREATE UNIQUE INDEX SCHOOLLIB/LSTUDENTS1 ON SCHOOLLIB/STUDENTS
(STUDENT#)
```

EXAMPLE

Using SQL to Create a View to Join Two Files

This example employs SQL to create an SQL view to join the data residing in two physical files. The first is a STUDENT file containing fields such as student number, name, address, birth date, and teacher, as shown in Figure 7.3. The second physical file contains information about schoolteachers, as shown in Figure 7.4. The view combines records from the two files, including only selected fields and concatenating the student's last and first names. The layout for the view, created as a join logical file, is shown in Figure 7.5.

File Layout

File: STUDENTS
Library: SCHOOLLIB

Field Name	Type	Length	Beginning Position	Ending Position	Column Heading
STUDENT#	Zoned	5 , 0	1	5	STUDENT#
FIRSTNAME	Char	12	6	17	FIRSTNAME
LASTNAME	Char	20	18	37	LASTNAME
ADDRESS	Char	30	38	67	ADDRESS
CITY	Char	15	68	82	CITY
STATE	Char	2	83	84	STATE
ZIP	Char	10	85	94	ZIP
BIRTHDATE	Date	10	95	104	BIRTHDATE
TEACHER	Zoned	3 , 0	105	107	TEACHER

Key
Arrival

Logical Files	Key	Unique?
LSTUDENTS1	STUDENT#	Yes

Figure 7.3: This STUDENT file is used to demonstrate SQL use.

```
                            File Layout

File:       TEACHERS
Library:    SCHOOLLIB

                              Beginning  Ending    Column
Field Name      Type   Length Position   Position  Heading
TEACHER#        Zoned   3 , 0     1          3      TEACHER#
TEACHERNAME     Char   30         4         33      TEACHERNAME
HIREDATE        Date   10        34         43      HIREDATE
PHONE           Char    8        44         51      PHONE




Key
TEACHER#        UNIQUE

Logical Files   Key            Unique?
NONE
```

Figure 7.4: This TEACHER file is used to demonstrate SQL use.

```
                            File Layout

File:       LSTUDENTS2
Library:    SCHOOLLIB

                               Beginning  Ending   Column
Field Name      Type    Length Position   Position Heading
STUDENT#        Zoned    5 , 0     1          5     STUDENT#
NAME            VarChar 34         6         41     NAME
TEACHER         Zoned    3 , 0    42         44     TEACHER
TEACH00001      Char    30        45         74     TEACHERNAME




Key
Arrival

Dependent Physical Files
STUDENTS
TEACHERS
```

Figure 7.5: This join logical file combines data from two physical files.

The SQL statement used to create the LSTUDENTS2 logical file is shown in Listing 7.2.

Listing 7.2: Source member DB010T uses SQL to create a view.

```
CREATE VIEW SCHOOLLIB/LSTUDENTS2
AS SELECT STUDENTS.STUDENT#,
RTRIM(STUDENTS.LASTNAME) || ', ' || STUDENTS.FIRSTNAME AS NAME,
        STUDENTS.TEACHER,
    TEACHERS.TEACHERNAME
FROM SCHOOLLIB/STUDENTS INNER JOIN SCHOOLLIB/TEACHERS
ON STUDENTS.TEACHER = TEACHERS.TEACHER#
```

WHAT THE EXAMPLE DOES

The example source member DB010T uses the CREATE VIEW SQL statement to create a join logical file, LSTUDENTS2. The CREATE VIEW statement specifies the fields from the two physical files that are to be shown. In addition to fields from the physical files, a derived field is created. The derived field, called NAME, is a concatenation of the student last name and first name, separated by a comma. When the logical file is created, it is not keyed.

HOW THE EXAMPLE WORKS

When executed, the CREATE VIEW statements listed in source member DB010T creates a logical file called LSTUDENTS2. The statement allows you to specify the fields to be included in the view, the files from which the fields are included, and any selection criteria used to determine which records are to be included.

The SELECT Clause

The SELECT clause identifies the field or fields that are to be included in the new logical file. Field names specified in the SELECT clause can be fields residing in the file named in the From clause or they can be derived values. An asterisk (*) is used to select all of the fields from the file being selected. Additionally, field names can be qualified with the file name to remove an ambiguity in field naming. Field names can be changed using an AS keyword on the field definition. The following is an example of the SELECT clause:

```
SELECT STUDENTS.STUDENT#,
    RTRIM(STUDENTS.LASTNAME) || ', ' || STUDENTS.FIRSTNAME AS NAME
```

The SELECT clause allows embedded functions to derive field values. The example employs the concatenation operator (||) and the Right Trim (RTRIM) function to derive a field that combines the student last name and first name, removing embedded spaces and inserting a comma. The new field is given the label NAME by the AS keyword.

Further, the SELECT clause allows you to specify how duplicate records are to be handled. To exclude all but one of a set of duplicate records, the word DISTINCT follows the SELECT clause. If not specified, the default value includes duplicate valued records. An example of using the DISTINCT keyword follows:

```
SELECT DISTINCT STUDENTS.STUDENT#,
   RTRIM(STUDENTS.LASTNAME) || ', ' || STUDENTS.FIRSTNAME AS NAME
```

The FROM Clause

The FROM clause allows you to identify the file or files that are the source of the included fields. When the FROM clause lists the name of a single file, the resulting file is based only on the listed file. If two or more files are listed without creating a join condition, the resulting file is based on the records in all listed files. If a join condition is established, the records in the resulting file are joined in a concatenated view.

When joining two files, the file listed first is treated as the primary, or leftmost, file. The subsequent files listed are the joined files. The JOIN keyword you use defines the relationship between the leftmost file and the joined file used to create the join. The JOIN keyword options are as follows.

Join or Inner Join

All records from the leftmost file meeting the join condition with one or more records in the join file are included. Records in the leftmost file that do not have a record meeting the join condition are not included. Records in the join file that do not match the leftmost file are also not included. The ON keyword allows you to specify the condition used to join the records.

Left Join or Left Outer Join

All records from the leftmost file are included in the resulting file regardless of whether there is a record in the join file meeting the join condition. All records that meet the join condition are joined. Records from the leftmost file that do not have a corresponding match with a record in the join file are joined using default or null values to represent the fields in the join file. The ON keyword allows you to specify the condition used to join the records.

Exception Join

Only records from the leftmost file that do not have a record in the join file meeting the join condition are returned. All leftmost file records are joined using default or null values to represent the fields in the join file. The ON keyword allows you to specify the condition used to join the records.

Cross Join

Every record in the leftmost file is joined to every record in the join-to file. The ON keyword is not used for cross-type joins.

The ON Keyword

The conditioning expression that determines the criteria for each join type is specified using the ON keyword. The example employs the ON keyword to specify that in order to join records from the STUDENT and TEACHER files, the teacher number fields must be equal, as shown in the following example:

```
FROM SCHOOLLIB/STUDENTS INNER JOIN SCHOOLLIB/TEACHERS
ON STUDENTS.TEACHER = TEACHERS.TEACHER#
```

The WHERE Clause

The WHERE clause allows you to specify selection criteria used to determine the inclusion of records in the logical file. You may condition the selection based on a comparison of the value of one field to another, a field to a constant value, a field to a function value, or a function value to a constant. SQL provides a number of built-in functions that allow you to avoid having to hard code comparison values. They include numerous date, timestamp, and string-handling functions. The example does not use the WHERE clause to provide selection criteria. However, if you wanted to include in the logical file only students whose last name begin with 'A', the WHERE clause would be coded as follows:

```
FROM SCHOOLLIB/STUDENTS INNER JOIN SCHOOLLIB/TEACHERS
ON STUDENTS.TEACHER = TEACHERS.TEACHER#
WHERE STUDENTS.NAME LIKE 'A%'
```

PERFORMING SIMPLE SQL SELECT QUERIES

The following three examples employ what is probably the single most powerful SQL statement used to query information from a file. The SELECT statement is used to generate a result file to be retrieved in an embedded SQL program or displayed in an interactive SQL session. A rich and powerful set of functions allows your query to return simple file records, summary data derived from records, and even complex joining of data from multiple files.

The examples use a typical school database, consisting of a STUDENT file, a TEACHER file, a TEST file, and a TEST SCORE file, as shown in Figure 7.6.

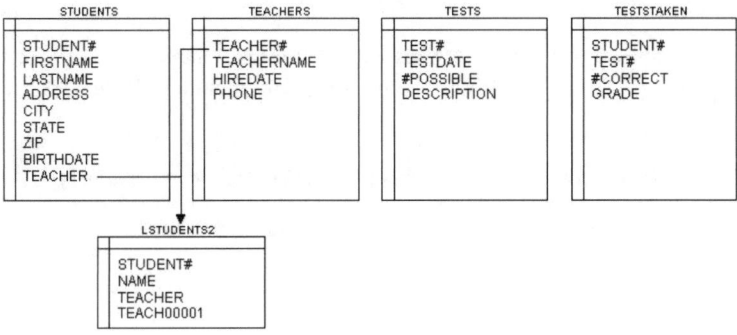

Figure 7.6: This school database is used to demonstrate SQL use.

The SELECT Statement

The SELECT statement is a type of query that retrieves information from a file based on desired criteria and returns the information in the form of a result table. The result table is either processed through embedded SQL in an HLL program or displayed using interactive SQL.

When used with the interactive SQL facility, initiated by the Start SQL (STRSQL) command, SELECT is a powerful ad hoc data analysis tool. A single statement allows you to specify the fields to retrieve, the file or files from which they originate, the selection criteria, the sort order, and even summarization options of the information to be queried. These specifications are supplied to the statement using clauses.

The SQL statements used to query data in the TESTSTAKEN file are shown in Listing 7.3.

Listing 7.3: Source member DB011T uses SQL to query data.

```
SELECT * FROM SCHOOLLIB/TESTSTAKEN ORDER BY TEST#, #CORRECT, STUDENT#

SELECT TEST#, #CORRECT, STUDENT# FROM SCHOOLLIB/TESTSTAKEN ORDER BY
TEST#, #CORRECT DESC,STUDENT#

SELECT TEST#, #CORRECT, STUDENT# FROM SCHOOLLIB/TESTSTAKEN WHERE
#CORRECT > 0 ORDER BY TEST#, #CORRECT DESC,STUDENT#
```

EXAMPLE

Using SQL to Perform a Simple Select Query Returning all Fields

The example, as shown in Figure 7.7, uses the SQL SELECT statement to retrieve student test scores from the TESTSTAKEN file. The returned data includes all fields from the file.

```
SELECT * FROM SCHOOLLIB/TESTSTAKEN ORDER BY TEST#, #CORRECT, STUDENT#
```

Figure 7.7: This SELECT statement returns all fields from the TESTSTAKEN file.

WHAT THE EXAMPLE DOES

When executed interactively using the STRSQL command, the example returns a resulting set of records, as shown in Figure 7.8.

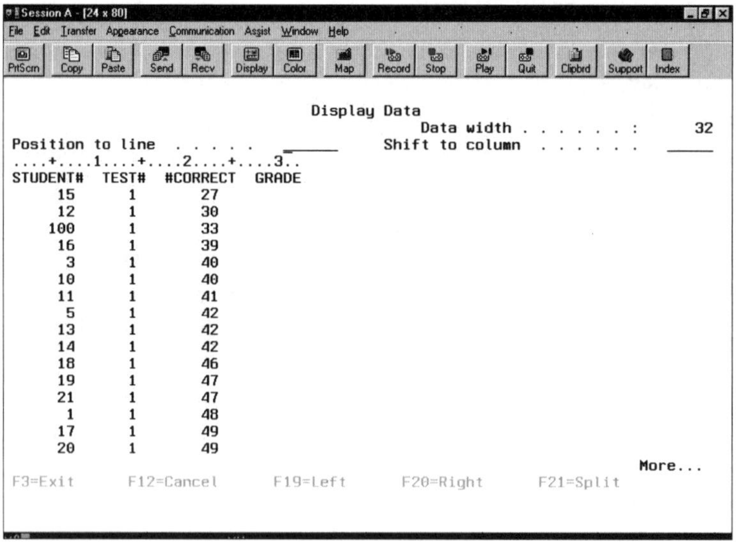

Figure 7.8: This output is displayed when the SELECT statement runs interactively.

HOW THE EXAMPLE WORKS

This query uses various SQL clauses to retrieve the specified data.

The SELECT Clause

The SELECT statement allows you to identify the field or fields that are to be included in the query. This definition is supplied in the SELECT clause of the Select statement. Field names specified can be fields residing in the file named or they can be derived values. An asterisk (*) is used to select all of the fields from the file being selected. Additionally, field names can be qualified with the file name to remove any ambiguity in field naming.

The FROM Clause

The SELECT statement allows you to identify the file or files that are the source of the included fields. The example includes a qualified file name to select the TESTSTAKEN file in the SCHOOLLIB library.

The ORDER BY Clause

The ORDER BY clause allows you to specify the order in which returned records are to be sorted. Each sort field specified can be sorted in ascending (ASC) or descending (DESC) order. When specified, the sort order must be a file field or derived function listed in the SELECT clause. It can be a field name, an ordinal value corresponding to a field, or the result of a built-in summary function. These functions allow you to sort the resulting data by the average, sum, minimum, or maximum value of a field within a group of records. You can also sort the records by record count for a group. The example sorts the resulting records by test number, number of correct answers, and then by student number.

EXAMPLE

Using SQL to Perform a Simple
Select Query Returning Selected Fields

The example, as shown in Figure 7.9, uses the SQL SELECT statement to retrieve student test scores from the TESTSTAKEN file. The returned data includes only the specified fields from the file.

```
SELECT TEST#, #CORRECT, STUDENT# FROM SCHOOLLIB/TESTSTAKEN
   ORDER BY TEST#, #CORRECT DESC,STUDENT#
```

Figure 7.9: This SELECT statement returns only selected fields from the TESTSTAKEN file.

WHAT THE EXAMPLE DOES

When executed interactively using the STRSQL command, the example returns a resulting set of records, as shown in Figure 7.10.

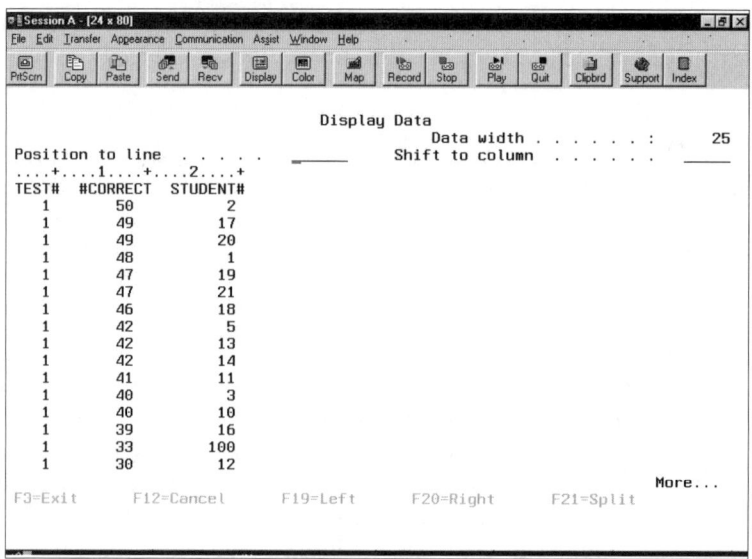

Figure 7.10: This output is displayed when the SELECT statement runs interactively.

HOW THE EXAMPLE WORKS

This query uses various SQL clauses to retrieve the specified data.

The SELECT Clause

The SELECT statement allows you to identify the field or fields that are to be included in the query. This definition is supplied in the SELECT clause of the SELECT statement. Field names specified can be fields residing in the named file or they can be derived values. An asterisk (*) is used to select all of the fields from the file being selected. Additionally, field names can be qualified with the file name to remove any ambiguity in field naming. The order in which fields are listed in the SELECT statement is the order in which they appear in the resulting data.

The FROM Clause

The SELECT statement allows you to identify the file or files that are the source of the included fields. The example includes a qualified file name to select the TESTSTAKEN file in the SCHOOLLIB library.

The ORDER BY Clause

The ORDER BY clause allows you to specify the order in which returned records are to be sorted. Each sort field specified can be sorted in ascending (ASC) or descending (DESC) order. When specified, the sort order must be a file field or derived function listed in the SELECT clause. It can be a field name, an ordinal value corresponding to a field, or the result of a built-in summary function. These functions allow you to sort the resulting data by the average, sum, minimum, or maximum value of a field within a group of records. You can also sort the records by record count for a group. The example sorts the resulting records by test number, number of correct answers in descending order, and then by student number.

EXAMPLE

Using SQL to Perform a Simple Select Query with Selection Criteria

The example, as shown in Figure 7.11, uses the SQL SELECT statement to retrieve student test scores from the TESTSTAKEN file. The returned data includes all fields from the file.

```
SELECT TEST#, #CORRECT, STUDENT# FROM SCHOOLLIB/TESTSTAKEN WHERE
#CORRECT > 0 ORDER BY TEST#, #CORRECT DESC,STUDENT#
```

Figure 7.11: This SELECT statement returns only selected records from the TESTSTAKEN file.

WHAT THE EXAMPLE DOES

When executed interactively using the STRSQL command, the example returns a resulting set of records, as shown in Figure 7.12.

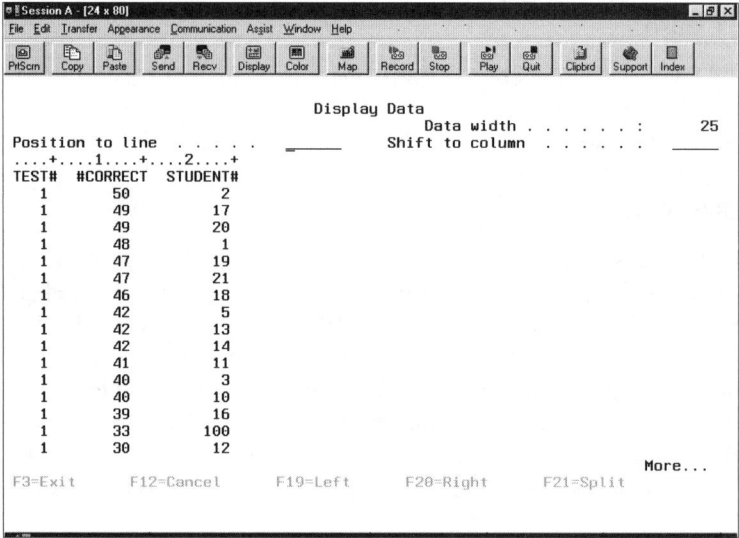

Figure 7.12: This output is displayed when the SELECT statement runs interactively.

HOW THE EXAMPLE WORKS

As in the previous examples, SQL clauses are used to define the desired data.

The SELECT Clause

The SELECT statement allows you to identify the field or fields that are to be included in the query. This definition is supplied in the SELECT clause of the SELECT statement. Field names specified can be fields residing in the file named or they can be derived values. An asterisk (*) is used to select all of the fields from the file being selected. Additionally, field names can be qualified with the file name to remove any ambiguity in field naming. The order in which fields are listed in the SELECT statement is the order in which they appear in the resulting data.

The FROM Clause

The SELECT statement allows you to identify the file or files that are the source of the included fields. The example includes a qualified file name to select the TESTSTAKEN file in the SCHOOLLIB library.

The WHERE Clause

The WHERE clause allows you to specify selection criteria used to determine the inclusion of records. You may condition the selection based on a comparison of the value of one field to another, a field to a constant value, a field to a function value, or a function value to a constant. SQL provides a number of built-in functions that allow you to avoid having to hard code comparison values. They include numerous date, timestamp, and string-handling functions. The example uses the WHERE clause to select only test records in which the number correct field is greater than zero.

The ORDER BY Clause

The ORDER BY clause allows you to specify the order in which returned records are to be sorted. Each sort field specified can be sorted in ascending (ASC) or descending (DESC) order. When specified, the sort order must be a file field or derived function listed in the SELECT clause. It can be a field name, an ordinal value corresponding to a field, or the result of a built-in summary function. These functions allow you to sort the resulting data by the average, sum, minimum, or maximum value of a field within a group of records. You can also sort the records by record count for a group. The example sorts the resulting records by test number, number of correct answers in descending order, and then by student number.

PERFORMING SQL SELECT QUERIES THAT JOIN FILES

The following three examples employ what is probably the single most powerful SQL statement used to query information from a file. The SELECT statement is used to generate a result file to be retrieved in an embedded SQL program or displayed in an interactive SQL session. A rich and powerful set of functions allows your query to return simple file records, summary data derived from records, and even complex joining of data from multiple files.

The examples use a typical school database, consisting of a STUDENT file, a TEACHER file, a TEST file, and a TEST SCORE file, as shown in Figure 7.13.

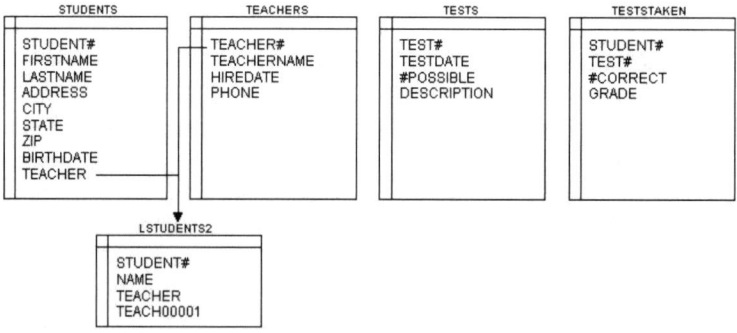

Figure 7.13: This school database is used to demonstrate SQL use.

The SELECT Statement

The SELECT statement is a type of query that retrieves information from a file based on desired criteria and returns the information in the form of a result table. The result table is either processed through embedded SQL in an HLL program or displayed using interactive SQL.

When used with the interactive SQL facility, initiated by the STRSQL command, SELECT is a powerful ad hoc data analysis tool. A single statement allows you to specify the fields to retrieve, the file or files from which they originate, the selection criteria, the sort order, and even summarization options of the information to be queried. These specifications are supplied to the statement using clauses.

The SQL statements used to query data in the school database files are shown in Listing 7.4.

Listing 7.4: Source member DB012T uses SQL to query data joining files.

```
SELECT TESTSTAKEN.TEST#,
       TESTS.DESCRIPTION,
       TESTSTAKEN.STUDENT#,
       TESTS.#POSSIBLE,
       TESTSTAKEN.#CORRECT,
       TESTS.TEST#
FROM   SCHOOLLIB/TESTSTAKEN INNER JOIN SCHOOLLIB/TESTS
       ON TESTSTAKEN.TEST# = TESTS.TEST#
ORDER BY  TESTSTAKEN.TEST#,
          TESTSTAKEN.#CORRECT DESC
```

**Listing 7.4: Source member *DB012T* uses
SQL to query data joining files (continued).**

```
SELECT TESTSTAKEN.TEST#,
       TESTS.DESCRIPTION,
       TESTSTAKEN.STUDENT#,
       TESTS.#POSSIBLE,
       TESTSTAKEN.#CORRECT,
       TESTS.TEST#
FROM
       SCHOOLLIB/TESTSTAKEN,
       SCHOOLLIB/TESTS
WHERE TESTSTAKEN.TEST# = TESTS.TEST#
ORDER BY TESTSTAKEN.TEST#,
         TESTSTAKEN.#CORRECT DESC


SELECT TESTSTAKEN.TEST#,
       TESTS.DESCRIPTION,
       TESTSTAKEN.STUDENT#,
       TESTS.#POSSIBLE,
       TESTSTAKEN.#CORRECT,
       LSTUDENTS2.NAME
FROM   SCHOOLLIB/TESTSTAKEN INNER JOIN SCHOOLLIB/TESTS
         ON TESTSTAKEN.TEST# = TESTS.TEST#
                             INNER JOIN SCHOOLLIB/LSTUDENTS2
         ON TESTSTAKEN.STUDENT# = LSTUDENTS2.STUDENT#


ORDER BY NAME,
         TESTSTAKEN.TEST#,
         TESTSTAKEN.#CORRECT DESC


SELECT TESTSTAKEN.TEST#,
       TESTS.DESCRIPTION,
       TESTSTAKEN.STUDENT#,
       TESTS.#POSSIBLE,
       TESTSTAKEN.#CORRECT,
       LSTUDENTS2.NAME
FROM   SCHOOLLIB/TESTSTAKEN,
       SCHOOLLIB/TESTS,
       SCHOOLLIB/LSTUDENTS2
WHERE  TESTSTAKEN.TEST# = TESTS.TEST# AND
       TESTSTAKEN.STUDENT# = LSTUDENTS2.STUDENT#
ORDER BY NAME,
         TESTSTAKEN.TEST#,
         TESTSTAKEN.#CORRECT DESC
```

→

**Listing 7.4: Source member DB012T uses
SQL to query data joining files (continued).**

```
SELECT NAME,
       TESTSTAKEN.TEST#,
       TESTS.DESCRIPTION,
       TESTS.#POSSIBLE,
       TESTSTAKEN.#CORRECT,
       DECIMAL((#CORRECT / #POSSIBLE)*100,3,0) AS PCT
FROM   SCHOOLLIB/TESTSTAKEN INNER JOIN SCHOOLLIB/TESTS
         ON TESTSTAKEN.TEST# = TESTS.TEST#
                              INNER JOIN SCHOOLLIB/LSTUDENTS2
         ON TESTSTAKEN.STUDENT# = LSTUDENTS2.STUDENT#
ORDER BY NAME,
         TESTSTAKEN.TEST#

SELECT NAME,
       TESTSTAKEN.TEST#,
       TESTS.DESCRIPTION,
       TESTS.#POSSIBLE,
       TESTSTAKEN.#CORRECT,
       DECIMAL((#CORRECT / #POSSIBLE)*100,3,0) AS PCT
FROM   SCHOOLLIB/TESTSTAKEN,
       SCHOOLLIB/TESTS,
       SCHOOLLIB/LSTUDENTS2
WHERE  TESTSTAKEN.TEST# = TESTS.TEST# AND
       TESTSTAKEN.STUDENT# = LSTUDENTS2.STUDENT#
ORDER BY NAME,
         TESTSTAKEN.TEST#
```

EXAMPLE

Using SQL to Perform a Select Query Joining Two Files

The example, as shown in Figure 7.14, uses the SQL SELECT statement to retrieve student test scores from the TESTSTAKEN file. To include information about each test, such as the description of the test and number of possible correct answers, the SELECT statement joins to the TESTS file. Two different methods are employed to join information from more than one file. Both SQL statements return the same results when executed. The returned data includes selected fields from both files.

WHAT THE EXAMPLE DOES

When executed interactively using the STRSQL command, the example returns a set of records, as shown in Figure 7.15.

```
SELECT TESTSTAKEN.TEST#,
       TESTS.DESCRIPTION,
       TESTSTAKEN.STUDENT#,
       TESTS.#POSSIBLE,
       TESTSTAKEN.#CORRECT,
       TESTS.TEST#
FROM   SCHOOLLIB/TESTSTAKEN INNER JOIN SCHOOLLIB/TESTS
       ON TESTSTAKEN.TEST# = TESTS.TEST#
ORDER BY  TESTSTAKEN.TEST#,
          TESTSTAKEN.#CORRECT DESC


SELECT TESTSTAKEN.TEST#,
       TESTS.DESCRIPTION,
       TESTSTAKEN.STUDENT#,
       TESTS.#POSSIBLE,
       TESTSTAKEN.#CORRECT,
       TESTS.TEST#
FROM
       SCHOOLLIB/TESTSTAKEN,
       SCHOOLLIB/TESTS
WHERE  TESTSTAKEN.TEST# = TESTS.TEST#
ORDER BY TESTSTAKEN.TEST#,
```

Figure 7.14: These SELECT statements return data from the TESTSTAKEN and TESTS files.

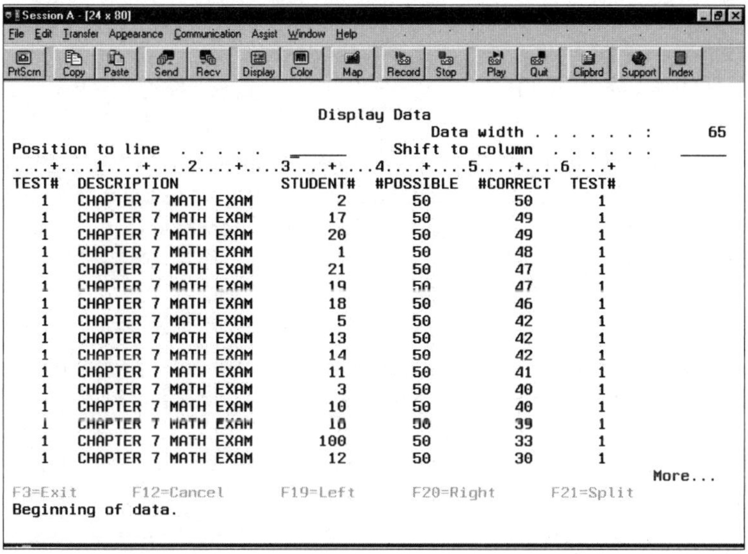

Figure 7.15: This output is displayed when either of the SELECT statements runs interactively.

HOW THE EXAMPLE WORKS

Two different examples are given that return data from more than one file by joining the records together. The first technique uses the JOIN keyword to combine records from two files. The second technique merely lists both files in the FROM clause, then joins the records using selection criteria in the WHERE clause. Both techniques return identical results. In general, it is more efficient to use the JOIN keyword technique.

The SELECT Clause

The SELECT statement allows you to identify the field or fields that are to be included in the query. This definition is supplied in the SELECT clause of the SELECT statement. Field names specified can be fields residing in the named files or they can be derived values. An asterisk (*) is used to select all of the fields from the file being selected. Additionally, field names can be qualified with the file name to remove any ambiguity in field naming.

The FROM Clause

The SELECT statement allows you to identify the file or files that are the source of the included fields. The example includes qualified file names to select the TESTSTAKEN and TESTS files in the SCHOOLLIB library.

In the first SELECT statement, the two files to be used are separated by the INNER JOIN keyword. This specifies that the second file listed is to be joined to the first file listed. The criteria to be used to join the records are then supplied using the ON keyword.

When joining two files, the file listed first is treated as the primary, or leftmost, file. The subsequent files listed are the joined files. The JOIN keyword you use defines the relationship between the leftmost file and the joined file used to create the join. The JOIN keyword options are as follows:

Join or Inner Join

All records from the leftmost file meeting the join condition with one or more records in the join file are included. Records in the leftmost file that do not have a record meeting the join condition are not included. Records in the join file that do not match the leftmost file are also not included. The ON keyword allows you to specify the condition used to join the records.

Left Join or Left Outer Join

All records from the leftmost file are included in the resulting file regardless of whether there is a record in the join file meeting the join condition. All records that meet the join condition are joined. Records from the leftmost file that do not have a corresponding match with a record in the join file are joined using default or null values to represent the fields in the join file. The ON keyword allows you to specify the condition used to join the records.

Exception Join

Only records from the leftmost file that do not have a record in the join file meeting the join condition are returned. All leftmost file records are joined using default or null values to represent the fields in the join file. The ON keyword allows you to specify the condition used to join the records.

Cross Join

Every record in the leftmost file is joined to every record in the join-to file. The ON keyword is not used for cross-type joins.

The ON Keyword

The conditioning expression that determines the criteria for each join type are specified using the ON keyword.

The second SELECT statement simply lists both files to be used separated by a comma. The criteria used to join the records are supplied in the WHERE clause.

The WHERE clause allows you to specify selection criteria used to determine the inclusion of records. Because the first SELECT statement uses the JOIN keyword to join the files, the WHERE clause is not used. If selection criteria unrelated to the joining of records were desired, they would be coded under the WHERE clause.

In the second SELECT statement, where you are joining records from more than one file, the join criteria are specified in the WHERE clause. You may condition the selection based on a comparison of the value of one field to another, a field to a constant value, a field to a function value, or a function value to a constant. SQL provides a number of built-in functions that allow you to avoid having to hard code comparison values. They include numerous date, timestamp, and string-handling functions. The example uses the Where clause to join the TESTSTAKEN file to the TESTS file based on the values in the test number fields that appear in both files.

The ORDER BY clause allows you to specify the order in which returned records are to be sorted. Each sort field specified can be sorted in ascending (ASC) or descending (DESC) order. When specified, the sort order must be a file field or derived function listed in the

SELECT clause. It can be a field name, an ordinal value corresponding to a field, or the result of a built-in summary function. These functions allow you to sort the resulting data by the average, sum, minimum, or maximum value of a field within a group of records. You can also sort the records by record count for a group. The example sorts the resulting records by test number, then by number of correct answers in descending order.

EXAMPLE

Using SQL to Perform a Select Query Joining Three Files

The example, as shown in Figure 7.16, uses the SQL SELECT statement to retrieve student test scores from the TESTSTAKEN file. To include information about each test, such as the description of the test and number of possible correct answers, the SELECT statement joins to the TESTS file. A third file, the logical file LSTUDENTS2, is also joined to access the student name. Two different methods are employed to join information from more than one file. Both SQL statements presented return the same results when executed. The returned data includes selected fields from all three files.

```
SELECT TESTSTAKEN.TEST#,
       TESTS.DESCRIPTION,
       TESTSTAKEN.STUDENT#,
       TESTS.#POSSIBLE,
       TESTSTAKEN.#CORRECT,
       LSTUDENTS2.NAME
FROM   SCHOOLLIB/TESTSTAKEN INNER JOIN SCHOOLLIB/TESTS
          ON TESTSTAKEN.TEST# = TESTS.TEST#
                            INNER JOIN SCHOOLLIB/LSTUDENTS2
          ON TESTSTAKEN.STUDENT# = LSTUDENTS2.STUDENT#

ORDER BY NAME,
         TESTSTAKEN.TEST#,
         TESTSTAKEN.#CORRECT DESC

SELECT TESTSTAKEN.TEST#,
       TESTS.DESCRIPTION,
       TESTSTAKEN.STUDENT#,
       TESTS.#POSSIBLE,
       TESTSTAKEN.#CORRECT,
       LSTUDENTS2.NAME
FROM   SCHOOLLIB/TESTSTAKEN,
       SCHOOLLIB/TESTS,
       SCHOOLLIB/LSTUDENTS2
WHERE  TESTSTAKEN.TEST# = TESTS.TEST# AND
       TESTSTAKEN.STUDENT# = LSTUDENTS2.STUDENT#
```

Figure 7.16: These SELECT statements return data from the TESTSTAKEN, TESTS, and LSTUDENTS2 files.

```
ORDER BY NAME,
          TESTSTAKEN.TEST#,
          TESTSTAKEN.#CORRECT DESC
```

Figure 7.16: These SELECT statements return data from the TESTSTAKEN, TESTS, and LSTUDENTS2 files (continued).

WHAT THE EXAMPLE DOES

When executed interactively using the STRSQL command, the example returns a resulting set of records, as shown in Figure 7.17.

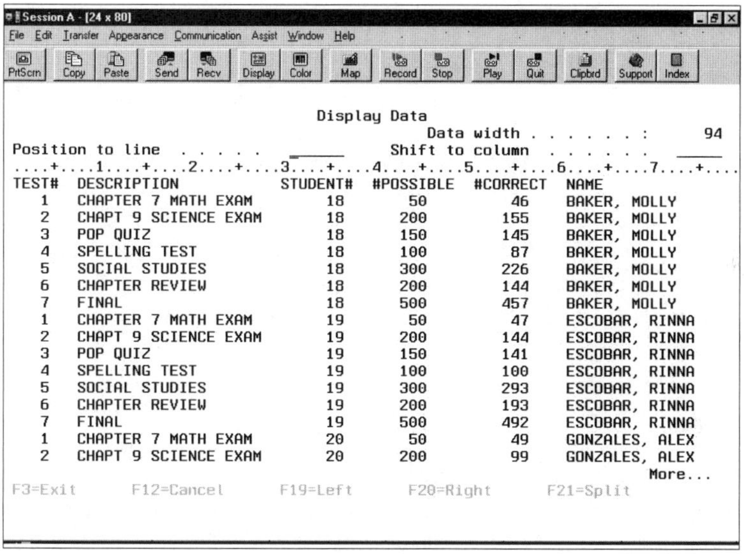

Figure 7.17: This output is displayed when either of the SELECT statements runs interactively.

HOW THE EXAMPLE WORKS

Two different examples are given that return data from multiple files by joining the records together. The first technique uses the JOIN keyword to combine records from three files. The second technique merely lists the files in the FROM clause, then joins the records using selection criteria in the WHERE clause. Both techniques return identical results. In general, it is more efficient to use the JOIN keyword technique.

The SELECT Clause

The SELECT statement allows you to identify the field or fields that are to be included in the query. This definition is supplied in the SELECT clause of the SELECT statement. Field names specified can be fields residing in the named files or they can be derived values. An asterisk (*) is used to select all of the fields from the file being selected. Additionally, field names can be qualified with the file name to remove any ambiguity in field naming.

The FROM Clause

The SELECT statement allows you to identify the file or files that are the source of the included fields. The example includes qualified file names to select the TESTSTAKEN, TESTS, and LSTUDENTS2 files in the SCHOOLLIB library.

In the first SELECT statement, files to be used are separated by the INNER JOIN keyword. This specifies that the file name following the JOIN keyword is to be joined to the first file name listed. The criteria used to join records are then supplied using the ON keyword.

When joining two files, the file listed first is treated as the primary, or leftmost, file. The subsequent files listed are the joined files. The JOIN keyword you use defines the relationship between the leftmost file and the joined file that is used to create the join. The JOIN keyword options are as follows:

Join or Inner Join

All records from the leftmost file meeting the join condition with one or more records in the join file are included. Records in the leftmost file that do not have a record meeting the join condition are not included. Records in the join file that do not match the leftmost file are also not included. The ON keyword allows you to specify the condition used to join the records.

Left Join or Left Outer Join

All records from the leftmost file are included in the resulting file regardless of whether there is a record in the join file meeting the join condition. All records that meet the join condition are joined. Records from the leftmost file that do not have a corresponding match with a record in the join file are joined using default or null values to represent the fields in the join file. The ON keyword allows you to specify the condition used to join the records.

Exception Join

Only records from the leftmost file that do not have a record in the join file meeting the join condition are returned. All leftmost file records are joined using default or null values to represent the fields in the join file. The ON keyword allows you to specify the condition used to join the records.

Cross Join

Every record in the leftmost file is joined to every record in the join-to file. The ON keyword is not used for cross-type joins.

The ON Keyword

The conditioning expression that determines the criteria for each join type are specified using the ON keyword.

The second SELECT statement simply lists the three files to be used separated by commas. The criteria used to join the records are then supplied in the WHERE clause.

The WHERE clause allows you to specify selection criteria used to determine the inclusion of records. Because the first SELECT statement uses the JOIN keyword to join the files, the WHERE clause is not used. If selection criteria unrelated to the joining of records were desired, they would be coded under the WHERE clause. In the second SELECT statement, where you are joining records from more than one file, the join criteria are also specified in the WHERE clause. You may condition the selection based on a comparison of the value of one field to another, a field to a constant value, a field to a function value, or a function value to a constant.

SQL provides a number of built-in functions that allow you to avoid having to hard code comparison values. They include numerous date, timestamp, and string-handling functions. The example uses the WHERE clause to join the TESTSTAKEN file to the TESTS file based on the values in the test number fields that appear in both files. It further joins the TESTSTAKEN file to the LSTUDENTS2 file based on the student number fields.

The ORDER BY clause allows you to specify the order in which returned records are to be sorted. Each sort field specified can be sorted in ascending (ASC) or descending (DESC) order. When specified, the sort order must be a file field or derived function listed in the SELECT clause. It can be a field name, an ordinal value corresponding to a field, or the result of a built-in summary function. These functions allow you to sort the resulting data by the average, sum, minimum, or maximum value of a field within a group of records. You can also sort the records by record count for a group. The example sorts the resulting records by student name, test number, and then by number of correct answers in descending order.

EXAMPLE

Using SQL to Perform a Select and Join Query Calculating an Average

The example, as shown in Figure 7.18, uses the SQL SELECT statement to retrieve student test scores from the TESTSTAKEN file. To include information about each test, such as the description of the test and number of possible correct answers, the SELECT statement joins to the TESTS file. A third file, the LSTUDENTS2 logical file, is also joined to access the student name. Two different methods are employed to join information from more than one file. Both SQL statements return the same results when executed. The returned data includes selected fields from all three files. The query also calculates the percentage of correct answers for each student test.

```
SELECT NAME,
       TESTSTAKEN.TEST#,
       TESTS.DESCRIPTION,
       TESTS.#POSSIBLE,
       TESTSTAKEN.#CORRECT,
       DECIMAL((#CORRECT / #POSSIBLE)*100,3,0) AS PCT
FROM   SCHOOLLIB/TESTSTAKEN INNER JOIN SCHOOLLIB/TESTS
       ON TESTSTAKEN.TEST# = TESTS.TEST#
                          INNER JOIN SCHOOLLIB/LSTUDENTS2
       ON TESTSTAKEN.STUDENT# = LSTUDENTS2.STUDENT#
ORDER BY NAME,
       TESTSTAKEN.TEST#


SELECT NAME,
       TESTSTAKEN.TEST#,
       TESTS.DESCRIPTION,
       TESTS.#POSSIBLE,
       TESTSTAKEN.#CORRECT,
       DECIMAL((#CORRECT / #POSSIBLE)*100,3,0) AS PCT
FROM   SCHOOLLIB/TESTSTAKEN,
       SCHOOLLIB/TESTS,
       SCHOOLLIB/LSTUDENTS2
WHERE  TESTSTAKEN.TEST# = TESTS.TEST# AND
       TESTSTAKEN.STUDENT# = LSTUDENTS2.STUDENT#
```

Figure 7.18: These SELECT statements return data from the TESTSTAKEN, TESTS, and LSTUDENTS2 files.

```
ORDER BY NAME,
         TESTSTAKEN.TEST#
```

Figure 7.18: These SELECT statements return data from the TESTSTAKEN, TESTS, and LSTUDENTS2 files (continued).

WHAT THE EXAMPLE DOES

When executed interactively using the STRSQL command, the example returns a resulting set of records, as shown in Figure 7.19.

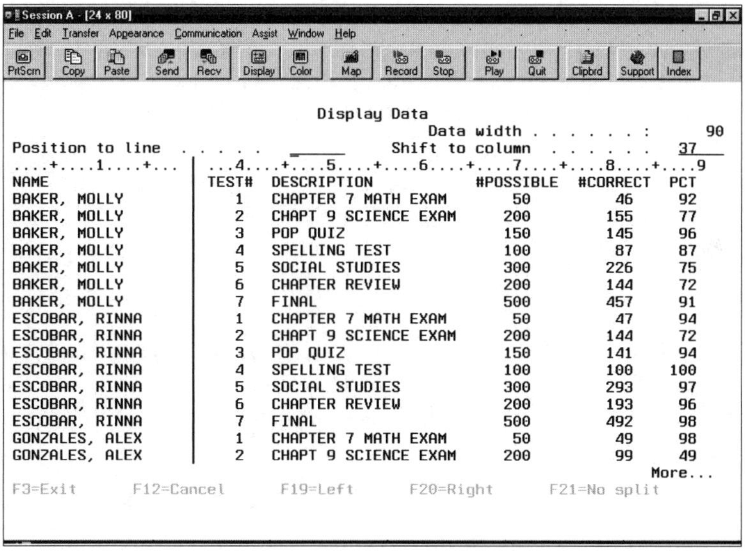

NAME	TEST#	DESCRIPTION	#POSSIBLE	#CORRECT	PCT
BAKER, MOLLY	1	CHAPTER 7 MATH EXAM	50	46	92
BAKER, MOLLY	2	CHAPT 9 SCIENCE EXAM	200	155	77
BAKER, MOLLY	3	POP QUIZ	150	145	96
BAKER, MOLLY	4	SPELLING TEST	100	87	87
BAKER, MOLLY	5	SOCIAL STUDIES	300	226	75
BAKER, MOLLY	6	CHAPTER REVIEW	200	144	72
BAKER, MOLLY	7	FINAL	500	457	91
ESCOBAR, RINNA	1	CHAPTER 7 MATH EXAM	50	47	94
ESCOBAR, RINNA	2	CHAPT 9 SCIENCE EXAM	200	144	72
ESCOBAR, RINNA	3	POP QUIZ	150	141	94
ESCOBAR, RINNA	4	SPELLING TEST	100	100	100
ESCOBAR, RINNA	5	SOCIAL STUDIES	300	293	97
ESCOBAR, RINNA	6	CHAPTER REVIEW	200	193	96
ESCOBAR, RINNA	7	FINAL	500	492	98
GONZALES, ALEX	1	CHAPTER 7 MATH EXAM	50	49	98
GONZALES, ALEX	2	CHAPT 9 SCIENCE EXAM	200	99	49

Figure 7.19: This output is displayed when either of the SELECT statements runs interactively.

HOW THE EXAMPLE WORKS

Two different examples are given that return data from multiple files by joining the records together. The first technique uses the JOIN keyword to combine records from three files. The second technique merely lists the files in the FROM clause, then joins the records using selection criteria in the WHERE clause. Both techniques return identical results. In general, it is more efficient to use the JOIN keyword technique.

The SELECT Clause

The SELECT statement allows you to identify the field or fields that are to be included in the query. This definition is supplied in the SELECT clause of the SELECT statement. Specified field names can be fields residing in the named files or they can be derived values. Derived fields may be created using standard arithmetic operators as well as with numerous built-in functions. The example calculates the percentage correct for each student test by dividing the number correct by the number possible. To set the percentage to a round number, the result is multiplied by 100. The DECIMAL function is then used to set the precision of the number to 3, with zero decimal positions. The derived field is named using the AS keyword. Additionally, all field names can be qualified with the file name to remove any ambiguity in field naming.

The FROM Clause

The SELECT statement allows you to identify the file or files that are the source of the included fields. The example includes qualified file names to select the TESTSTAKEN, TESTS, and LSTUDENTS2 files in the SCHOOLLIB library.

In the first SELECT statement, the files to be used are separated by the INNER JOIN keyword. This specifies that the file name following the JOIN keyword is to be joined to the first file name listed. The criteria to be used to join the records are then supplied using the ON keyword.

When joining two files, the file listed first is treated as the primary, or leftmost, file. The subsequent files listed are the joined files. The JOIN keyword you use defines the relationship between the leftmost file and the joined file that is used to create the join. The JOIN keyword options are as follows.

Join or Inner Join

All records from the leftmost file meeting the join condition with one or more records in the join file are included. Records in the leftmost file that do not have a record meeting the join condition are not included. Records in the join file that do not match the leftmost file are also not included. The ON keyword allows you to specify the condition used to join the records.

Left Join or Left Outer Join

All records from the leftmost file are included in the resulting file regardless of whether there is a record in the join file meeting the join condition. All records that meet the join condition are joined. Records from the leftmost file that do not have a corresponding match with a record in the join file are joined using default or null values to represent the fields in the join file. The ON keyword allows you to specify the condition used to join the records.

Exception Join

Only records from the leftmost file that do not have a record in the join file meeting the join condition are returned. All leftmost file records are joined using default or null values to represent the fields in the join file. The ON keyword allows you to specify the condition used to join the records.

Cross Join

Every record in the leftmost file is joined to every record in the join-to file. The ON keyword is not used for cross-type joins.

The ON Keyword

The conditioning expression that determines the criteria for each join type is specified using the ON keyword.

The second SELECT statement simply lists the three files to be used separated by commas. The criteria used to join the records are then supplied in the WHERE clause.

The WHERE clause allows you to specify selection criteria used to determine the inclusion of records. Because the first SELECT statement uses the JOIN keyword to join the files, the WHERE clause is not used. If selection criteria unrelated to the joining of records were desired, they would be coded under the WHERE clause.

In the second SELECT statement, where you are joining records from more than one file, the join criteria are also specified in the WHERE clause. You may condition the selection based on a comparison of the value of one field to another, a field to a constant value, a field to a function value, or a function value to a constant. SQL provides a number of built-in functions that allow you to avoid having to hard code comparison values. They include numerous date, timestamp, and string-handling functions. The example uses the WHERE clause to join the TESTSTAKEN file to the TESTS file based on the values in the test number fields that appear in both files. It further joins the TESTSTAKEN file to the LSTUDENTS2 file based on the student number fields.

The ORDER BY clause allows you to specify the order in which returned records are to be sorted. Each sort field specified can be sorted in ascending (ASC) or descending (DESC) order. When specified, the sort order must be a file field or derived function listed in the SELECT clause. It can be a field name, an ordinal value corresponding to a field, or the result of a built-in summary function. These functions allow you to sort the resulting data by the average, sum, minimum, or maximum value of a field within a group of records. You can also sort the records by record count for a group. The example sorts the resulting records by student name, and then by test number.

PERFORMING SQL SELECT QUERIES THAT SUMMARIZE DATA

The following two examples employ what is probably the single most powerful SQL statement to query information from a file. The SELECT statement is used to generate a result file to be retrieved in an embedded SQL program or displayed in an interactive SQL session. A rich set of functions allows your query to return simple file records, summary data derived from records, and complex joining of data from multiple files.

The examples use a typical school database, consisting of a STUDENT file, TEACHER file, TEST file, and TEST SCORE file, as shown in Figure 7.20.

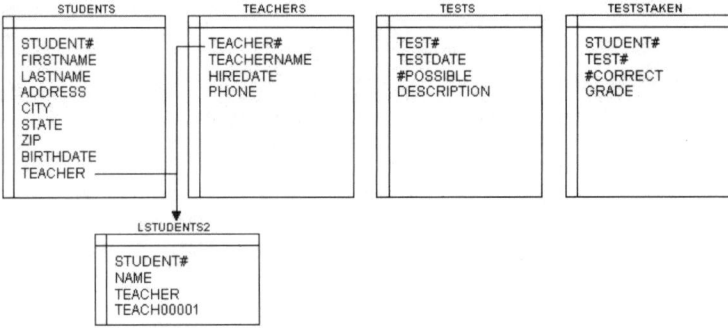

Figure 7.20: This school database is used to demonstrate SQL use.

The SELECT Statement

The SELECT statement is a type of query that retrieves information from a file based on desired criteria and returns the information in the form of a result table. The result table is either processed through embedded SQL in an HLL program or displayed using interactive SQL.

When used with the interactive SQL facility, initiated by the STRSQL command, SELECT is a powerful ad hoc data analysis tool. A single statement allows you to specify the fields to retrieve, the file or files from which they originate, the selection criteria, the sort order, and even summarization options of the information to be queried. These specifications are supplied to the statement using clauses.

The SQL statements used to query data in the school database files are shown in Listing 7.5.

Listing 7.5: Source member *DB013T* uses SQL to query summary data.

```
SELECT TEACHERNAME,
       COUNT(*) AS #_OF_STUDENTS
FROM   SCHOOLLIB/LSTUDENTS2
GROUP BY TEACHERNAME
ORDER BY TEACHERNAME

SELECT NAME,
       DECIMAL(AVG((#CORRECT / #POSSIBLE))*100,3,0) AS AVG_PCT
FROM   SCHOOLLIB/TESTSTAKEN,
       SCHOOLLIB/TESTS,
       SCHOOLLIB/LSTUDENTS2
WHERE TESTSTAKEN.TEST# = TESTS.TEST# AND
      TESTSTAKEN.STUDENT# = LSTUDENTS2.STUDENT#
GROUP BY NAME
ORDER BY AVG_PCT DESC
```

EXAMPLE

Using SQL to Count the Number of Records in a Group

The example, as shown in Figure 7.21, uses the SQL SELECT statement to count the number of student records assigned to each teacher. The returned data includes the teacher name and derived student record count.

```
SELECT TEACHERNAME,
       COUNT(*) AS #_OF_STUDENTS
FROM   SCHOOLLIB/LSTUDENTS2
GROUP BY TEACHERNAME
ORDER BY TEACHERNAME
```

Figure 7.21: This SELECT statement summarizes data from the LSTUDENTS2 file.

WHAT THE EXAMPLE DOES

When executed interactively using the STRSQL command, the example returns a resulting set of records, as shown in Figure 7.22.

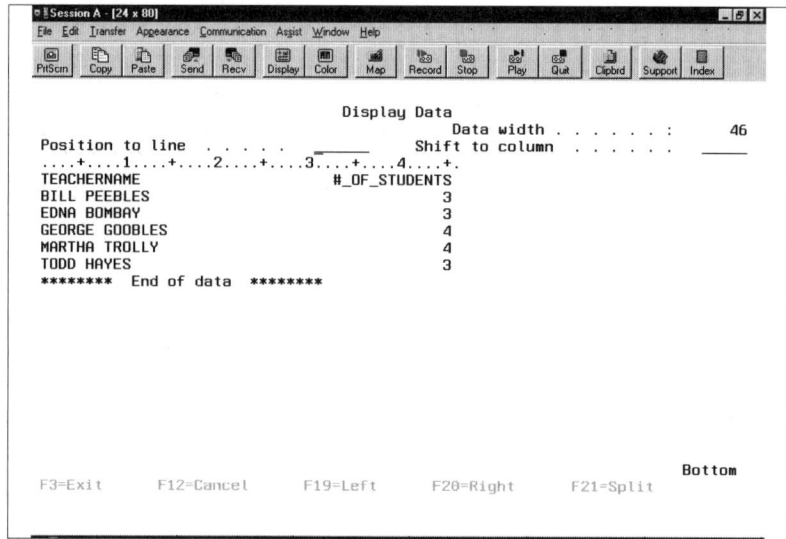

```
Session A - [24 x 80]
File  Edit  Transfer  Appearance  Communication  Assist  Window  Help

PrtScrn  Copy  Paste  Send  Recv  Display  Color  Map  Record  Stop  Play  Quit  Clipbrd  Support  Index

                        Display Data
                                  Data width . . . . . . :     46
     Position to line  . . . . .  _____       Shift to column  . . . . . .  _____
     ....+....1....+....2....+....3....+....4....+.
     TEACHERNAME                   #_OF_STUDENTS
     BILL PEEBLES                        3
     EDNA BOMBAY                         3
     GEORGE GOOBLES                      4
     MARTHA TROLLY                       4
     TODD HAYES                          3
     ********  End of data  ********




                                                          Bottom
     F3=Exit     F12=Cancel     F19=Left     F20=Right     F21=Split
```

Figure 7.22: This output is displayed when the SELECT statement runs interactively.

HOW THE EXAMPLE WORKS

This query uses various SQL clauses to retrieve the specified data.

The SELECT Clause

The SELECT statement allows you to identify the field or fields that are to be included in the query. This definition is supplied in the SELECT clause of the SELECT statement. Field names specified can be fields residing in the named files or they can be derived values. The summary function Count returns a count of records meeting the selection criteria for each group of records. Additionally, field names can be qualified with the file name to remove any ambiguity in field naming.

The FROM Clause

The SELECT statement allows you to identify the file or files that are the source of the included fields. The example includes a qualified file name to select the LSTUDENTS2 file in the SCHOOLLIB library.

The GROUP BY Clause

The GROUP BY clause allows you to define the result file as a summary file. In the clause, you list the fields for which you want to group and summarize records. It is conceptually similar to defining level break fields in RPG. The example uses the GROUP BY clause to group the resulting records by teacher name. Any summary functions used in the SELECT clause will then output totals by teacher name.

The ORDER BY Clause

The ORDER BY clause allows you to specify the order in which returned records are to be sorted. Each specified sort field can be sorted in ascending (ASC) or descending (DESC) order. When specified, the sort order must be a file field or derived function listed in the SELECT clause. It can be a field name, an ordinal value corresponding to a field, or the result of a built-in summary function. These functions allow you to sort the resulting data by the average, sum, minimum, or maximum value of a field within a group of records. You can also sort the records by record count for a group. The example sorts the resulting records by teacher name.

EXAMPLE

Using SQL to Produce Summary Totals for a Group of Records

The example, as shown in Figure 7.23, uses the SQL SELECT statement to summarize data by student name. The statement calculates the average percentage correct for all tests taken by each student. The returned data includes the student name and derived average of all student test scores.

```
SELECT NAME,
       DECIMAL(AVG((#CORRECT / #POSSIBLE))*100,3,0) AS AVG_PCT
FROM   SCHOOLLIB/TESTSTAKEN,
       SCHOOLLIB/TESTS,
       SCHOOLLIB/LSTUDENTS2
WHERE TESTSTAKEN.TEST# = TESTS.TEST# AND
      TESTSTAKEN.STUDENT# = LSTUDENTS2.STUDENT#
GROUP BY NAME
ORDER BY AVG_PCT DESC
```

Figure 7.23: This SELECT statement summarizes data from the student database files.

WHAT THE EXAMPLE DOES

When executed interactively using the STRSQL command, the example returns a resulting set of records, as shown in Figure 7.24.

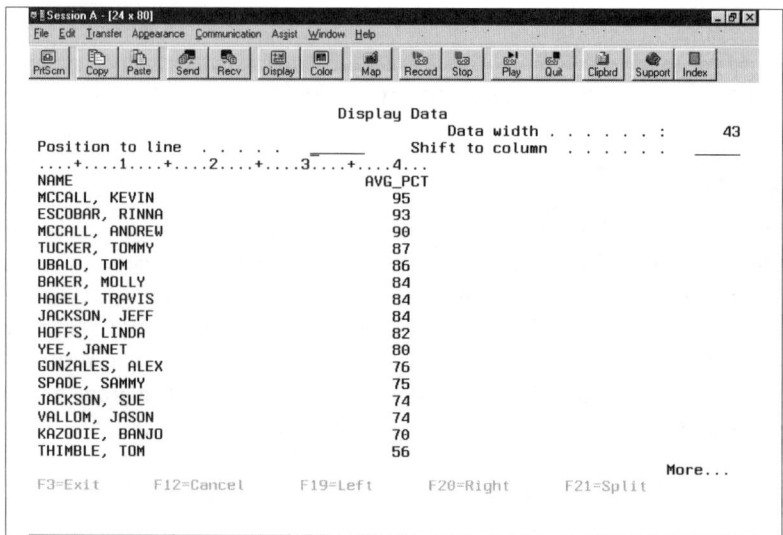

Figure 7.24: This output is displayed when the SELECT statement runs interactively.

HOW THE EXAMPLE WORKS

This query uses various SQL clauses to retrieve the specified data.

The SELECT Clause

The SELECT statement allows you to identify the field or fields that are to be included in the query. This definition is supplied in the SELECT clause of the SELECT statement. Specified field names can be fields residing in the named files or they can be derived values. Derived fields may be created using standard arithmetic operators as well as with numerous built-in functions. The example calculates the percentage correct for each student test by dividing the number correct by the number possible. To set the percentage to a round number, the result is multiplied by 100. The DECIMAL function is then used to set the precision of the number to 3, with zero decimal positions. The summary function Average (AVG) returns the average value of records meeting the selection criteria for each group of records. The derived field is named using the AS keyword. Additionally, field names can be qualified with the file name to remove any ambiguity in field naming.

The FROM Clause

The SELECT statement allows you to identify the file or files that are the source of the included fields. The example includes qualified file names to select the TESTSTAKEN, TESTS, and LSTUDENTS2 files in the SCHOOLLIB library.

The WHERE Clause

The WHERE clause allows you to specify selection criteria used to determine the inclusion of records. In the case where you are joining records from more than one file, the join criteria are also specified in the WHERE clause. You may condition the selection based on a comparison of the value of one field to another, a field to a constant value, a field to a function value, or a function value to a constant. SQL provides a number of built-in functions that allow you to avoid having to hard code comparison values. They include numerous date, timestamp, and string-handling functions. The example uses the Where clause to join the TESTSTAKEN file to the TESTS file based on the values in the test number fields that appear in both files. It further joins the TESTSTAKEN file to the LSTUDENTS2 file based on the student number fields.

The GROUP BY Clause

The GROUP BY clause allows you to define the result file as a summary file. In the clause, you list the fields for which you want to group and summarize records. It is conceptually similar to defining level break fields in RPG. The example uses the GROUP BY clause to group the resulting records by student name. Any summary functions used in the SELECT clause will then output totals by student name.

The ORDER BY Clause

The ORDER BY clause allows you to specify the order in which returned records are to be sorted. Each sort field specified can be sorted in ascending (ASC) or descending (DESC) order. When specified, the sort order must be a file field or derived function listed in the SELECT clause. It can be a field name, an ordinal value corresponding to a field, or the result of a built-in summary function. These functions allow you to sort the resulting data by the average, sum, minimum, or maximum value of a field within a group of records. You can also sort the records by record count for a group. The example sorts the resulting records by average test score in descending order.

INSERTING RECORDS WITH SQL

The following two examples employ the SQL INSERT statement to add records to a file. The Insert statement can add a single record when given field values, and it can perform a mass add to populate a file.

The examples use a typical school database, consisting of a STUDENT file, TEACHER file, TEST file, and TEST SCORE file, as shown in Figure 7.25.

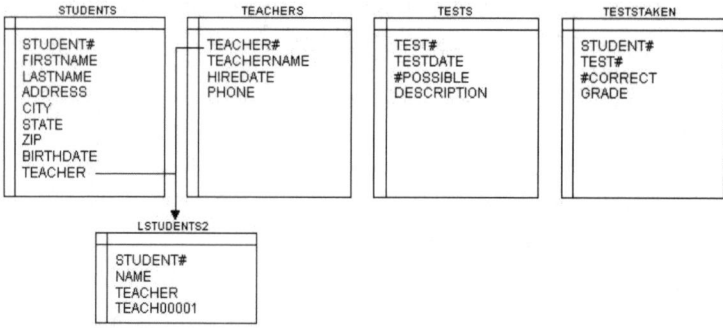

Figure 7.25: This school database is used to demonstrate SQL use.

The INSERT Statement

The INSERT statement adds one or more new records to a file. The statement is either processed through embedded SQL in an HLL program or using interactive SQL.

The most common uses of the INSERT statement allow you to add a single record to a file using field values you supply or add records as the result of a SELECT statement. When using a SELECT statement, called a subquery, the field values derived from one or more other files provide the field values for new records added.

The SQL statements used to add records to the school database files are shown in Listing 7.6.

Listing 7.6: Source member DB014T uses SQL to add new file records.

```
INSERT INTO SCHOOLLIB/TEACHERS (TEACHER#, TEACHERNAME, HIREDATE,
PHONE) VALUES(20, 'GARY HOWLETT', '1985-05-10', '555-1212')
```

**Listing 7.6: Source member *DB014T*
uses SQL to add new file records (continued).**

```
CREATE TABLE SCHOOLLIB/STDNTSCORE
(TEACHER CHAR (30) NOT NULL WITH DEFAULT,
 STUDENT CHAR (35) NOT NULL WITH DEFAULT,
 TEST CHAR (20) NOT NULL WITH DEFAULT,
 POSSIBLE NUMERIC (3, 0) NOT NULL WITH DEFAULT,
 CORRECT NUMERIC (3, 0) NOT NULL WITH DEFAULT)


INSERT INTO SCHOOLLIB/STDNTSCORE
(TEACHER, STUDENT, TEST, POSSIBLE, CORRECT)
 SELECT TEACHERNAME,
        NAME,
        DESCRIPTION,
        #POSSIBLE,
        #CORRECT
 FROM SCHOOLLIB/TESTSTAKEN,
      SCHOOLLIB/TESTS,
      SCHOOLLIB/LSTUDENTS2
 WHERE TESTSTAKEN.TEST# = TESTS.TEST# AND
         TESTSTAKEN.STUDENT# = LSTUDENTS2.STUDENT#
```

EXAMPLE

Using SQL to Add a Single Record to a File

The example shown in Figure 7.26 uses the SQL INSERT statement to add a single new record to the TEACHERS file

```
INSERT INTO SCHOOLLIB/TEACHERS (TEACHER#, TEACHERNAME, HIREDATE,
PHONE) VALUES(20, 'GARY HOWLETT', '1985-05-10', '555-1212')
```

Figure 7.26: This INSERT statement adds a record to the TEACHERS file.

WHAT THE EXAMPLE DOES

When executed interactively, the example adds a new record to the teachers file using the supplied field values.

HOW THE EXAMPLE WORKS

This query uses various SQL clauses to retrieve the specified data.

The INTO Clause

The INSERT statement allows you to identify the target file that will receive one or more new records. Optionally, field names are specified to identify the fields that are to receive supplied values. If field names are not specified, it is assumed that you will supply values for all fields in the file. The example lists each of the fields in the TEACHERS file.

The VALUES Clause

The SELECT statement allows you to identify the file or files that are the source of the included fields. The example includes a qualified file name to select the LSTUDENTS2 file in the SCHOOLLIB library.

The GROUP BY Clause

The VALUES clause allows you to supply values used to populate each of the specified fields for the new record. The number of values specified must equal the number of fields listed in the INSERT statement. The values are supplied based on their ordinal position. That is, the first value listed is associated with the first field name listed and so forth. The example uses the VALUES clause to supply values for each of the field values for the record being added to the file.

EXAMPLE

Using SQL to Add Multiple Records to a File

The example, as shown in Figure 7.27, creates a new file, then uses the SQL INSERT statement to add new records to it based on values queried from other school database files.

WHAT THE EXAMPLE DOES

The file, STDNTSCORE, is loaded with the records appearing in the TESTSTAKEN, TESTS, and LSTUDENTS2 files. Field values are derived from the three files being joined.

```
CREATE TABLE SCHOOLLIB/STDNTSCORE
(TEACHER CHAR (30) NOT NULL WITH DEFAULT,
 STUDENT CHAR (35) NOT NULL WITH DEFAULT,
 TEST CHAR (20) NOT NULL WITH DEFAULT,
 POSSIBLE NUMERIC (3, 0) NOT NULL WITH DEFAULT,
 CORRECT NUMERIC (3, 0) NOT NULL WITH DEFAULT)


INSERT INTO SCHOOLLIB/STDNTSCORE
(TEACHER, STUDENT, TEST, POSSIBLE, CORRECT)
 SELECT TEACHERNAME,
        NAME,
        DESCRIPTION,
        #POSSIBLE,
        #CORRECT
 FROM SCHOOLLIB/TESTSTAKEN,
      SCHOOLLIB/TESTS,
      SCHOOLLIB/LSTUDENTS2
 WHERE TESTSTAKEN.TEST# = TESTS.TEST# AND
       TESTSTAKEN.STUDENT# = LSTUDENTS2.STUDENT#
```

Figure 7.27: This INSERT statement adds records to the STDNTSCORE file.

HOW THE EXAMPLE WORKS

When executed, the CREATE TABLE statement used in the example creates a physical file called STDNTSCORE. Files created using the SQL CREATE TABLE statement are not significantly different than those created using specifications keyed into a source member using DDS.

The COLUMN Definition

The CREATE TABLE statement accepts one or more column definitions to specify the name and attributes of each field. A table column definition allows you to provide a field name, data type, length, default value, null capability, constraint and primary key, or unique key. The first field defined in the example student test score is the teacher name. It is a 30-character field that does not accept null values and has a default value of blanks. The field is defined as follows:

```
TEACHER CHAR (30) NOT NULL WITH DEFAULT,
```

The INTO Clause

The INSERT statement allows you to identify the target file that is to receive one or more new records. Optionally, field names are specified to identify the fields that are to receive supplied values. If field names are not specified, it is assumed that you will supply values for all fields in the file. The example lists each of the fields in the STDNTSCORE file.

The Subquery

In addition to adding a single record to a file, the INSERT statement can allow you to write multiple records in a single statement. The written records are derived as the result of a SELECT query. As you will recall from previous examples in this chapter, the SQL SELECT statement queries a file or files and returns a set of records meeting the desired criteria. While previous examples have focused on using SELECT as a standalone SQL statement, it can also be used as an embedded clause used to supply other statements with source data. The INSERT statement allows you to specify a SELECT query, called a subquery, as the source of new records to add to a target file.

This example uses a SELECT query to gather data from three files, using the data as the source of each record written to the STDNTSCORE file. The field names returned by the SELECT statement, TEACHERNAME, NAME, DESCRIPTION, #POSSIBLE, and #CORRECT, are mapped to the field names specified in the INSERT statement based on their ordinal position. In other words, the TEACHERNAME field maps to the first field on the INSERT statement, NAME to the second, DESCRIPTION to the third, and so forth.

DELETING RECORDS WITH SQL

The following three examples employ the SQL DELETE statement to remove records from a file. The DELETE statement can remove a single record when given selection criteria, and it can perform a mass delete to remove multiple records.

The examples use a typical school database, consisting of a STUDENT file, TEACHER file, TEST file, and TEST SCORE file, as shown in Figure 7.28.

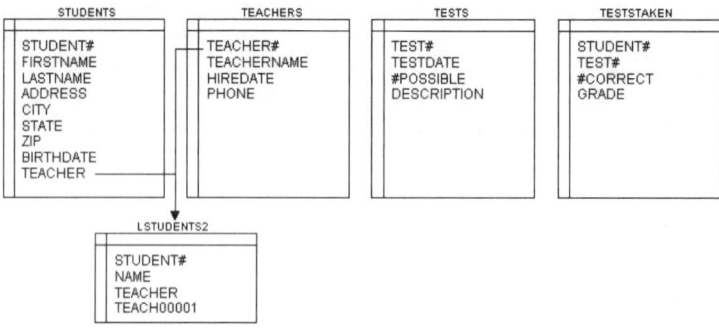

Figure 7.28: Example of typical database.

The DELETE Statement

The DELETE statement removes one or more records from a file. The statement is either processed through embedded SQL in an HLL program or using interactive SQL.

The DELETE statement accepts criteria that allow you to specify the record or records that are to be deleted. Further, the statement allows you to use a SELECT statement, called a subquery, to derive the deletion criteria.

The SQL statements used to delete records from the school database files are shown in Listing 7.7.

Listing 7.7: Source member DB016T uses SQL to delete file records.

```
DELETE FROM SCHOOLLIB/TESTSTAKEN
WHERE GRADE = 'F'


DELETE FROM SCHOOLLIB/TEACHERS


DELETE FROM SCHOOLLIB/TESTSTAKEN F1
WHERE F1.STUDENT# NOT IN
     (SELECT F2.STUDENT# FROM SCHOOLLIB/STUDENTS F2)
```

EXAMPLE

Using SQL to Delete Records Based on a Selection

As shown in Figure 7.29, the example uses the SQL DELETE statement to selectively remove records from a file based upon specific criteria.

```
DELETE FROM SCHOOLLIB/TESTSTAKEN
WHERE GRADE = 'F'
```

Figure 7.29: This DELETE statement removes records from TEST SCORE file.

WHAT THE EXAMPLE DOES

The example deletes all of the records from the TEST SCORE file having a grade of 'F'.

HOW THE EXAMPLE WORKS

This query uses various SQL clauses to retrieve the specified data.

The FROM Clause

The DELETE statement allows you to identify the file from which records are to be deleted. The specified file may be a physical file (table) or a logical file (view).

The WHERE Clause

The WHERE clause allows you to specify the selection criteria used to determine the deletion of records. You may condition the selection based on a comparison of the value of one field to another, a field to a constant value, a field to a function value, or a function value to a constant. SQL provides a number of built-in functions that allow you to avoid having to hard code comparison values. They include numerous date, timestamp, and string-handling functions. The example uses the WHERE clause to delete test score records having a value of 'F' in the grade field.

EXAMPLE

Using SQL to Delete All Records in a File

As shown in Figure 7.30, the example uses the SQL DELETE statement to clear a file.

```
DELETE FROM SCHOOLLIB/TEACHERS
```

Figure 7.30: This DELETE statement removes all records from a TEACHER file.

WHAT THE EXAMPLE DOES

Because the example uses a DELETE statement without conditioning criteria, all records are deleted from the TEACHERS file.

HOW THE EXAMPLE WORKS

This query uses various SQL clauses to retrieve the specified data.

The FROM Clause

The DELETE statement allows you to identify the file from which records are to be deleted. The specified file may be a physical file (table) or a logical file (view).

The WHERE Clause

The WHERE clause allows you to specify selection criteria used to determine the deletion of records. Be careful, however, because when the WHERE clause is omitted, all records are deleted.

EXAMPLE

Using SQL to Delete Records Based on Query Results

The SQL DELETE statement allows you to delete records from a file based upon the query results of another file.

WHAT THE EXAMPLE DOES

The example, as shown in Figure 7.31, uses the SQL DELETE statement to delete records from the TEST file based on the results of a query analyzing the contents of the STUDENT file.

```
DELETE FROM SCHOOLLIB/TESTSTAKEN F1
WHERE F1.STUDENT# NOT IN
    (SELECT F2.STUDENT# FROM SCHOOLLIB/STUDENTS F2)
```

Figure 7.31: This DELETE statement removes records based on subquery results.

HOW THE EXAMPLE WORKS

The DELETE statement allows you to identify the file from which records are to be deleted. The specified file may be a physical file (table) or a logical file (view).

The FROM Clause

The FROM clause allows you supply an alternative name for the qualified file name. When using fields from multiple files, especially where duplicate naming occurs, the field name must be qualified by the name of the file. Correlation naming simplifies this process by allowing you to assign a shorter name to each file. The example assigns the correlation name F1 as an alternative name to the full file name of SCHOOLLIB/ TESTTAKEN and F2 as a correlation name for SCHOOLLIB/STUDENTS.

The WHERE Clause

The WHERE clause allows you to specify selection criteria used to determine the deletion of records. You may condition the selection based on a comparison of the value of one field to another, a field to a constant value, a field to a function value, or a function value to a constant. SQL provides a number of built-in functions that allow you to avoid having to hard code comparison values. They include numerous date, timestamp, and string-handling functions. Field values can also be compared against the results of an embedded subquery. Be careful, however, because when the WHERE clause is omitted, all records are deleted.

The Subquery

In addition to deleting records based on simple field-to-field comparisons, the DELETE statement allows you to delete records based on the results of a selection query. As you will recall from previous examples in this chapter, the SQL SELECT statement queries a file or files and returns a set of records meeting the desired criteria. While previous examples have focused on using SELECT as a standalone SQL statement, it can also be used as an embedded clause used to supply other statements with source data. The DELETE statement allows you to specify a SELECT query, called a subquery, as the source of comparison values to determine whether records are to be deleted. The WHERE clause employs special operators called *predicates* to facilitate comparisons against query results. Predicates allow you to perform comparisons more complex than simple operators, such as equal to, greater than, and less than. Comparing a field against wildcard values, a list of values, and a range of values are examples of what can be accomplished using predicates. All predicates support use of the NOT operator to compare the negative state of the comparison.

The BETWEEN Predicate

The BETWEEN predicate allows you to perform a comparison against a range of values. The following is an example use of the BETWEEN predicate:

```
WHERE BIRTHDATE BETWEEN '1960-01-01' AND '1965-01-01'
```

The EXISTS Predicate

The EXISTS predicate allows you to test for a True or False condition based on a selection subquery. If any records satisfy the selection criteria of the subquery, the EXISTS predicate evaluates to True. If no records are selected by the query, the condition is False. The following is an example use of the EXISTS predicate:

```
WHERE EXISTS (SELECT * FROM STUDENTS WHERE STUDENT# = 00001)
```

The IN Predicate

The IN predicate allows you to perform a comparison against a list of values. The list of values can be hard coded or a set of single-column records returned by a subquery. The following is an example use of the IN predicate using hard-coded values:

```
WHERE STATE IN('WA' 'OR' 'MT' 'ID')
```

In addition to hard-coded values, a subquery can be used to supply a list of comparison values. The following is an example:

```
WHERE STATE IN(SELECT STATECODE FROM STATEFILE)
```

The LIKE Predicate

The LIKE predicate allows you to perform a comparison against a string pattern. The comparison value can be a combination of string characters, wildcard characters, and placeholders used to search for the occurrence of the value within a string. The following is an example use of the LIKE predicate:

```
WHERE NAME LIKE 'MA%'
```

The NULL Predicate

The NULL predicate allows you to test a field for a NULL value. If the field contains a Null value, the comparison evaluates as True. The following is an example use of the NULL predicate:

```
WHERE NAME IS NULL
```

This example uses a SELECT query to gather a list of student numbers from the STUDENTS file. The resulting list is used as the basis of a list search using the In predicate to determine which records are to be deleted. If the student number field of the TEST SCORE file, TESTSTAKEN, is not found in the list of student numbers from the student file, STUDENTS, the record is deleted.

UPDATING RECORDS WITH SQL

The following examples employ the SQL UPDATE statement to change existing records in a file. The UPDATE statement can alter a single record when given selection criteria, and it can perform a mass update to change multiple records.

The examples use a typical school database, consisting of a STUDENT file, TEACHER file, TEST file, and TEST SCORE file, as shown in Figure 7.32.

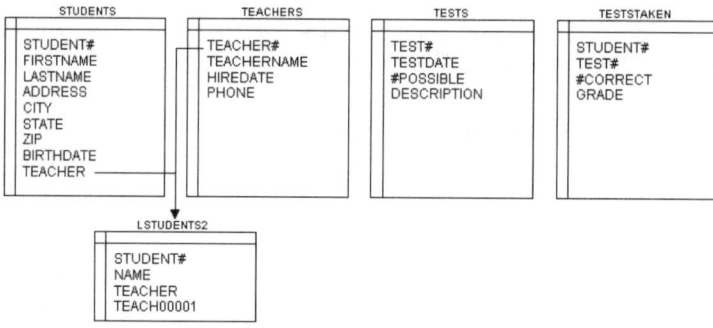

Figure 7.32: This school database is used to demonstrate SQL use.

The UPDATE Statement

The UPDATE statement changes field values for one or more records in a file. The statement is either processed through embedded SQL in an HLL program or using interactive SQL.

The UPDATE statement accepts criteria that allow you to specify the record or records that are to be changed. Further, the statement allows you to use a SELECT statement, called a subquery, to determine whether a record is to be changed. The fields to be changed and the new field values are supplied to the statement using the SET clause.

The SQL statements used to update records in the school database files are shown in Listing 7.8.

Listing 7.8: Source member DB015T uses SQL to update file records.

```
UPDATE SCHOOLLIB/STUDENTS
SET FIRSTNAME = UCASE(FIRSTNAME), LASTNAME = UCASE(LASTNAME)

UPDATE SCHOOLLIB/TESTSTAKEN F1
SET GRADE = 'A'
WHERE EXISTS
(SELECT * FROM SCHOOLLIB/TESTS F2
WHERE F1.TEST# = F2.TEST# AND
      #POSSIBLE   0 AND
      DECIMAL((#CORRECT / #POSSIBLE) *100,3,0) > 89)

UPDATE SCHOOLLIB/TESTSTAKEN F1
SET GRADE = 'B'
WHERE EXISTS
(SELECT * FROM SCHOOLLIB/TESTS F2
WHERE F1.TEST# = F2.TEST# AND
      #POSSIBLE   0 AND
      DECIMAL((#CORRECT / #POSSIBLE) *100,3,0) > 79 AND
      DECIMAL((#CORRECT / #POSSIBLE) *100,3,0) < 90)

UPDATE SCHOOLLIB/TESTSTAKEN F1
SET GRADE = 'C'
WHERE EXISTS
(SELECT * FROM SCHOOLLIB/TESTS F2
WHERE F1.TEST# = F2.TEST# AND
      #POSSIBLE   0 AND
      DECIMAL((#CORRECT / #POSSIBLE) *100,3,0) > 69 AND
      DECIMAL((#CORRECT / #POSSIBLE) *100,3,0) < 80)

UPDATE SCHOOLLIB/TESTSTAKEN F1
SET GRADE = 'D'
WHERE EXISTS
(SELECT * FROM SCHOOLLIB/TESTS F2
WHERE F1.TEST# = F2.TEST# AND
      #POSSIBLE   0 AND
      DECIMAL((#CORRECT / #POSSIBLE) *100,3,0) > 59 AND
      DECIMAL((#CORRECT / #POSSIBLE) *100,3,0) < 70)

UPDATE SCHOOLLIB/TESTSTAKEN F1
SET GRADE = 'F'
WHERE EXISTS
(SELECT * FROM SCHOOLLIB/TESTS F2
WHERE F1.TEST# = F2.TEST# AND
      #POSSIBLE   0 AND
      DECIMAL((#CORRECT / #POSSIBLE) *100,3,0) < 60)
```

EXAMPLE

Using SQL to Change All Records in a File to Uppercase

The SQL UPDATE statement allows the updating of a single record or, as shown in this example, it allows a change to one or more fields in all of the records in a file.

WHAT THE EXAMPLE DOES

The example, as shown in Figure 7.33, uses the SQL UPDATE statement to change the STUDENT NAME fields of all records in the STUDENTS file to uppercase.

```
UPDATE SCHOOLLIB/STUDENTS
SET FIRSTNAME = UCASE(FIRSTNAME), LASTNAME = UCASE(LASTNAME)
```

Figure 7.33: This UPDATE statement changes student name fields to uppercase.

HOW THE EXAMPLE WORKS

This query uses various SQL clauses to retrieve the specified data.

The UPDATE Clause

The UPDATE statement allows you to identify the file that is to be changed. The specified file may be a physical file (table) or a logical file (view).

The SET Clause

The SET clause allows you to specify the fields in the file you want to change. Additionally, you supply the desired field value, which can be a hard-coded value or a derived value resulting from built-in functions. SQL provides a number of built-in functions that allow you to avoid having to hard code values. They include numerous date, timestamp, and string-handling functions. The example employs the uppercase function (UCASE) to capitalize all characters in the specified fields.

The WHERE Clause

The WHERE clause allows you to specify selection criteria used to determine which records are to be changed. Be careful, however, because when the WHERE clause is omitted, all records are changed.

EXAMPLE

Using SQL to Update Records Based on Query Results

The SQL UPDATE statement allows you to change field values in a file based upon the query results of another file.

WHAT THE EXAMPLE DOES

The example, as shown in Figure 7.34, uses the SQL UPDATE statement to calculate student test scores, and then assign and update a letter grade based on the calculated value.

```
UPDATE SCHOOLLIB/TESTSTAKEN F1
SET GRADE = 'A'
WHERE EXISTS
(SELECT * FROM SCHOOLLIB/TESTS F2
WHERE F1.TEST# = F2.TEST# AND
      #POSSIBLE   0 AND
      DECIMAL((#CORRECT / # POSSIBLE) *100,3,0) > 89)
```

Figure 7.34: This UPDATE statement assigns letter grades based on subquery results.

HOW THE EXAMPLE WORKS

The UPDATE statement allows you to identify the file that is to be changed. The specified file may be a physical file (table) or a logical file (view).

Correlation File Naming

The UPDATE clause allows you to supply an alternative name for the qualified file name. When using fields from multiple files, especially where duplicate naming occurs, the field name must be qualified by the name of the file. Correlation naming simplifies this process by allowing you to assign a shorter name to each file. The example assigns the correlation name F1 as an alternative name to the full file name of SCHOOLLIB/TESTTAKEN and F2 as a correlation name for SCHOOLLIB/TESTS.

The SET Clause

The SET clause allows you to specify the fields in the file you want to change. Additionally, you supply the desired field value, which can be a hard-coded value or be a derived value resulting from built-in functions. SQL provides a number of built-in functions that allow you to avoid having to hard code values. They include numerous date, timestamp, and string-handling functions. The example sets the value of the grade field to an 'A' for all records meeting the specified criteria.

The WHERE Clause

The WHERE clause allows you to specify selection criteria used to determine which records are to be changed. You may condition the selection based on a comparison of the value of one field to another, a field to a constant value, a field to a function value, or a function value to a constant. SQL provides a number of built-in functions that allow you to avoid having to hard code comparison values. They include numerous date, timestamp, and string-handling functions. Field values can also be compared against the results of an embedded subquery. Be careful, however, because when the WHERE clause is omitted, all records are changed.

The Subquery

In addition to changing records based on simple field-to-field comparisons, the UPDATE statement allows you to change records based on the results of a selection query. As you will recall from previous examples in this chapter, the SQL SELECT statement queries a file or files and returns a set of records meeting the desired criteria. Previous examples have focused on using SELECT as a standalone SQL statement, but it can also be used as an embedded clause used to supply other statements with source data. The UPDATE statement allows you to specify a SELECT query, called a subquery, as the source of comparison values to determine whether records are to be changed. The WHERE clause employs special operators called predicates to facilitate comparisons against query results. Predicates allow you to perform comparisons more complex than simple operators, such as equal to, greater than, and less than. Comparing a field against wildcard values, a list of values and a range of values are examples of what can be accomplished using predicates. All predicates support use of the NOT operator to compare the negative state of the comparison.

The BETWEEN Predicate

The BETWEEN predicate allows you to perform a comparison against a range of values. The following is an example use of the BETWEEN predicate:

```
WHERE BIRTHDATE BETWEEN '1960-01-01' AND '1965-01-01'
```

The EXISTS Predicate

The EXISTS predicate allows you to test for a True or False condition based on a selection subquery. If any records satisfy the selection criteria of the subquery, the EXISTS predicate evaluates to True. If no records are selected by the query, the condition is False. The following is an example use of the EXISTS predicate:

```
WHERE EXISTS (SELECT * FROM STUDENTS WHERE STUDENT# = 00001)
```

The IN Predicate

The IN predicate allows you to perform a comparison against a list of values. The list of values can be hard coded or a set of single-column records returned by a subquery. The following is an example use of the IN predicate using hard-coded values:

```
WHERE STATE IN('WA' 'OR' 'MT' 'ID')
```

In addition to hard-coded values, a subquery can be used to supply a list of comparison values. The following is an example:

```
WHERE STATE IN(SELECT STATECODE FROM STATEFILE)
```

The LIKE Predicate

The LIKE predicate allows you to perform a comparison against a string pattern. The comparison value can be a combination of string characters, wildcard characters, and placeholders used to search for the occurrence of the value within a string. The following is an example use of the LIKE predicate:

```
WHERE NAME LIKE 'MA%'
```

The NULL Predicate

The NULL predicate allows you to test a field for a NULL value. If the field contains a NULL value, the comparison evaluates as True. The following is an example use of the NULL predicate:

```
WHERE NAME IS NULL
```

This example uses a complex SELECT query to determine which of the records in the TEST file should be assigned a grade of 'A'. The numbers needed to calculate the student test scores are retrieved from the TESTS file. The subquery SELECT statement's WHERE clause calculates each test score, including only those higher than 89 percent. The EXISTS predicate specifies that if the record passes the subquery criteria, the grade is changed to an 'A'.

EMBEDDED SQL

To this point, all of the SQL examples presented have centered on using SQL as a standalone database tool. Another powerful implementation of SQL allows you to integrate SQL into your traditional RPG software applications. If you have purchased and installed the licensed product DB2/400 Query Manager and SQL Development Kit, you can embed and execute SQL statements within an RPG or other high-level language program.

Native database access techniques such as chaining and reading in an RPG program are generally more efficient than SQL for single record-level processing. The advantages offered by SQL are realized when you are processing sets of records or when grouping functions are required.

When executing embedded SQL statements, there are two implementations from which to choose: static statements and dynamic statements.

Static Embedded SQL

A static SQL statement is one that is defined when the program is compiled. All of the files and fields used are established and resolved before the program executes. The statements coded in the program undergo an SQL precompilation process that checks the syntax and prepares the statements for execution. Static SQL statements are generally simpler to code and maintain than their dynamic counterparts.

Dynamic Embedded SQL

A dynamic SQL statement is one that is defined and created while the program executes. Unlike static statements, files and fields are not established and resolved before the program executes. Because statements are not prepared by the precompiler, greater responsibility falls in the lap of the programmer.

General Embedded Syntax

Embedded SQL statements in an RPG program are coded in the Calculation specifications. They can be coded within the main line logic, within a subroutine, or within a procedure. Each and every individual SQL statement coded must be preceded by the keywords EXEC and SQL and followed by the keywords END and EXEC.

EXAMPLE

Using Static Embedded SQL to Select and Process Records

The example uses SQL embedded in an RPG module to select and process records.

WHAT THE EXAMPLE DOES

The example, as shown in Listing 7.9, uses the SQL SELECT statement within an ILE RPG program to retrieve records from a TEACHER file. Records are read and processed one-at-a time and printed on a report.

Listing 7.9: ILE RPG member DB017R uses static embedded SQL.

```
FQPRINT    O    F  132        Printer OFLIND(*InOF)
DTeach#         S             3S 0
DTeachName      S             30
D@Title1        C                   'Teacher File Rpt'
D@Head1         C                   'Teacher #'
D@Head2         C                   'Teacher Name'
 *
C/Exec SQL
C+ DECLARE TEACHERCSR CURSOR FOR SELECT Teacher#, TeacherName
C+   FROM SCHOOLLIB/TEACHERS ORDER BY Teacher#
C/End-Exec
 *
C/Exec SQL
C+ OPEN TEACHERCSR
C/End-Exec
 *
C                   Except    Header1
 *
C                   DoW       SQLCOD = 0
C/Exec SQL
C+ FETCH NEXT FROM TEACHERCSR INTO :Teach#, :TeachName
C/End-Exec
C                   If        SQLCOD = 0
```

Listing 7.9: ILE RPG member DB017R
uses static embedded SQL (continued).

```
C                       Except    Detail1
C                       Endif
C                       Enddo
 *
C/Exec SQL
C+      CLOSE TeacherCSR
C/End-Exec
 *
C                       Return
OQprint     E                 Header1        2 01
O                             @Title1              32
O                                                  70 'Page:'
O                             Page1          z     76
O           E                 Header1      1 1
O                             @Head1               10
O                             @Head2               29
O           E                 Detail1      1
O                             Teach#               10
O                             TeachName            47
```

HOW THE EXAMPLE WORKS

When working with embedded SQL, an important mechanism to understand is the SQL cursor. As you will recall from previous examples, an SQL SELECT statement is a powerful tool for querying data from files and retrieving the resulting records. A cursor provides a way for your program to access the records that have been retrieved as a result of an SQL SELECT statement. The cursor maintains the program's positioning within the resulting set of records. By manipulating the cursor position, you determine which record in the set is the current record. Embedded SQL currently supports two types of cursors: serial cursors and scrollable cursors. The type of cursor you define determines the capabilities of movement and positioning within the cursor.

Serial Cursors

Serial cursors allow your program forward-looking access only. That is, your program may advance the cursor forward to the next record but can never move backward. Once the end of the records has been reached, the only way to re-read a record is to close and then reopen the cursor.

Scrollable Cursors

Scrollable cursors allow your program to position the cursor with a great deal of flexibility. Your program may read records multiple times, moving backward or forward at will.

Because of the performance overhead associated with scrollable cursors, they should be used only when your program needs the flexibility they offer.

Cursor-Related Statements

Four SQL statements are commonly used in conjunction with cursors.

The DECLARE Cursor Statement

To use a cursor in an embedded SQL program, it must first be declared. The DECLARE CURSOR statement defines and names the cursor. Additionally, it includes the SELECT statement that specifies the records to be retrieved.

The OPEN Statement

The OPEN statement opens a cursor, allowing your program to access it. When a cursor is opened, the SELECT statement specified on the DECLARE CURSOR is executed.

The FETCH Statement

The FETCH statement is used to retrieve one or more records from the cursor. Additionally, it determines the current cursor position relative to the set of records it references. The positioning capability of the FETCH statement is determined by the type of cursor that has been declared.

The CLOSE Statement

The CLOSE statement explicitly closes an open cursor. This is necessary when you are using a serial cursor and you want to re-read records. Depending on the value of the Close SQL Cursor (CLOSQLCSR) parameter supplied to the SQL precompile step, the system may automatically close your cursors for you.

The RPG Example Program

The example program begins by declaring the SQL cursor. The DECLARE CURSOR statement, as shown in Figure 7.35, defines a cursor named TEACHERCSR. The cursor performs an SQL SELECT statement that retrieves the teacher number and teacher name fields from the SCHOOLLIB/TEACHERS file. Because the statement does not specify a WHERE clause, all records in the file are returned. Records are returned sorted by teacher number, as specified by the ORDER BY clause. For more detailed information about the SELECT statement, see the examples presented earlier in this chapter.

It's important to understand that the field names listed within the SELECT statement are not referenced in the program. The names are supplied only to specify fields you want to return from the file. The actual data isn't supplied to the program through these field names; rather, they're assigned to the field names you supply on the FETCH statement.

```
C/Exec SQL
C+ DECLARE TEACHERCSR CURSOR FOR SELECT Teacher#, TeacherName
C+   FROM SCHOOLLIB/TEACHERS ORDER BY Teacher#
C/End-Exec
```

Figure 7.35: The DECLARE CURSOR statement defines the query SELECT cursor TEACHERCSR.

After the cursor has been declared, it is opened using the OPEN statement. The OPEN statement, as shown in Figure 7.36, opens the TEACHERCSR cursor. When opened, the SQL SELECT statement defined by the DECLARE CURSOR executes. The resulting set of records is returned to the cursor.

```
C/Exec SQL
C+ OPEN TEACHERCSR
C/End-Exec
```

Figure 7.36: The OPEN statement opens the TEACHERCSR cursor and executes the SELECT statement.

After the cursor is opened, the program uses a Do While control structure to fetch records from the cursor until an error condition, such as end-of-data, is encountered. Figure 7.37 shows the control structure logic. When the cursor is opened, the positioning of the cursor is automatically set to before the first record in the record set. The SQL FETCH statement, using the NEXT keyword, positions the current record of the cursor to the next record. The fields named in the cursor declare are returned to your program through host variables specified on the FETCH statement. The host variables used to receive values are specified by the INTO clause. These fields, always preceded by a colon, must be previously defined in the program. Their attributes and position within the INTO clause must match those of the fields listed in the DECLARE CURSOR statement.

As you will notice, the field SQLCOD has not been defined anywhere in the program, yet its value controls the logic of the program. The field SQLCOD is one of several fields that are automatically included in your program by the SQL precompiler. The SQLCOD field is used by the system to provide return codes to you for performed SQL operations. If the value is zero, there is not an error condition. For a complete list of SQL return codes, please refer to the manual *DB2 for AS/400 SQL Programming* (SC41-5611-02).

```
C                      DoW        SQLCOD = 0
C/Exec SQL
C+ FETCH NEXT FROM TEACHERCSR INTO :Teach#, :TeachName
C/End-Exec
C                      If         SQLCOD = 0
C                      Except     Detail1
C                      Endif
C                      Enddo
```

Figure 7.37: The DO WHILE construct fetches records until an error is encountered.

When the FETCH statement successfully returns a record, the program performs an EXCEPT op code to print the line of detail on a report.

When all records have been processed, the program closes the TEACHERCSR cursor before ending. This step is usually not required, but it is good practice in case the CLOSE SQL CURSOR option specified when the precompile is performed is not set to the desired or expected value.

EXAMPLE

Using Static SQL to Flexibly Select and Process Records

The example, as shown in Listing 7.10, uses a complex SQL SELECT statement within an ILE RPG program to retrieve records joined from three different files from a school database. Records are read, processed one at a time, and printed on a report.

WHAT THE EXAMPLE DOES

When the program is called, it receives a parameter that determines which student test grade is to be printed on a report. For example, passing a parameter of 'A' causes only student tests with a grade of 'A' to print. The coding technique used differs slightly from the previous example, isolating all embedded SQL statements into subroutines. This technique improves the readability of the program mainline logic.

Listing 7.10: ILE RPG member *DB018R* uses static embedded SQL.

```
FQPRINT    O   F  132         Printer OFLIND(*InOF)
DStudentNm     S              34
DTestDesc      S              20
DTestPct       S               3S 0
```

⟶

Listing 7.10: ILE RPG member DB018R uses static embedded SQL (continued).

```
DGradeIn          S              1
D@Head1           C                       'Student'
D@Head2           C                       'Test'
D@Head3           C                       'Pct Correct'
 *
C      *Entry      PList
C                  Parm                    GradeIn
 *
C                  Exsr      DeclareCsr
C                  Exsr      OpenCsr
 *
C                  Except    Header1
 *
C                  DoW       SQLCOD = 0
C                  Exsr      FetchRcd
 *
C                  If        SQLCOD = 0
C                  Except    Detail1
C                  Endif
C                  Enddo
 *
C                  Exsr      CloseCsr
 *
C                  Return
 *-----------------------------------------------------------
 *  DeclareCsr - Declare an SQL Select cursor
 *-----------------------------------------------------------
C      DeclareCsr  Begsr
 *
C/Exec SQL
C+ DECLARE SCORECSR CURSOR FOR
C+    SELECT    NAME,
C+              DESCRIPTION,
C+              DECIMAL((#CORRECT / #POSSIBLE) * 100, 3, 0) AS PCT
C+    FROM      TESTSTAKEN,
C+              TESTS,
C+              LSTUDENTS2
C+    WHERE     TESTSTAKEN.TEST# = TESTS.TEST# And
C+              TESTSTAKEN.STUDENT# = LSTUDENTS2.STUDENT# And
C+              GRADE = :GradeIn
C+    ORDER BY PCT DESC,
C+              NAME
C/End-Exec
 *
C                  Endsr
 *-----------------------------------------------------------
 *  OpenCsr - Open SQL Cursor
 *-----------------------------------------------------------
```

**Listing 7.10: ILE RPG member DB018R
uses static embedded SQL (continued).**

```
C       OpenCsr      Begsr
 *
C/Exec SQL
C+ OPEN SCORECSR
C/End-Exec
 *
C                    Endsr
 *_____
 *  FetchRcd - Get next record from Cursor
 *_____
C       FetchRcd     Begsr
 *
C/Exec SQL
C+ FETCH NEXT FROM SCORECSR INTO :StudentNm, :TestDesc, :TestPct
C/End-Exec
 *
C                    Endsr
 *_____
 *  CloseCsr - Close SQL Cursor
 *_____
C       CloseCsr     Begsr
 *
C/Exec SQL
C+    CLOSE SCORECSR
C/End-Exec
 *
C                    Endsr
 *_____
OQprint    E          Header1       2 01
O                                           50 'Student Tests - Grade'
O                      GradeIn               52
O                                           70 'Page:'
O                      Page1         z       76
O          E          Header1      1  1
O                      @Head1                10
O                      @Head2                29
O                      @Head3                66
O          E          Detail1       1
O                      StudentNm             34
O                      TestDesc              45
O                      TestPct       z       62
```

HOW THE EXAMPLE WORKS

The example uses the same set of files representing a school database as many previous examples, as shown in Figure 7.38.

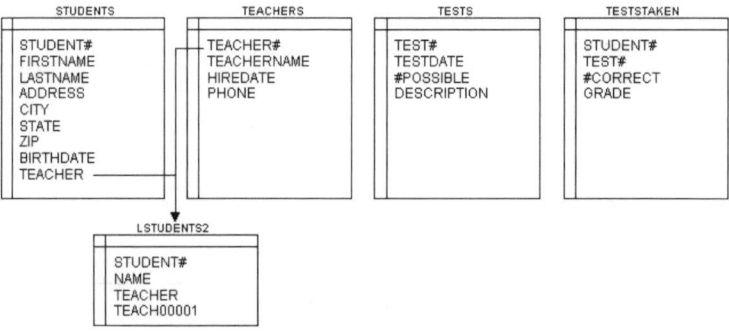

Figure 7.38: This school database is used to demonstrate embedded SQL functions.

The SQL Cursor

When working with embedded SQL, an important mechanism to understand is the SQL cursor. As you will recall from previous examples, an SQL SELECT statement is a powerful tool for querying data from files and retrieving the resulting records. A cursor provides a way for your program to access the records that have been retrieved as a result of an SQL SELECT statement. The cursor maintains the program's positioning within the resulting set of records. By manipulating the cursor position, you determine which record in the set is the current record. Embedded SQL currently supports two types of cursors: serial cursors and scrollable cursors. The type of cursor you define determines the capabilities of movement and positioning within the cursor.

Serial Cursors

Serial cursors allow your program forward-looking access only. That is, your program may advance the cursor forward to the next record, but can never move backward. Once the end of the records has been reached, the only way to re-read a record is to close and then reopen the cursor.

Scrollable Cursors

Scrollable cursors allow your program to position the cursor with a great deal of flexibility. Your program may read records multiple times, moving backward or forward at will. Because of the performance overhead associated with scrollable cursors, they should be used only when your program needs the flexibility they offer.

Cursor-Related Statements

Four SQL statements are commonly used in conjunction with cursors.

The DECLARE CURSOR Statement

To use a cursor in an embedded SQL program, it must first be declared. The DECLARE CURSOR statement defines and names the cursor. Additionally, it includes the SELECT statement that specifies the records to be retrieved.

The OPEN Statement

The OPEN statement opens a cursor, allowing your program to access it. When a cursor is opened, the SELECT statement specified on the DECLARE CURSOR statement is executed.

The FETCH Statement

The FETCH statement is used to retrieve one or more records from the cursor. Additionally, it determines the current cursor position relative to the set of records it references. The positioning capability of the FETCH statement is determined by the type of cursor that has been declared.

The CLOSE Statement

The CLOSE statement explicitly closes an open cursor. This is necessary when you are using a serial cursor and want to re-read records. Depending on the value of the Close SQL Cursor (CLOSQLCSR) parameter supplied to the SQL precompile step, the system may automatically close your cursors for you.

The RPG Example Program

The example program begins by declaring the SQL cursor. Declaration of the cursor is coded in the subroutine DECLARECSR. The DECLARE CURSOR statement, as shown in Figure 7.39, defines a cursor named SCORECSR. The cursor performs an SQL SELECT statement that retrieves the student name and test description fields from the files LSTUDENTS2 and TESTS. Additionally, the test percentage correct is calculated by dividing the number possible by the number correct. The built-in decimal function is used to set the precision of the calculation to a three-digit zoned numeric. The AS clause assigns a field name, PCT, to the calculated result.

The statement specifies a WHERE clause to select only tests from the TESTSTAKEN file having a letter grade that matches the value passed to the program as an input parameter in the GRADEIN field. The WHERE clause selects records where the value of the grade field in the TEST file matches the value of the host variable. Host variable field names are always preceded by a colon.

```
C       DeclareCsr    Begsr
 *
C/Exec SQL
C+ DECLARE SCORECSR CURSOR FOR
C+      SELECT    NAME,
C+                DESCRIPTION,
C+                DECIMAL((#CORRECT / #POSSIBLE) * 100, 3, 0) AS PCT
C+      FROM      TESTSTAKEN,
C+                TESTS,
C+                LSTUDENTS2
C+      WHERE     TESTSTAKEN.TEST# = TESTS.TEST# And
C+                TESTSTAKEN.STUDENT# = LSTUDENTS2.STUDENT# And
C+                GRADE = :GradeIn
C+      ORDER BY PCT DESC,
C+                NAME
C/End-Exec
 *
C                    Endsr
```

Figure 7.39: The DECLARE CURSOR statement defines the query SELECT cursor SCORECSR.

Additionally, the WHERE clause performs comparisons that join records from the three files. Records are returned sorted by the derived percentage in descending order, followed by the student name, as specified by the ORDER BY clause. For more detailed information about the SELECT statement, see the examples presented earlier in this chapter.

It is important to understand that the field names listed within the SELECT statement are not referenced in the program. The names are supplied only to specify the fields you want to return from the file. The actual data is not supplied to the program through these field names; rather, they are assigned to the field names you supply on the FETCH statement.

After the cursor has been declared, it is opened using the OPEN statement. The OPEN statement, as shown in Figure 7.40, opens the cursor SCORECSR. When opened, the SQL SELECT statement defined by the DECLARE CURSOR executes. The resulting set of records is returned to the cursor.

```
C       OpenCsr       Begsr
 *
C/Exec SQL
C+ OPEN SCORECSR
C/End-Exec
 *
C                    Endsr
```

Figure 7.40: The OPEN statement opens the SCORECSR cursor and executes the SELECT statement.

After the cursor is opened, the program uses a Do While control structure to fetch records from the cursor until an error condition, such as end-of-data, is encountered. Figure 7.41 shows the control structure logic. When the cursor is opened, the positioning of the cursor is automatically set to before the first record in the record set. The subroutine, FETCHRCD, is shown in Figure 7.42. The SQL FETCH statement, using the NEXT keyword, positions the current record of the cursor to the next record. The fields named in the cursor declare are returned to your program through host variables specified on the FETCH statement. The host variables used to receive values are specified by the INTO clause. These fields, always preceded by a colon, must be previously defined in the program. Their attributes and position within the INTO clause must match those of the fields listed in the DECLARE CURSOR statement.

As you will notice, the field SQLCOD has not been defined anywhere in the program, yet its value controls the logic of the program. The field SQLCOD is one of several fields that are automatically included in your program by the SQL precompiler. The SQLCOD field is used by the system to provide return codes to you for the performed SQL operations. If the value is zero, there is not an error condition.

```
C                      DoW        SQLCOD = 0
C                      Exsr       FetchRcd
  *
C                      If         SQLCOD = 0
C                      Except     Detail1
C                      Endif
C                      Enddo
```

Figure 7.41: The Do While construct fetches records until an error is encountered.

```
C     FetchRcd       Begsr
  *
C/Exec SQL
C+ FETCH NEXT FROM SCORECSR INTO :StudentNm, :TestDesc, :TestPct
C/End-Exec
  *
C                     Endsr
```

Figure 7.42: The FETCH statement retrieves fields from the cursor and loads them into host fields.

When the FETCH statement successfully returns a record, the program performs an EX-CEPT op code to print the line of detail on a report. When all records have been processed, the program closes the SCORECSR cursor before ending. This step is usually not required, but it is good practice to use it in case the Close SQL Cursor option specified when the precompile is performed is not set to the desired or expected value.

Appendix

Software Loading Instructions

For your convenience, the source code presented in this book may be uploaded to your AS/400 from the accompanying CD-ROM. To install the code, you will need a personal computer attached to your AS/400 and file-transfer software such as Client Access.

If you prefer not to install the source members to your AS/400, each member is stored as a text file that can be copied and pasted from your Windows-based emulator. Each text file's extension identifies the type of AS/400 source member it represents.

Step-By-Step Instructions

1. Sign on to your AS/400 and, if one does not already exist, create a library called MCHANDBOOK:

```
CRTLIB LIB(MCHANDBOOK) TEXT('THE PROGRAMMER''S HANDBOOK')
```

2. If one does not already exist, create a source file called SOURCE in the MCHANDBOOK library with a record length of 112 bytes:

```
CRTSRCPF FILE(MCHANDBOOK/SOURCE) RCDLEN(112) TEXT('EXAMPLE
SOURCE')
```

3. Using a file-transfer program, such as Client Access File Transfer or FTP, transfer the file HNDBOOK2 from the CD to the SOURCE file in the MCHANDBOOK library:

```
From:   D:\HNDBOOK2    (Where D is the letter of your CD drive)
To:     MCHANDBOOK/SOURCE(HNDBOOK2)
```

4. Again using a file-transfer program such as Client Access File Transfer, transfer the files INST2C and INST2R from the CD to the SOURCE file in the MCHANDBOOK library:

```
From:   D:\INST2C    (Where D is the letter of your CD drive)
To:     MCHANDBOOK/SOURCE(INST2C)
```

```
From:   D:\INST2R    (Where D is the letter of your CD drive)
To:     MCHANDBOOK/SOURCE(INST2R)
```

5. Add the MCHANDBOOK library to your library list:

```
ADDLIBLE MCHANDBOOK
```

6. Compile the installation programs in the MCHANDBOOK library:

```
CRTCLPGM PGM(MCHANDBOOK/INST2C) SRCFILE(MCHANDBOOK/SOURCE)
CRTRPGPGM PGM(MCHANDBOOK/INST2R) SRCFILE(MCHANDBOOK/SOURCE)
```

7. Run the extract program INST2C. This will install the example source members into the SOURCE file:

```
CALL MCHANDBOOK/INST2C
```

Finally, if you have any comments about this book, I'd love to hear from you. My email address is markmccall@sprintmail.com.

Chapter 1 — Modular Coding Techniques

MOD001R.RPG	/COPY Compiler Directive
MOD002R.RPG	/COPY Copybook #1
MOD003R.RPG	/COPY Copybook #2
MOD004R.RPG	Internal Subroutine
MOD005R.RPG	Dynamic Subprogram Caller
MOD006R.RPG	Dynamic Subprogram
MOD007R.RPG	Subprocedure
MOD008R.RPG	Service Program Caller
MOD009R.RPG	Service Program Procedure

Chapter 2 — Built-In Functions

BIF001R.RPG	%ABS Function
BIF002R.RPG	%ADDR Function
BIF003R.RPG	%CHAR Function
BIF004R.RPG	%DEC and %DECH Functions
BIF005R.RPG	%DECPOS Function
BIF006R.RPG	%DIV and %REM Functions
BIF007R.RPG	%EDITC, %EDITFLT, and %EDITW Functions
BIF008R.RPG	%ELEM Function
BIF009R.RPG	%EOF Function
BIF010R.RPG	%EQUAL Function
BIF011R.RPG	%ERROR and %STATUS Functions
BIF012R.RPG	%FOUND Function
BIF013R.RPG	%INT and %INTH Functions
BIF014R.RPG	%LEN and %SIZE Functions

Chapter 3 — Exit Programs

Chapter 4 — Application Programming Interfaces

API006R.RPG	QUSLSPL API Example
API007R.RPG	CEERAN0 API Example
API008R.RPG	CEEDAYS and CEEDATE API Example

Chapter 5 — Database Constraints

DB001C.CL	Add a Check Constraint #1
DB002C.CL	Add a Check Constraint #2
DB003C.CL	Add a Check Constraint #3
DB004C.CL	Add a Check Constraint #4
DB005C.CL	Add a Referential Integrity Constraint

Chapter 6 — Database Triggers

DB006C.CL	Add a Trigger to a File #1
DB006R.RPG	Auto-Generate a Key Value Trigger Program
DB007C.CL	Add a Trigger to a File #2
DB007R.RPG	Security Monitor Trigger Program
DB008C.CL	Add a Trigger to a File #3
DB008R.RPG	Data Validation Trigger Program

Chapter 7 — Using SQL

DB009T.SQL	Create Library and Physical File
DB010T.SQL	Create Join Logical View
DB011T.SQL	Single File Select Queries
DB012T.SQL	Multiple File Select Queries
DB013T.SQL	Summary Queries
DB014T.SQL	Insert Queries
DB015T.SQL	Update Queries
DB016T.SQL	Delete Queries
DB017R.RPG	Embedded SQL #1
DB018R.RPG	Embedded SQL #2

INDEX

Note: Boldface numbers indicate illustrations.

Note: Boldface numbers indicate illustrations.

Getting Down to e-business with AS/400

by Bob Cancilla

Gain an understanding of the issues, concepts, and technologies necessary to implement an AS/400-based e-business solution with the help of this new book from Bob Cancilla. From planning for e-business to selecting an ISP, you'll learn through examples from those companies that have successfully deployed mission-critical e-business applications with the IBM AS/400. You'll also learn about the many products that work together to make the AS/400 a Web server, how to develop a project plan, and how to design and build an e-business Web site. While many other books touch on individual Internet-related technologies, *Getting Down to e-business with AS/400* puts all the pieces together! 448 pages. Level: Novice, Intermediate, and Advanced.

BOOK 5014 ....$89
ISBN 1-58347-010-7

e-RPG: Building AS/400 Web applications with RPG

by Bradley V. Stone

Learn to develop fully functional e-business solutions using nothing more than your existing knowledge of RPG and the Web facilities already included in OS/400. All you need is *e-RPG: Building AS/400 Web applications with RPG*, a revolutionary new book from Midrange Computing.

With *e-RPG*, you'll discover how to program RPG to drive the Web applications you want to develop...all without having to learn Java, Visual Basic, Perl, or even Visual RPG! When you have completed this book, you will be able to build Web applications using RPG, create Web pages in HTML, enhance the interactivity of Web pages with JavaScript (not to be confused with the Java programming language), set up the AS/400 as an HTTP server, use RPG to create Common Gateway Interface (CGI) programs, write an RPG program to output dynamic HTML to a browser, and more.

e-RPG: Building AS/400 Web applications with RPG comes with a CD-ROM that contains full source for examples given in the book, including binder language source for service programs, /COPY prototype source, DDS for physical file, logical file and external data structure, HTML source, HTML images, module source, and complete RPG source for all e-RPG programs. The book and CD-ROM give you everything you need to use your knowledge of RPG and the power of the AS/400 to develop robust e-business solutions. 368 pages. Level: Novice to Intermediate.

BOOK 5015 ....$99
ISBN 1-58347-008-5

AS/400 Primer—Third Edition

by Ernie Malaga, Doug Pence, and Ron Hawkins

Increase understanding of the AS/400 and boost productivity with *AS/400 Primer—Third Edition*, the new book from Midrange Computing. A must for every AS/400 professional, this comprehensive, newly revised, 30-chapter volume is perfect for novice and intermediate programmers as well as for system administrators and operators. In simple, straightforward style, the authors not only explain core AS/400 concepts but also show you—step-by-step—how to perform 30 essential AS/400 functions, including installation, troubleshooting, administration, operations, programming, and 25 other tasks!

Updated by Doug Pence and Ron Hawkins, this third edition of the *Primer* contains page after page of enhanced information covering programming in RPG IV, new system values, ILE concepts, important new system security information, running the AS/400 as an Internet server, and much more! You'll definitely find *AS/400 Primer—Third Edition* to be a learning tool and valuable reference for years to come. 550 pages. Level: Novice, Intermediate, and Advanced.

BOOK 5012 ....$99
ISBN 1-883884-59-4

AS/400 TCP/IP Handbook

TCP/IP Networking Concepts, Configurations, Services, and Programming for the AS/400 Server Environment

by Chris Peters

Understand the protocol that is the heart of Internet and intranet communications and position youself to take full advantage of the AS/400's potential with *AS/400 TCP/IP Handbook*.

This is the most complete TCP/IP book on the market. It has the concepts and background material that traditional AS/400 professionals need as they start their Internet development journey. This handbook details all of the significant TCP/IP utilities available on the AS/400—providing all the information you need for your development in one source. Plus, Sockets technology is explained in detail through the use of a full-feature, production-quality TCP/IP Sockets server program with ILE RPG. This book is truly the single source for AS/400 TCP/IP programming information. 400 pages. Level: Novice, Intermediate, and Advanced.

❑ BOOK 5008 .... $99
ISBN 1-58347-005-0

The Modern RPG IV Language—Second Edition

by Robert Cozzi, Jr.

Now you can exploit all the enhanced functionality that IBM has built into RPG IV. The long awaited update to Cozzi's masterpiece on RPG IV shows how to take full advantage of the powerful features and functions added to the language since 1996. If you program in RPG IV, this book will be indispensable to your productivity and your career.

The Modern RPG IV Language—Second Edition takes you through the language from the very foundations to the most advanced techniques. At the core of this book are the chapters on built-in functions (BIFs) and op codes. Cozzi details each BIF and provides valuable information on more than 30 op codes and provides a syntax table that gives you the information you need at a glance, plus an explanation of the hows and whys of usage. And this isn't just a book on theory and rules; Cozzi includes over 100 charts and tables that show you how the rules apply. He also includes samples of the functions and operations in real-life code—more than 350 individual examples! 592 pages. Level: Novice, Intermediate, and Advanced.

❏ BOOK C5005 ....$99
ISBN 1-58347-002-6

The Modern RPG [III] Language with Structured Programming—Fourth Edition

by Robert Cozzi, Jr.

Whether you're a new programmer or an old hand, this best-selling book will help you write the kind of code that sets you apart from the crowd—powerful RPG code that's easy to use, enhance, and expand. You'll increase your professional value as you apply the principles and ready-to-use solutions that have made *The Modern RPG [III] Language with Structured Programming* the world's most popular RPG III book.

You'll learn about structured programming concepts—from design to implementation—so that you can easily write, debug, and maintain truly modern modular programs. Cozzi explains how to code and implement traditional RPG database file processing so that you will no longer be constricted by the RPG cycle. He even includes information on database file processing with embedded SQL. 458 pages. Level: Novice, Intermediate, and Advanced.

BOOK 531 ....$69
ISBN 0-9621825-0-8

Introduction to RPG IV

by Robert Cozzi, Jr.

Now you can come up to speed quickly on the basics of programming in RPG IV, the modern, modular AS/400 programming language that has gained acceptance worldwide. All you need is this easy-to-follow book from Bob Cozzi, the world's leading authority on RPG programming. Rich with practical examples and sample code, this book provides step-by-step guidance for writing structured programs in RPG IV. You'll find out how to create simple, powerful programs with just a few lines of code.

Completely up-to-date with all new RPG IV features, this book tells you everything you need to understand the modern constructs of RPG IV, including figurative and named constants, operation extenders, and free-format expressions. You'll discover how to perform basic programming tasks, such as opening files, processing data, communicating with the user, controlling work flow, and calling other programs. You'll even learn how to set up a development environment, including the integration of RPG IV and DDS! This book opens the door to the world of programming in RPG IV. 304 pages. Level: Novice.

❏ BOOK 577 ....$59
ISBN 1-883884-46-2

Re-engineering RPG Legacy Applications

by Paul Tuohy

Now you can use IBM's recent enhancements to the AS/400, OS/400, and RPG to immediately increase the reliability of your legacy applications, improve programmer productivity, and build a firm basis for the future of your business. This book and companion CD-ROM provide a tutorial aimed at showing you how to modernize your applications by taking you through a re-engineering of a sample application step-by-step. Author Paul Tuohy covers conversion of RPG IV programs as well as re-engineering them to take full advantage of RPG IV and ILE. He also covers triggers, referential integrity, and APIs so that your applications can take advantage of all the new technology that is available today. This book will be a valuable aid as you evaluate your legacy applications and then move into re-engineering.

Putting your company's IT resources in a condition of stasis while technology moves on may be a costly business mistake. It is possible and profitable to derive some of the benefits of new technology from within a legacy application. Best of all, re-engineering gives you the opportunity to learn new programming concepts and acquire new skills. 528 pages. Level: Intermediate to Advanced.

BOOK 5009 ....$99
ISBN 1-58347-006-9

Other Best-sellers of Related Interest

The RPG Programmer's Guide to RPG IV and ILE

by Richard Shaler and Robin Klima

Aimed at the experienced RPG programmer, this book will quickly take you from your RPG III skills to writing powerful RPG IV programs. It addresses the differences between RPG III and RPG IV so that you can quickly become a productive RPG IV programmer.

The book contains extensive code examples that compare the two RPG languages and introduces the ILE capabilities that can be used to your advantage. There are two new chapters on subprocedures. The authors have added a chapter on conditional compiler objects to show you how the old directives have been enhanced and what new directives are available. They have also added a chapter on implementing object-oriented concepts in RPG. There are also appendixes with utilities and programs that you can add to your copybook and learn from.

368 pages. Level: Intermediate to Advanced.

❑ BOOK 588 ....$79
ISBN 1-883884-56-X

Power RPG IV

Advanced Concepts, Tips, & Techniques, Including ILE

by Doug Pence and Ron Hawkins

Before you write your next RPG IV program, make sure you're using the most powerful code-saving features this potent new language has to offer. This book from Doug Pence and Ron Hawkins gives you practical, hands-on tips, hints, and shortcuts that will save you time and increase the reliability of the code you write. The book includes a valuable chapter devoted to date handling. It also contains a chapter on ILE concepts, exploring this vital feature of RPG IV. You get explanations of softcoding function keys, new ways to use the QCMDEXC command processing API, new APIs for ILE, and new utilities to help you work with ILE. Built-in functions, such as %ELEM, %TRIML, %TRIMR, and %TRIM, also are explained in detail. *Power RPG IV* comes with a free diskette containing 11 useful AS/400 utilities. 477 pages. Level: Intermediate to Advanced.

❑ BOOK 560 .... $99
ISBN 1-883884-32-2

Subfiles for RPG Programmers

A Comprehensive User Guide

by Michael Catalani

Does the word *subfile* scare you? Fear no more! *Subfiles for RPG Programmers* explains everything you need to know about subfiles in simple and concise detail. Whether you're a novice subfile programmer or a seasoned pro, you'll find this book to be an invaluable resource.

Subfiles for RPG Programmers begins with concepts such as subfile record formats and subfile loading, then progresses to more advanced applications. DDS, of course, is at the heart of subfiles, so the author thoroughly explains the DDS keywords and how they apply to subfile programming. He explains and shows you examples of how the RPG code and the DDS work together to make a subfile function with all its built-in power. The more advanced subfile techniques are covered here, too: coding for multiple subfiles on the screen, using OPNQRYF and subfiles, coding message subfiles, and coding window techniques.

To increase your understanding and retention of the information, all theory is backed up with easy-to-understand working program examples. *Subfiles for RPG Programmers* is V2R3-ready and comes with a diskette of all working lprogram examples. 505 pages. Level: Intermediate.

❑ BOOK 517 ....$99
ISBN 1-883884-18-7

5 Easy Ways to Order!

FAX
this order form to 760-931-9935, 24 hours a day, 365 days a year.

MAIL
your order to 5650 El Camino Real, Suite 225, Carlsbad, CA 92008.

EMAIL
your order to *custsvc@midrangecomputing.com*.

PHONE
toll-free 1-800-477-5665 (Mon. to Fri., 6 a.m. to 5 p.m. PST).

ONLINE
ordering is available at *www.mc-store.com*.

Other Best-sellers of Related Interest

The AS/400 & Microsoft® Office Integration Handbook

by Brian Singleton with Colleen Garton

This book takes a detailed look at how you can integrate applications in the Microsoft Office 97 product suite with data from your AS/400. Unravel secrets such as how to use your AS/400's output with your PC's data formatting tools or how to make attractive, professional reports with AS/400 data the easy way. Learn the secret of using visual query tools to point and click the creation of sophisticated information output and how to analyze and summarize the detailed (and often cumbersome) reports from your AS/400. Discover how you can combine the presentation capabilities of Microsoft Office with the database capabilities of the AS/400 to provide your company with the best of both worlds.

In the first sections of the book, Singleton introduces you to the essential knowledge you need to use Client Access as you integrate AS/400 data with the Microsoft Office applications. He covers installing and configuring Client Access, how to provide a seamless method of AS/400 integration with Microsoft Office using ODBC, the network drive functionality of Client Access, and the Client Access data transfer function.

The remaining sections of the book cover the veritable Swiss Army knife functions of Microsoft Office. 320 pages. Level: Novice, Intermediate, and Advanced.

❏ BOOK 587..$79
ISBN 1-883884-49-7

The AS/400 Owner's Manual for V4

by Mike Dawson

Midrange Computing's all-time best-selling manual is now V4R2-ready! Designed for AS/400 professionals at all levels, *The AS/400 Owner's Manual for V4* walks you through hundreds of AS/400 tasks from the perspective of how most shops actually work. Cutting through the dozens of parameters and options of AS/400 commands, *The AS/400 Owner's Manual for V4* takes you directly to the results you need. Offering much more than brief, to-the-point instructions, it also includes valuable descriptions that examine why AS/400 managers, administrators, operators, and programmers do certain things on the machine and how the AS/400 works internally. This edition is completely up-to-date for Version 4 of OS/400 and contains a new chapter about the Internet and TCP/IP. Wire-bound and concise, *The AS/400 Owner's Manual for V4* is the perfect workstation tool for anyone who does AS/400 operations, administration, or management. 464 pages. Level: Novice, Intermediate, and Advanced.

❏ BOOK 5000..$59
ISBN 1-58347-001-8

Java® Application Strategies for the AS/400

An Introduction to AS/400 Java Development Strategies for RPG Programmers
by Don Denoncourt

At last! Here's a book that lays out real-world strategies for the development of AS/400 Java applications! *Java® Application Strategies for the AS/400* is the new book written specifically for RPG programmers to help them understand the structure and intent of the Java programming language as well as why Java applications developed with the structure techniques used in RPG applications are doomed to fail.

You will learn about the structure and the intent of the Java programming language and standard strategies for object-oriented design (OOD), strategies for interoperating Java applications with your legacy applications, and strategies and frameworks for the development of business classes. You will also find out how to develop Java GUIs complete with a replacement paradigm for AS/400 subfiles.

The book includes a FREE companion CD-ROM that contains the source code presented in the book, the complete source for Midrange Computing's object-to-relational framework classes, and a .jar file that contains the package of Java classes for Midrange Computing's object-to-relational classes. 448 pages. Level: Intermediate to Advanced.

❏ BOOK 591..$79
ISBN 1-883884-61-6

AS/400 Associate System Operator Certification Study Guide

by Steve Murray
Rochester Community and Technical College

This is the first study guide designed specifically for AS/400 professionals preparing for IBM's new Associate System Operator certification exam. This guide takes you through the basics of AS/400 operation from concepts to work management, providing the help you need to successfully complete the IBM Associate System Operator certification exam 000-052. Hands-on lab exercises reinforce the chapter topics and prepare the reader to operate an AS/400 system. Whether you need individual or group operator training, you will find this book to be an excellent resource. 384 pages. Level: Novice to Intermediate.

❏ BOOK 5010..$119
ISBN 1-58347-007-7

ORDER FORM

5 Easy Ways to Order!

BILL TO:

Name _____

Title _____

Company_____

Address _____

City _____ State_____ ZIP _____

YTQBZ

SHIP TO (if different from above):

Name _____ Title _____

Company _____

Address _____

City/State/ZIP _____

FAX
this order form to 760-931-9935, 24 hours a day, 365 days a year.

MAIL
your order to 5650 El Camino Real, Suite 225, Carlsbad, CA 92008.

EMAIL
your order to *custsvc@ midrangecomputing.com.*

PHONE
toll-free 1-800-477-5665 (Mon. to Fri., 6 a.m. to 5 p.m. PST).

ONLINE
ordering is available at *www. mc-store.com.*

ITEMS ORDERED:

Item No.	Description	Price	Quantity	Total Price

ADDITIONAL INFORMATION:

Daytime Phone (required to process order):

( ) - _____

Fax ( ) - _____

Email _____

Subtotal	
Add 7.75% sales tax (CA residents only), 6.25% sales tax (TX residents only), or 6% sales tax (NJ residents only). Residents of Canada add 7% GST.	
Shipping/Handling—$6.25 per item (ground, continental United States only)	
Total	

* Note: All prices are United States only. Please call for orders and prices outside the United States. Prices subject to change.

BILLING INFORMATION:

☐ Payment Enclosed (Make check payable to Midrange Computing.)

CREDIT CARD: ☐ VISA ☐ MasterCard ☐ American Express ☐ Discover

Card # _____ Exp. Date _____

BILL ME: P.O. # _____

Signature (required)_____

Priority code: YUQAZ

Y04HBPAA